Encore Performance

WATCH VIDEOS OF VICKI'S TAP PUPS WHILE YOU READ

ATRIA AUTHORS ON YOUR SMART PHONE

Tag images like the one above are placed throughout *Encore Performance* to bring videos of the Tap Pups directly to your smart phone.

To watch these videos, simply download the free Microsoft tag app at http:gettag.mobi.

Then hold your phone's camera a few inches away from the tag images, and you'll immediately be brought to the video.

View the tag above to watch the Tap Pups perform to "42nd Street."

CLICK IT. READ IT.

Or you can watch the videos on Vicki's Tap Pups' YouTube channel at: www.youtube.com/vickistappups.

Encore Performance

HOW ONE WOMAN'S PASSION HELPED
A TOWN TAP INTO HAPPINESS

Vicki G. Riordan and Brian S. Riordan

ATRIA BOOKS

New York   London   Toronto   Sydney   New Delhi

ATRIA BOOKS

A Division of Simon & Schuster, Inc.
1230 Avenue of the Americas
New York, NY 10020

First Atria Books hardcover edition April 2012

ATRIA BOOKS and colophon are trademarks of Simon & Schuster, Inc.

The following photographs are reprinted by permission: page 2 (bottom)—Sterling Commercial Photos; page 3 (top) and page 4 (both)—Charles Gehret Photography.

For information about special discounts for bulk purchases, please contact Simon & Schuster Special Sales at 1-866-506-1949 or business@simonandschuster.com.

The Simon & Schuster Speakers Bureau can bring authors to your live event. For more information or to book an event, contact the Simon & Schuster Speakers Bureau at 1-866-248-3049 or visit our website at www.simonspeakers.com.

Designed by Agnieszka Stachowicz

Manufactured in the United States of America

10 9 8 7 6 5 4 3 2 1

Library of Congress Cataloging-in-Publication Data
Grubic Riordan, Vicki.
Encore performance : how one woman's passion helped a town tap into happiness / Vicki Grubic Riordan.
p. cm.
1. Grubic Riordan, Vicki. 2. Tap dancers—United States—Biography. 3. Women tap dancers—United States—Biography. I. Title.

GV1785.R57A3 2012
792.7'8092—dc23
[B]   2011040923

isBn 978-1-4516-4349-7
isBn 978-1-4516-7307-4 (ebook)

TO ALL BABY BOOMERS,
MAY WE NEVER LOSE OUR RHYTHM

PROLOGUE

I STAND IN THE WINGS, WAITING FOR MY CURTAIN CALL.
When the moment comes, I walk out.

Ahead of me, spotlights are flashing pink, blue, white, and aqua. A giant video camera on a boom is swirling overhead. The music is so loud I can feel its vibrations under my feet. Directly in front of me, an audience of seventeen hundred people is already standing, cheering and applauding. The energy they give off is like a force field.

Instinctively I turn around. I want to see my dancers. They're lined up in dozens of rows behind me. I give them a giant smile—and they beam right back at me. I know we're all thinking the same thing: "We did it!"

I put my hands in the air and start to move. A second later, every one of the nearly three hundred dancers onstage is moving in sync with me, stepping from side to side to the music, arms above their heads. I turn to face the audience again, and all arms go up in the air along with us.

This moment, right here, right now, is something everyone should experience at least once in their life. It's not Broadway. It's not Madison Square Garden. It's not even close. But it makes us feel like rock stars.

This is Harrisburg, the state capital of Pennsylvania. The date is June 12, 2011, and I'm standing onstage with the largest adult tap dance group in America. It's a group that I founded fourteen years ago with just seventeen dancers. Now there are more than five hundred of us. Even with my back to my dancers, I can feel their excitement, their collective glow, and their pride pouring over me and the audience in waves. I'm like a general leading an army, except that instead of boots, we're all wearing black-and-white spectator tap shoes. The members of my army are mostly women, and their average age is sixty.

Behind me are mothers, grandmothers, teachers, doctors, nurses, attorneys, insurance agents, CPAs, therapists, owners of boutiques, salons, and businesses, not to mention a ton of retirees. Our ages range from the youngest at twenty-three to the oldest at eighty. We're tall, short, skinny, wide, and every shape in between. We're ordinary women, with the best kind of ordinary lives, and yet this afternoon, we're shining in the spotlight. The audience is giving us a standing ovation. We're celebrities in our hometown.

How did all this get started? How did Harrisburg go from state capital to tap capital? When I founded this group I never could have dreamed I'd end up on this stage today. Back then, my classes were held in school cafeterias, and we'd have to dance over cookie crumbs. Today, I have my own gorgeous tap studio and cultural center; we've opened for stars like Joan Rivers, Chubby Checker, and Patti LaBelle; and for the third year running, we've taken over Harrisburg's biggest and grandest theater, The Forum, for our annual spring show.

In the wings, I look for Brian, my son. I give him a wink to let him know how much he counts. More than anyone, Brian knows all the years and the hard work that led up to this moment. Ten years ago, it was Brian who reminded me who I really was and what I was meant to do. None of this could have happened today if I didn't start looking at my life with that fresh perspective.

I'm sixty-four now and since I retired from my nine-to-five job, I've been living with a passion and a sense of commitment that few people would expect from someone my age. What's true of me is true for so many of my dancers standing behind me. For most of these women, coming to tap class was terrifying at first. It's not so easy to be fifty or sixty years old and to try something new, something challenging and out of your comfort zone. At "our age" the assumption is that we should move aside quietly and fade into the background. People don't expect women our age to be stepping out center stage and performing, and they certainly don't think we'll be any good at it. Today we've shattered all expectations, not just for the audience but for ourselves.

Like the dancers in my classes, tap has filled a void in me that I hadn't realized existed. For so many years, I'd put dance on the back burner. When my generation was growing up, dance wasn't just a pastime, it was everything. It was what we did and who we were, but we put it behind us when we became adults. Now we're finding our rhythm together again and it's amazing what that's done for us. These days, we're not so naïve to think that we have all the time in the world ahead of us. But we're smart enough to know that after years of raising children and always putting everyone else first, this is our moment to do something strictly for ourselves. Today, it's our kids and our husbands who are in the audience cheering *us* on. It's our time to shine.

Part of what makes this so exciting is that it's so unexpected. Ten years ago, if you'd told me that I'd be here with all these dynamic dancers onstage in this theater, I never would have believed you. This is my story, but it's also the story of some of these amazing women—and a handful of men—who have come along with me for the ride. We were once the ones who wondered if we were running out of time but, as it turns out, the best was yet to come.

• •

MEET VICKI AND HER TAP PUPS

www.youtube.com/vickistappups

• •

Encore Performance

Chapter 1

•••

Sunday, June 12, 2011
8:35 AM

EVEN BEFORE I TURN THE CORNER TO THE THEATER, I CAN SEE THEM ARRIVING.

They're streaming along the sidewalks, carrying carefully ironed costumes in plastic dry cleaning bags, loaded down with coolers and folded lawn chairs. They're in groups, or two by two, chatting and smiling, coming from every possible direction. A few of the ladies see me and try to wave, but they're carrying too much stuff, so they have to jump up and down to say hello. I give a short honk of the horn, a quick wave, and a big smile.

On any other day of the week, these streets would be busy with state workers making their way to the giant gray municipal buildings just behind us. This is Harrisburg, Pennsylvania, and like any state capital across the country, it's a city where people work in departments with a capital *D*, where the jobs start at nine and end at five—a workaday universe of offices and cubicles and business suits. But today Harrisburg has glamour. Today the city belongs to these women.

Most of the ladies live within a few miles of here. Many of them will be walking these same sidewalks to the office on Monday. Some are stay-at-home moms with small children. Some are empty nesters with grown children. Many are retired. Some have lived here all their lives; others have moved here from states across the country. The majority of them are grand-mothers, although there are some in their twenties and thirties too. In al-most every way, the ladies carrying their costumes are like any other women you'd find living in any midsized city anywhere in America, but with one important exception: every one of them is a tap dancer.

In Harrisburg, we're part of the culture. If you ask people here if they know about our group, the answer is usually "Yes, I'm a tap dancer," or "Yeah, my mom is a dancer," or "I've seen those ladies in the Saint Patrick's Day Parade." I know dancers who practice their riffs while pushing their shopping carts in the supermarket, because the hard tile floors are perfect for tapping. One lady taps while she walks her dog each morning. When she passes the same elementary school, all the kids give her the thumbs-up. It's not unusual to see a dancer perfecting a routine while standing by an elevator, or waiting for a bus, or sitting at a table at a restaurant. There's not another city in the country that's home to so many adult tappers. We're the town that loves to tap.

Today is the morning of June 12, the most important day on our calen-dar. It's our annual spring show, when we perform for our family, friends, and fans, raising thousands of dollars for charity. As I pull up in my car, I see my dancers filing up to the giant iron doors along six separate pathways in the shape of a sunburst—Busby Berkeley couldn't have choreographed it better. I glance at my watch. In less than six hours, it'll be showtime. My son Brian climbs out of the passenger's seat, and we begin unloading big plastic containers filled with all the dancers' accessories: pink and black feather hair clips; chiffon scarves in aqua, black, white, red, and polka dot; pink sequined wristbands; silver and red sequined hatbands; and red sequined gloves. With the boxes piled high in our arms, we join the stream of dancers going inside.

As we push open the double doors to the backstage area, the sound of tapping and voices just explodes. Dancers are everywhere: chatting, taking photographs. Others are lined up down the long hallway, practicing their arm movements, and the clatter of their taps is ricocheting off the walls. One group is using a storage area as a dressing room; the rest are using the bathrooms, the green room, and the locker rooms to lay out makeup bags, costume bags, and curling irons. The four men who will be dancing along-side all these ladies today have their own dressing room, otherwise known as the men's bathroom. I adore these guys—and so do all of my ladies. These men are here strictly for the love of tapping, and they're not intimidated by doing it alongside all these women.

In the long, wide corridor behind the stage, the ladies have already staked out their areas for the day. They've unfolded their lawn chairs and are sitting along the walls, tailgating on the marble floors. They're prepar-ing for a long day of rehearsals before showtime, with breakfast from the big open coolers at their feet. Everyone is wearing comfortable clothes, sweats, and T-shirts. The costumes come later. Backstage looks like a large outdoor family reunion.

Brian and I leave our boxes of accessories next to the green room and head for the stage. As we walk out from the wings, we see that the production crew has already set up the giant nine-and-a-half-foot V-shaped light in the center of the stage. During the show, the V will flash white and aqua—our signature colors. V for Vicki, my name; V for Vicki's Tap Pups, our group.

It was my students who came up with the name Tap Pups. A month after I started teaching my first adult tap class in 1997, Brian took me to see the Philadelphia production of the Tap Dogs, an Australian men's tap group. I was instantly taken with them and talked incessantly about the Tap Dogs to my class. After our first year together, my original seventeen dancers presented me with a birthday gift. The card read, "We realize we will never be as good as your Tap Dogs, but we can at least be your Tap Pups." My gift was a T-shirt that read, "Vicki's Tap Pups."

The name stuck.

As I look out across the huge circular auditorium, with its four tiers of seats, I see different groups of dancers pacing out their steps for the show, arms linked, feet flying. No one looks up. No one wants to forget a step. For nine months now, these ladies have been coming to their classes once a week, some twice a week, or more, to perfect the routines they'll be performing today. Seven levels of dancers appearing in fourteen different numbers, each with a different style, different costumes, and different challenges. Now that the big day is finally here, it's easy to spot the ladies who are nervous. They're the ones spending every spare second going over the choreography, as if their lives depended on it.

In the small hallway that leads to the stage door, I see a group from one of my New Beginner classes helping one another remember a complex sequence they'll be performing this afternoon. In the middle of the six of them stands Jana, fifty-four years old, a tall woman with straight, bobbed blonde hair and long, graceful arms. Although she's just one dancer out of many, Jana's story is true of so many of my Tap Pups.

Ever since she was a little girl, Jana always knew that she'd like to learn to tap-dance, but as a child, she'd never gotten that chance. By the time Jana was old enough to make her own decisions in life, she found herself too busy juggling family, work, and home to make time for her own interests. Only when she was older, and when her children left home, did she realize that this was her time. Maybe she could finally do something for herself. But what activities were there for Jana? For women like us? Not much. She kept hearing experts on TV telling her that she needed to find a passion in order to be fulfilled, but for many reasons, Jana didn't feel confident that she could try something new. Besides, she never thought of herself as much of a "joiner"—she preferred doing things alone, or with her family.

At this point, Jana had no idea that tap classes for adults even existed. Like most people, she assumed tap lessons were for little girls. Then fate took over.

Jana works as an occupational therapist, helping people recuperate from injuries and surgeries. Last summer she was meeting with one of her clients, a woman in her seventies named Elsa, who had recently beaten breast cancer. Jana always asks new patients about their hobbies so that she can get a better idea of how they spend their time. It turned out that Elsa was a tap dancer.

The very next day, Jana met with another new client, Joan. She was also taking tap lessons. Two tap dancers in the same week! This piqued Jana's interest.

She didn't think too much more about it until a few days later she met with a client named Jeanne. This lady was also—you guessed it—a Tap Pup.

"You're my third client this week who's a tap dancer!" Jana exclaimed.

"I don't have much rhythm," Jana told the lady in her consulting chair. "I don't know if I would be able to keep up."

Jeanne, who was in her sixties, assured her, "Don't worry! Vicki breaks everything down for you. Trust me, you're going to love it. Everyone does."

Later that day, Jana sent me a note requesting information about my classes.

I can still picture her on her first day of class last September. It was a Tuesday night, and Jana arrived at my studio wide eyed and clutching her black-and-white tap shoes in their box, looking like she couldn't wait another minute to put them on. I've been teaching tap to adults for fourteen years now, but I still get a kick out of seeing the new dancers' faces as they lace up their tap shoes for the first time. Jana was no exception. She wore the kind of smile you'd expect to see on a child opening presents on Christmas morning.

Jana took a few tentative steps, like she was walking across hot coals, and her smile faded. Then she got a little bolder—*click, click, click*—and her smile returned. The class hadn't even begun, but Jana had already learned the first lesson of being a Tap Pup: it feels good to make noise.

Right away, I asked the dancers to form three long lines in front of me from one side of the room to the other. Jana chose a spot in the back line.

"I'm about to say the four words you've been waiting a lifetime to hear," I announced to my new beginners. "WELCOME TO TAP CLASS!" Everyone laughed and class began.

For most people, tapping doesn't come easily. There's a reason you never see tap routines on *So You Think You Can Dance*: it takes a lot longer than a week to master even the most simple combination. In order to get that true, solid tap sound, you have to find the "sweet spot" right in the middle of the ball of your foot. And to do this, you have to shift the weight to your toes instead of your heels. It feels completely unnatural at first. When you walk, you always hit your heels first, but when you tap, you have to lead with the balls of your feet instead.

Most of the New Beginners were struggling as they took their first steps, which is natural, seeing as they were wearing tap shoes for the very first time. By contrast, Jana was picking up everything I showed her quite easily and by the end of the hour, she was tapping naturally. She left class that night pink in the face from working so hard, smiling from ear to ear.

Jana came back to class week after week, making new friends and quietly pushing herself. Tap is so complex, it makes people want to try it again and again, to figure it out. It's a challenge, but in a good way. When you're tapping, you're completely focused on the intricacy of what you're doing. There's something about the connection between your mind and the sounds of your taps that allows you to forget everything else. It's hard to think about what you're going to make for dinner, or the boss who made you feel bad at work, or the guy who didn't call you back. All you can focus on is the steps. It's like meditation in motion.

It's also a lot of fun. Remember that famous scene with Gene Kelly in *Singin' in the Rain*? Remember the smile on his face even though he's soaked to the skin? Well, in the movie, he says it's because he's in love. But I think it's simply because he's tap dancing. Nothing else gets the endorphins flowing in quite the same way. When you're tapping, you're completely in the moment. When it's working—and it was definitely working for Jana—it just flows.

As we got closer to the date of this year's spring show, I knew that I wanted to put Jana in the front row so that the other dancers could follow her footwork when it came time to perform. One evening, I went over to Jana and told her quietly that I wanted her to move to the front line.

"Really?" she asked.

"Yes. I want you to go to your new spot each week when you arrive." I put my hand on her shoulder and walked her to the front line, moving different dancers from one line to another to make room for her. Jana was blushing, but she was smiling too.

"Class, from now on, Jana will be dancing in the front line," I told them. "She's doing so well that I want you to be able to watch her feet as well as watch mine. No pressure, Jana!"

Jana beamed, and the class laughed. Until now they had no idea that Jana was such a good dancer, because she was always in the back row, but by the end of the session, Jana had proved her worth.

Afterward, Jana came to find me in my office.

"Vicki, I have to tell you something," she said. "When I arrived at class this evening, I was planning to tell you that I needed to quit."

"Oh, no!" I replied. "Why? You've been doing so well!"

Jana explained that her husband had recently undergone knee surgery and her mother-in-law was not well. She was taking care of both of them right now, and she felt she didn't have enough energy for tap too.

"But now that you've put me in the front row, I can't quit!" she told me. "I love to tap. And if you think I have potential, then I'm going to stay."

"Jana, you belong here," I replied.

I had no idea she was thinking of leaving, but by putting her in the front row, I'd helped Jana to realize that tap was important to her, that it made her feel good, and that she was good at it.

That night, Jana became a true Tap Pup. She stumbled upon her passion.

ONCE upon a time, I made my own very first tap sound.

I was just three years old when my mother took me by my hand to my first dance class. That was sixty-one years ago, but I can still remember looking up at a white building with a bright pink door on what seemed to be the steepest hill in Harrisburg. I could hardly wait to see what was behind it. Later my mom told me that she had to scrape pennies together to afford those classes, but at the time, I had no idea about her sacrifice. All I knew was that the pink door looked like the entrance to fairyland, and when I stepped inside, I entered another world. It was a place that felt about as exciting and glamorous as anything I could imagine.

At first I took tap and ballet. Eventually, I also took classes in jazz, acrobatics, and baton twirling, but from the beginning, tap was my favorite. Tap was unlike any other form of dance. Tap was fast. It was exciting. Ballet felt so slow and dull by comparison. Most important, tap came with the coolest shoes. When I put them on my feet, I wasn't just moving in rhythm, I was making noise. From an early age, I knew that the crisp, clean sound of a steel tap on a hard floor is one of the best sounds in the world. As a young girl growing up at a time when little girls were expected to be quiet and demure, tap taught me that it was okay to put my foot down. It gave me permission to be bold. "The louder the better!" our tap teacher told us.

When you're a child, you don't have to think much about which activities you enjoy the most. You don't wonder to yourself, "What's my passion in life?" You just *know*. So at age three, I knew that I loved to dance. Sunday afternoons, my aunt Dutch would come over. She was my mom's sister, and because she never had her own children, Aunt Dutch was like a second mother to me. As soon as she entered the door, we'd go into the dining room and roll up the rug. Then my mother would open the lid to the portable record player, pop a record onto the spindle, drop the needle on the disc, and after a fuzzy *click*, the music would begin.

We usually listened to Glenn Miller, but we also played Perry Como and Tommy Dorsey—one of the big band–era classics. At the sound of the music, my mom and my aunt started snapping their fingers. Then their feet would begin to move, and before I knew it, they were hopping, turning, and jumping. They could jitterbug better than anyone I've ever seen. I can still see them, their faces lit up, their eyes shining.

At first I'd sit on the couch with my knees pulled up to my chin, watching and taking in everything. I loved to see my mom and aunt laughing like two little girls as they danced. Before long, they'd hold out their hands and beckon for me to join them, and I'd begin jitterbugging right alongside them. Aunt Dutch was single, so she was a regular at the ballrooms around town and in Philadelphia. Whenever she learned a new step, she'd teach it to my mom and me, always taking the lead. She'd hold out her hand, and I'd take it, using my other hand to hit her open palm, bouncing back, and spinning around. Then my mom and I would cross over, while Dutch released us and twirled.

Eventually all three of us would collapse on the sofa in happy exhaustion. I never wanted those afternoons to end. Looking back, I realize that dance was the way that I played at home. I was an only child. While other kids were out in the backyard with their brothers and sisters, I was dancing in the living room with my aunt and my mom.

I was born in 1946 in a small town called Steelton, just a few miles from Harrisburg and the theater where we're performing today. Steelton was literally a steel town back then—the entire town revolved around the mill. My family lived in one of the row homes on the hill overlooking the Bethlehem Steel Company plants. From my bedroom window, I could see the trains making their daily deliveries of coal, and the smokestacks that overshadowed the plants pushing smoke up into the sky. At the end of each shift, the whistles blew, and hundreds of men came pouring out of the gates, each one carrying a metal lunch box, wearing a hard hat, and bearing a face black with soot.

Steelton was a true melting pot. Our neighbors were Irish, German, Italian, Serbian, Slovenian, African-American, and Croatian like my dad. The mill was a hub of constant activity and a source of pride for everyone, because all of our fathers and uncles worked there. When you drove into Steelton in those days, you saw a sign that read: Steelton, the Little Town with a Big Heart.

After the working day was over, there were four main sources of local entertainment: the taverns on every corner of Front Street; the high school sporting events where everyone gathered to watch football and basketball; the many churches; and the social clubs. Steelton had a social club for practically every ethnic group in town. The Croatians had the St. Lawrence Club; the Italians had the Italian Club; the Germans had the Dutch Club; the Slovenians had the St. Aloysius Club; and the Serbians had Serb Hall. Each of these places held regular dances, featuring everything from big band to polka nights.

Some people were tavern people, some were sports people, some were church people, some were dance people, and some were a combination. Although my mother loved to dance, overall, you could say that my parents were definitely on the sports side. When my dad, Victor Grubic, first set eyes on my mother, Charlotte Brubacher, in 1945, she was the only woman competing in the local steelworkers men's bowling league. My mother was wearing a stylish bowling dress that she'd specially ordered out of a catalogue from the Midwest, set off with a bright red manicure and matching red lipstick.

My dad wasn't intimidated at all. He took one look at the girl bowling like a dream and turned to a friend to say, "I'm going to marry that woman."

Charlotte went on to win the bowling league that year with the highest season average of 177. And sure enough, three months after first meeting, she and my dad married. They would have wed even sooner if the priest hadn't insisted that they wait for the end of Lent. Charlotte had always been a very independent person, but when she met Vic, she fell hard. My mom said she felt so safe in his arms that she let down her guard and trusted a man for the first time in her life.

Vic was twelve years older than Charlotte, tall and strong with black hair and a striking dimple in his chin. He was six foot one, and once upon a time, he'd been a star athlete: a brilliant bowler, baseball pitcher, and amateur boxer. But then, in 1941, World War II erupted. Like millions of men across the United States, he was drafted into the army, and his life took another course. He was injured in Italy. Shrapnel lodged in his back and right leg, and although he recovered initially, soon after I was born in 1946, the damage caused a disc in his spine to slip. After he underwent surgery, he was back to bowling and led a healthy life for more than a year, until the disc went a second time, and his doctors told him he'd never walk again. Although it took Vic three years, he proved them wrong and got back on his feet, but he knew he would never bowl, pitch, or box again. And so my father kept involved in sports by coaching. It was his gift. He could look at people and tell them exactly what they were doing wrong and how to fix it.

From the beginning, my dad recognized that my mom was a superb athlete and began coaching her not only in bowling but also in softball and basketball too. While five months pregnant with me, my mom entered and won her first circuit competition, the Harrisburg Ladies City Bowling Tournament. Later he coached her women's softball team, the Harrisburg Roverettes, and soon they were competing all over the state. They were the team to beat. In most marriages at that time, the wives helped the husbands fulfill their dreams. In my parents' marriage, the reverse was true. My dad believed in my mom's talent and did whatever he could to nurture it.

In fact, Vic was so obsessed with sports that when I was born, he brought my mother a brand-new bowling bag as a gift—he didn't even think to bring flowers. Of course, my dad would have loved a son, a little Vic Jr. to coach, so he was admittedly a little disappointed to find himself the father of a girl. Then, a few days after my arrival, he was given new hope. It was the hospital's responsibility to print the birth announcement in the local newspaper, and for some reason, when my announcement appeared in the *Harrisburg Telegraph*, they made a mistake:

To Mr. and Mrs. Victor Grubic, a son.

My dad raced back to the hospital, clutching the newspaper.

"Are you sure they've given us the right baby?" he asked Charlotte. "It says in the paper we had a boy!"

"Vic, for heaven's sakes," my mother replied. "You saw her with your own eyes. You know we have a little girl!"

My mother tells me that it didn't take me very long to win over my dad. When my parents brought me home a few days later, I fell asleep wrapped up in my tiny bundle of blankets, safe in my dad's arms. From that moment on, he was smitten. He didn't want to put me down. After a while, my mother actually had to beg him to lay me in my crib, but my dad loved for me to fall asleep lying on his chest, and that's what I did for the first two years of my life.

Early on, my dad decided it didn't matter that I was a girl—he was going to coach me anyway. At three, I knew how to make a proper pocket in a mitt by oiling the glove and wedging in a softball. I became the bat girl on my mom's softball team, and loved wearing my miniature version of their uniform. But as much as I enjoyed all the attention, I knew from an early age this wasn't my world. I hated getting dirty, I cried when I scraped my knees, and when the ball came my way, I really just wanted to duck.

Luckily for me, my mother recognized my love of dance and told my dad that she wanted to take me to classes. Growing up during the Depression, my mom had always dreamed of taking ballet or tap classes, but dance classes cost a quarter then. She came from a family of six siblings, and that was money her parents couldn't spare. My mom wanted to give me every opportunity she'd missed. Dissatisfied with my first dance school (the one with the pink door), she moved me to another one and then another one after that, until she finally settled on the Bette Weeks Winn Academy of Dance in Harrisburg. My mother had high standards, and Miss Bette—who had once been a professional dancer—was an exceptional teacher.

I loved my Saturday morning classes, and from the beginning, my teachers started putting me in the front row so that everyone could follow my steps. From then on, I was always dancing. My mom never had to nag me to practice. After school, I'd run down to our basement, pull out my dance shoes, and go through my steps on the concrete floor.

When I was seven, my teacher wanted me to dance with the older girls. This meant attending class after school three days a week. My mother worked as a secretary for the United Steelworkers union, and my dad, forced to leave his job at the steel mill due to his back injury, was working as a security guard. Neither of them could drive me to Harrisburg on a weekday afternoon. But that didn't stop my mother. She decided that at the age of seven, I was old enough to take the bus on my own. The weekend before

I was to start my new classes, we took a bus together, and she showed me where I had to get off in Market Square and how to transfer to another bus that would take me to my class. The journey took thirty minutes, but even at age seven, I wasn't nervous. It was an adventure. And nothing was going to stop me from getting to dance class.

I was taking six hours of classes a week: tap, jazz, ballet, baton, acrobatics, and at this point, trampoline too. Taking so many classes was becoming expensive, and my parents weren't wealthy by any stretch of the imagination, but my mother was smart. She went to Miss Bette and offered to keep her books in return for my lessons—bookkeeping was a part of my mother's job—so that I could take as many classes as I liked. Mom could see that I'd found something that I loved to do and she was going to do everything in her power to encourage that.

From a very young age, I loved to perform. When I was seven, my mom took me to an audition for a local talent show, *TV Teen Time* hosted by Ron Drake. This was a big deal. In 1953 TV was still a new phenomenon in Steelton. We were one of the first families in town to get a television set, not because we had more money than anyone else but because my mom was so good at managing the money that we did have. I remember being in the second grade and sitting in the car with my parents when my dad turned around and said to me, "Vicki, in about an hour, we are having a television set delivered to our house!" I was so excited. When the TV did arrive, I raced around the house, waving my hands and screaming with excitement. It was a large brown floor model with a tiny screen and rabbit ears on top. In the end, we saw snow on that TV more than anything else—we had to constantly hit the top of it to get any reception—but even so, watching it was always magical to me.

Now I was auditioning to appear on that same TV. The tryouts were held at WHP-TV, the first television studio in Harrisburg. After I showed the producers my little routine, I was given a contract to dance on the program once a month. For the next year, on the day of the live show, I got to leave school early, and my mom would drive me to the TV station. When we arrived, I'd get dressed in one of the many costumes from my dance recitals. I still have a photo of myself in a half-moon hat with ruffles around the brim, a big bow under my chin, and wearing a satin pink-and-silver polka-dot dress with frills that my mother made for me. She even bought an extra pair of black tap shoes and painted them silver to match my outfit. As much as I loved my costume, my favorite part of the experience was coming home and hearing what my dad had to say about my performance: "Hey, princess, you made me proud again."

After my appearances with Ron Drake, we got a call from *Uncle Josh*, a local Saturday morning cartoon show that featured guest performers between *Casper the Friendly Ghost* and the *Roadrunner*. The best part was that it was taped in front of a live audience of children my age. I remember feeling about as proud of myself as can be, dancing away in front of them. "I love cartoons," I remember thinking. "And here I am on a cartoon show!"

After my TV appearances, I was hooked. I kept finding ways to get up in front of an audience and dance. One night when I was about nine years old, I was at a drive-in movie with my uncle Whitey and my cousins when at intermission, Bill Haley and His Comets' "Shake, Rattle and Roll" played over the speakers.

"Vicki, they're playing your song!" called out my uncle, who came to all my recitals and knew that I'd danced to that tune. "Get in front of my car and do your dance. I'll put the car lights on you."

Without skipping a beat, I popped out of the car and started dancing in front of the headlights. Before long, all the cars around us turned on their headlights too, and when I finished, the crowd clapped and honked their horns. I took my bow and climbed back in the backseat. Life was good!

If my dad was frustrated that I didn't share his love of sports, he didn't show it. At every dance recital, I'd look out and see him in the front row: a big guy with tears streaming down his face as he proudly watched his little girl dance. Right by his side sat my mom, beaming. Although my dad had no interest in dancing until I came along, he recognized that I was doing something that I loved, and he appreciated that. It would have been so much easier for him if I'd gone the sporting route, but he knew it wasn't my passion. My mom was such a talented athlete that I never could have lived up to her achievements. Instead dance helped me carve out my identity in a family that was defined by sports, and that made me feel good about myself.

Some of my happiest childhood memories, though, take place after the annual recital was over. My parents were always extremely careful with money, but they'd make an exception this one time each year and take me to Sam's Ice Cream Parlor in Harrisburg. The three of us always ordered the same sundae, our favorite: vanilla ice cream with hot fudge, wet nuts, whipped cream, and a cherry on top. I'd scoop up tiny spoonfuls, making each mouthful last as long as I could, while Mom and Dad told me in detail everything they liked about the show: the songs, my nonstop smiling, each costume I wore (which took awhile, because I was usually in about fourteen different routines), how they noticed that my arms were always extended about an inch above all the others. Thanks to my parents, I was able to relive every moment of the recital, and this was just as much of a treat as the sundae.

Through their love and their example, they showed me that it's a very good thing to have a passion and to express yourself by doing something you love. During my childhood, my mom continued to be a success in sports. When I was twelve, she did something that no one else in Steelton had ever done before: she qualified for a world bowling championship. In 1958 my parents traveled to Chicago so that my mother could compete in the World's Invitational Match Game Championship, leaving me home with

Aunt Dutch. On Friday, December 12, my aunt took me to my mom's regular bowling league in Harrisburg to watch the final game of the tournament on TV. That night, all bowling stopped at the alley so that everyone could watch my mom. When she rolled the winning ball, the entire bowling alley erupted in applause. Aunt Dutch picked me up and put me on her shoulders while all these people clapped and cheered for my mother. Somebody called the bowling alley that night to tell Aunt Dutch that work at the steel mill had been put on hold so that all of Steelton could watch Mom; they'd even blown the mill whistles to celebrate her victory. When my mom returned home, they held a parade along Front Street in her honor, and the day was declared "Charlotte Grubic Day." The mayor gave her a key to the town, telling her that she'd put Steelton on the map. After that, my mother signed a contract with the Ebonite bowling ball company to tour the country. The tagline for the tour was "Bowl the Ball the World's Champ Bowls." My dad and I went with her. We'd never even been in an airplane before, and all of a sudden, we were traveling first class in a new 707 jet. I even got to go to Disneyland. This was a big deal for a family from Steelton. My mother was a celebrity, not just in our hometown but also nationally. I was so proud to be Charlotte Grubic's daughter.

Not everyone is fortunate enough to find something she loves from such an early age. Or if she does, she might not have parents who are willing to take the trouble (or who have the means) to encourage it. My mom and dad did everything they could to support my passion and allowed me to be unapologetic about who I was and what I loved. The pleasure that both my parents took in my dancing and performing gave me the confidence and poise to hold my head up, not just as a little girl but also during the hard times that were soon to come my way.

Chapter 2

• • •

Sunday, June 12, 2011

9:00 AM

"FIFTEEN MINUTES TO REHEARSAL!" I CALL OUT TO THE LADIES AS I CIRCLE AROUND BACKSTAGE AGAIN.

Before the curtain goes up this afternoon, we're running through our entire program one last time just to make sure that everyone feels confident and prepared for showtime.

Over in the green room—the big, square, carpeted room at the back of the theater—my most advanced dancers are chatting and sharing coffee. They're the first ones performing today, but they've been onstage so many times before that they seem calm and relaxed, at least compared to the nervous New Beginners.

"Nearly time, ladies!" I say. They look up and smile.

Right in the middle of the group, lacing up her shoes, is Joan. At eighty, she's the oldest dancer performing today. She's put together beautifully—as she always is—her short, light brown hair with golden highlights set to perfection, makeup on, ready to go.

Joan first called me about attending my classes five years ago.

"Which level are you interested in?" I asked.

"Well, the Advanced, of course," she replied.

I paused. To be honest, I don't hear many seventy-five-year-olds saying that they want to be in my Advanced class, let alone with that much confidence! Joan asked if I auditioned dancers for the Advanced class. I don't usually, but given my concerns that she might be better off in a less challenging class, I asked her to meet me at the studio the following evening.

"Wow!" I thought the moment I saw Joan walk through the door. She was tall and trim, and perfectly put together. She walked carrying her head high, with her arms swinging, just like a dancer.

After Joan put on her tap shoes, she joined me in the middle of the room.

"Let's do the first time step," I said. Time steps are combinations of tap steps that create a rhythm. You repeat a time step over and over, just like a drummer playing along with a band. Every dance studio has its own signature spin on time steps, so you can never be certain if someone is going to be familiar with yours.

As it turned out, I didn't even have to show Joan our time steps, because she was already dancing right alongside me.

"Wow, that was great!" I said.

"Well, of course it was," Joan replied with a smile. "I told you, I've been dancing for years."

Just to make sure, I asked Joan to do some pick-ups with me. Pick-ups are an advanced step where you pull back on one foot, making sure to hear the heel and toe sound before hopping up and landing with a clean, clear tap on the ball of your foot. It's tough to execute—I have a few dancers in my Advanced class who still struggle with pick-ups. Joan rattled off hers like nobody's business.

"I think you passed!" I laughed, giving her a hug. "You go straight to Advanced!"

Joan started coming to my Wednesday night class, never missing a week. To see her keeping up with dancers twenty and thirty years younger was inspiring for everyone. When she danced, she was ageless. Joan raised the bar and gave all of us hope. If we could dance as well as she did when we reached her age, we'd be very happy women. Her doctor tells her that her blood pressure is normal and her bones are strong. "Whatever you do, keep tapping" is his advice.

As I got to know Joan a little better, she was eager to share her tap story with me. Every dancer has one, and after hearing Joan's, I admired her even more. When Joan talked about her younger years, her eyes lit up. It turned out that she grew up in the Harrisburg area with her twin sister, Jean. As little girls, Jean and Joan went to tap classes, and they loved to dance. They had a natural ability to keep in step with each other, and when they danced standing opposite each other, it was like they were looking into a mirror. At twelve, the sisters appeared on the popular radio talent show *Ted Mack's Original Amateur Hour*, the sound of their "twin taps" broadcast across the country.

After Joan and Jean graduated high school, they went to work for Bell Telephone as secretaries. Evenings and weekends, they'd still find ways to dance, performing in local talent shows in movie theaters, dancing during intermission and between double bills. At twenty, Joan and her sister even tried out for the Rockettes. Although they didn't make the cut (they couldn't kick to the regulation height), they had the unforgettable experience of auditioning on the stage of New York's Radio City Music Hall.

The twins kept dancing and performing until they turned twenty-four, at which point dance faded out of their lives. Neither Joan nor Jean ever married or had children. They lived together and worked together, as close as two people could be. It wasn't until they were fifty-six and eligible for retirement that they decided it was time to dust off their tap shoes again. For ten years, they took classes at a local studio, but then the unthinkable happened. In 1997, at the age of sixty-six, Jean developed cancer and passed away. Joan's heart was broken. The two were so close—in sixty-six years, they had barely spent more than a night apart from each other. After her sister died, Joan stopped going to tap classes.

Then, in 2006, Joan came across a township newsletter with an announcement about the Tap Pups. By now my classes were really taking off, and word was getting around. Taking a deep breath, Joan picked up the phone and bravely called me. She knew it wasn't going to be easy tapping without Jean by her side, but she felt that she owed it to her sister to give it a shot.

The first class was a big surprise for Joan. She'd thought dancing without her sister would make her feel too sad, but in fact, the opposite was true. When she was dancing, her sadness slipped away. Those steps were like a lifeline for Joan. They were in her bones. They connected her to her childhood. Tap actually brought her back to the person she'd been as a young girl and woman, dancing with her sister by her side.

The night I first learned Joan's story, I remember putting my arm around her shoulder.

"I bet your sister is looking down on you in class," I told her. "She must be so excited to see you dancing again."

"Yes," Joan said, smiling. "And I bet she thinks I'm an idiot for waiting so long to come back to it!"

Joan understands that it's too late to make the Rockettes. It doesn't matter that she'll probably never dance on Broadway. Although we strive for professionalism in the Tap Pups, the word "amateur" is absolutely appropriate here: in Latin, it simply means a person who does something for love. What's important is that Joan has found a way to reconnect with her love of dance as part of a unified group. When Joan danced with her sister, the happiness she felt was doubled, because she knew that Jean felt the same way. Now Joan is surrounded by friends who share her passion, and although nothing could ever replace her sister, her happiness has come back, magnified.

WHEN I was growing up, I always felt most happy and most comfortable when I was in a dance studio. No wonder then, that aside from my mother and father, the person who had the most influence on me as a child was my tap teacher, Bette Weeks Winn.

Miss Bette had bleached Jean Harlow–white hair, pulled back from her face in a tight bun, with big white plastic glasses on her nose, and her lips painted bright red. Short and thin as a rail, she usually wore shorts with an elastic waistband loose enough to accommodate a little round beer belly. To her students, she looked fifty years old, although she might have been ten years younger or ten years older; like most little children, we couldn't guess her age. What we did know was that Miss Bette was fascinating to us. The word around town was that she had been born into a well-to-do family in Philadelphia and that her parents wanted her to become a prima ballerina. Miss Bette had other ideas. As a young woman, she moved to New York City and hit the Broadway circuit as a professional dancer. At five foot three, she wasn't tall enough for the Rockettes kick line, but because she was such a fabulous dancer, the show's producers made her a tap soloist instead. From Broadway, she went into vaudeville, eventually settling in Harrisburg. There she met her husband and founded her school, Bette Weeks Winn Academy of Dance. Miss Bette's school was in uptown Harrisburg, but that didn't stop my mother from signing me up for classes. My mom was determined that I would receive the best instruction, and that meant Miss Bette.

Tap was Miss Bette's forte. She had no interest in teaching ballet, baton, or acrobatics—she hired other instructors to teach those classes for her. Miss

Bette was a tap teacher, and as a teacher, she was strict. When she came into the classroom, all chatting stopped. There was no laughing, no being silly, no chewing gum. If our underwear showed beneath our leotards, we had to go to the dressing room and correct it. When it came to our steps, Miss Bette wanted her tappers to be clear and precise. She wanted us to be professional. Often she came to class with a little pointer in her hand, and if we didn't straighten our legs when doing our Rockette kicks, we'd get a little jab under the knee. From Miss Bette, we learned to strive for perfection.

I'm sure that many of her students found her a little intimidating at times, but I loved Miss Bette. She was one of the best dancers I've ever seen; her feet and skinny legs moved at such speed that they practically blurred beneath her white shorts. I loved her dancing, I loved that she expected the best of us, and above all, I loved her recitals. Each year, at our annual recital, Miss Bette pulled out all the stops. The whole town would come out to watch those performances at Reservoir Park, on one of the highest hills in Harrisburg. We performed in a large white band shell that had a proscenium arch in a half circle illuminated with hundreds of shimmering lightbulbs. In the middle of the stage, Miss Bette set up a big black box with the words "Stars of Tomorrow" painted in glittering silver and white. Each year during the opening number, we'd start dancing, then our instructor would emerge from inside the box, decked out in a cocktail dress, with a full skirt with crinolines underneath. She'd step down to join our kick line and the crowd always roared its approval.

Perched on a raised platform at the back of the stage, the Eddie Huber Band provided live accompaniment. Eddie, one of Miss Bette's friends from her vaudeville days, was a pianist, backed up by his drummer and trumpeter. I can still picture him: fingers flying across the keyboard, legs pounding up and down on the pedals like he was dancing along with us, his face bright red, and always a Scotch on the rocks on top of the piano, quivering in time to the music.

Miss Bette consistently choreographed the most fabulous routines for us, with more than fifty numbers for every recital. Every individual dance had a theme. Miss Bette had us in hats and feathers, down on our haunches, kicking our legs out like Russian Cossacks. The next time you saw us, we were dancing with toy sabers, battling one another onstage; or swaying in hula skirts; or marching about dressed as Christmas presents, with our arms and legs sticking out of cardboard boxes. I remember dancing on roller skates with the back wheels locked, like Fred Astaire and Ginger Rogers in *Shall We Dance*. In my very favorite routine, we danced out onstage carrying little wooden suitcases and then set them down and tapped right on top of them.

In many ways, I had a fairly ordinary childhood. I spent time with my parents and my cousins. I went to school. I did my homework. But when the recital came around, my life was the opposite of ordinary. Dancing in front of an audience meant getting dressed up and looking my best. It was an event. I was actually allowed to wear makeup: red lipstick and rouge, so that even the people in the back row would be able to see me smiling. I felt happy, glamorous, and special.

There was one rule during showtime: no matter what happened, we had to keep dancing. I remember being eight years old and performing a solo to the song "Hernando's Hideaway." I was about to start a complicated series of eight fast turns, but when I pivoted to the right, my left shoe fell off and flew across the stage! I didn't stop dancing; I didn't even blink. I carried on, even with one shoe on and one shoe off. "Just keep dancing!" I told myself. When my solo was over, the crowd was on its feet. Afterward Miss Bette gave me a hug and exclaimed, "I told you if something happens, the show must go on!" Looking back, I can see that she wasn't just teaching us to dance, she was teaching us how to be confident and to keep calm in any circumstance. To this day, I have no problem getting up in front of people and speaking or performing, and I credit Miss Bette for that.

I was a good little dancer. Maybe I could have gone professional. But from an early age, I knew this wasn't my destiny. Everyone told me there was one major obstacle standing in my way if I wanted to be a dancer on Broadway. To dance in musicals, you needed to dance, act, *and* sing. And although my acting abilities were fine, singing was another matter. I couldn't carry a tune to save my life. Every time I opened my mouth to sing a note, it was completely off-key. Although a career in the chorus line clearly wasn't going to be an option for me, I don't remember feeling disappointed about this. I was a young girl who loved to dance, and so I kept dancing for dancing's sake. Maybe it helped me to enjoy my classes even more—I wasn't dancing to make it big; I was dancing because it made me happy.

I knew I was a good dancer and that I loved to perform, but as it turned out, there was something else I needed to do even more than that.

When I was a little girl, my grandmother lived nearby, and her house had a small front porch. I remember sitting there with my cousins, and when the neighborhood kids came by, more often than not, they'd ask me to teach them some of the steps I'd learned at dance class. I'd hop up and start showing them my moves. A tap step, an arabesque from ballet, a cartwheel. One year, when I was about eight or nine, I'd gone with my cousin Denny to a carnival in town. We'd each won a long orange-and-yellow-striped wooden cane at the fairground, and I decided to incorporate it into a dance routine. When our friends on the block saw our canes, they ran off to win the exact same prize so that they could be in Vicki's "recital." I choreographed a routine for us, and coached everyone to learn the steps and dance in unison. Later that day, we performed for our parents, along with anyone else we could drag in off the street. I guess you could say this was my first ever "spring show."

Most of the children in my hometown came from big families with four or five kids. The little houses on the narrow streets of Steelton were crammed so closely together that when I would eat my cereal at the break-fast table, I could chat with the boy next door without ever having to open the window. As children we had the run of the streets. Nothing was off-limits. At nine thirty in the evening, the town's curfew alarm sounded and we all went home. It was such a small town, and we lived so close to one another, that we all felt connected.

Most parents from Steelton couldn't pay for extra activities like dance class. I was an only child, and as a result, my parents only had to find enough money for one. I was always conscious that I was lucky enough to have a little bit more than my cousins and neighbors. This motivated me to share what I had with the other children I knew—including my dancing. It was the most natural thing in the world for me to go from enjoying dance to helping others enjoy it too.

Miss Bette was quick to notice the teacher in me and to nurture it. One day when I was about nine years old, she asked me to stay after class because she needed to ask me something. Miss Bette never joked around or engaged much in conversation with her students, so when she singled me out, I leapt to attention.

"Will you help me teach little Debbie?" she asked me.

Miss Bette explained that Debbie Waltz was a little girl in the four-year-old class and she was struggling because she'd started classes a month later than the other girls.

"There are too many other students in class for me to give her the one-on-one attention she needs," said Miss Bette. "Can you stay behind to take her through the basics and get her up to speed?"

Over the next few weeks, I taught Debbie in the studio's dressing room before class. I was in fourth grade at the time, only five years older than Debbie, but Miss Bette had taught me so well that I knew my steps like they were written in my bones. Step-by-step, I showed her how to move her feet. I stood beside her, holding her hand to make sure she was steady and because I felt that this would help her to pay better attention to me. I showed her how to move her head and her arms and how to combine this with her footwork.

After only a few sessions, Debbie began to put the steps together. She found her tap feet and was smiling from ear to ear. It's a moment I'll never forget.

When Mrs. Waltz saw that her daughter was improving, she asked me to come over to their house to give Debbie extra lessons. She asked my mother if she could pay me, and after that, I made $1 a class. Little Debbie started to enjoy her classes, and she began listening closely to Miss Bette. Now that she was no longer struggling, she started taking every kind of dance the academy offered. Her confidence soared. During our recital, Miss Bette always put the best girl up front so that the others could follow her footwork. The year after I started teaching her, Debbie Waltz was front and center, tapping to "Animal Crackers in My Soup," the song made famous by Shirley Temple.

At the early age of nine, I learned how good it feels to help someone become a dancer and to earn your own money while doing it. Teaching Debbie was my first paying job, and that dollar bill in my pocket as her mom drove me home made me feel like a millionaire.

Before long, I got a chance to teach my entire class. One day when I was around eleven, I arrived for my tap lesson, but Miss Bette was nowhere to be seen. One of the other instructors told me to go into the bar across the street to find her. Neither of my parents drank, so I'd never been in a bar before. It was smoky and dark inside, and I found Miss Bette in a corner with a beer in hand.

"Miss Bette," I said, "it's time for class."

She looked up, then looked at her beer again.

"Go back and start teaching for me," she said. "I'll be over in a few minutes."

At the time, I couldn't figure out why Miss Bette needed to stay in the bar. Obviously, Miss Bette just wanted to finish her beer.

I ran back to the studio and started to teach the class at the same point where she'd left off the week before. I remember feeling like this was a huge responsibility, but at the same time I was very comfortable with the role, even though it only lasted a few minutes. None of the other students seemed to mind that Miss Bette was late, and so we just got to work. When our teacher came back into class, I jumped back into the line. That afternoon, when she walked over to me and put her hand on my shoulder, I knew it was her private way of thanking me.

As I transitioned into junior high school, everything that I learned from Miss Bette became even more valuable to me. When I was in seventh grade, I was chosen for my school's majorette squad. At the first practice, the head majorette came up to me, wrapped her arm around my shoulder, and asked, "Vicki, why don't you go to that tree over there and come up with a new routine for us?" Although she was a senior, she must have known that I was the only girl on the squad with formal training.

I was so excited that a senior—and the head majorette, to boot—had picked me to help her that I ran straight over to the tree and got to work. A half hour later, I ran back over to the girls and began teaching them the steps. Our new routine featured plenty of twirling, but I made sure that I added some extra dance moves to help us stand out on the football field.

Life was good. I loved my dancing, loved being a majorette, and I was finding that I loved to teach others to dance.

And then it hit.

I was fourteen, and my mom was at an all-star bowling tournament in San Bernardino, California, when she got a call from her boss.

"Char, I think you better come home now," he said. "Vic's been taken ill."

Dad had passed out at work and was rushed to the hospital. He was jaundiced. The doctors were sure that he had kidney stones, and so they went ahead and scheduled the operation. My mom rushed home that same day.

"Everything's going to be fine," the doctor told us.

The day of my dad's surgery, we trusted that the doctor was right and felt optimistic. We kissed my dad, wished him luck, and went back downstairs to figure out how to distract ourselves while he was in surgery.

"Why don't we go shopping?" my mom asked.

Pomeroys, our local department store, was only a few blocks from the hospital, and Mom had some money left over from her world championship winnings. That day, we bought a brand-new living room set, complete with lamps, curtains, a bench, an ottoman, and a sectional couch: a beautiful, low, modern model that was dark brown with tan- and cream-striped accents. We knew that Daddy would love it. The two of us hurried back to the hospital so we could be there when he was brought out of surgery. We wanted to tell him about the new furniture!

The doctor came looking for us shortly after we returned, and the expression on his face told us that something was terribly wrong. It wasn't kidney stones after all. It was liver cancer, and it was advanced. He was in a coma.

Two weeks after he'd entered the hospital, we got a call in the middle of the night telling us that he had passed. In the days after my father's death, I couldn't process that he was gone and that I was never going to see him again. The morning after his viewing, there was a massive snowstorm, and we had to wait three days before we could bury him. The day of the funeral, all of my dad's colleagues came to pay their respects. They arrived straight from work, and when they walked into the funeral home, they were still wearing their uniforms. They looked just like my father did every day when he went to work as a security guard. So where was *my* dad? Where had *he* gone?

At first there were so many people at the house, bringing us food and offering condolences, that I felt more confused than sad. It was only when they all went back to their lives and my mom went back to work that I found myself coming home from school to an empty house for the first time in my life. My dad's job had allowed him to finish work midafternoon. After school each day, we'd spend the afternoon together. We'd talk, go out in the yard to throw a softball around, or watch American Bandstand on TV together. My father had been a hands-on dad at a time when most men didn't even change diapers. He'd been so present in my life that those long afternoons at home alone were like a knife to my heart.

I was old enough to know that I had to be strong for my mother. I didn't want to add to her sadness by crying in front of her. But when I came home from school each day and found Dad's favorite chair in the living room sitting empty, I lay down on our new couch—the one I'd helped my mother pick out the day of his surgery—and let the tears flow without stopping.

After my dad died, my world stopped turning. I'd lost my hero. I didn't know who I was without my father. I'm still trying to figure that out.

Chapter 3

• • •

Sunday, June 12, 2011

9:15 AM

I WALK PAST THE BATHROOM AT THE FAR LEFT OF THE STAGE, ON MY WAY TO DO ONE FINAL CHECK ON THE T-SHIRTS THE DANCERS WILL BE WEARING DURING THE SHOW TODAY. THROUGH THE DOORWAY, I SEE ANNI AND BETSY COMPARING EYE SHADOW IN THE BATHROOM MIRROR. BETSY LOOKS UP AT ME AND GRINS. SHE IMMEDIATELY HOLDS OUT HER HANDS AND WIGGLES HER FINGERS SO THAT I CAN SEE HER BRIGHT RED MANICURE.

"Anni did it for me," she says.

"I love it," I tell her, as I wave my fingers in the air, showing her my own red nails.

Our costumes for the show are simple. No skinny leotards for us—not at our age. We wear black dress pants, with a strip of black sequins down the side, colored T-shirts, and different accessories for each routine. To help us stand out onstage, I also ask that all the ladies put on bright red nail polish, red lipstick, and gold hoop earrings.

Of course, some dancers protest about the regulation makeup and jewelry:

"I never wear makeup!"

"I don't have pierced ears!"

"They probably don't even sell gold hoop clip-on earrings!"

"I don't even wear lipstick, and now I have to wear red!"

"Just do it for me," I say. "You can wipe that red lipstick off your face, and the gold hoops come off your ears. But when you're onstage, you'll feel the difference: you're going to feel glamorous, ready to perform." In other words, it doesn't matter what your personal style is or how old you are; when everyone wears the same accents, everyone feels part of the same team. And although there are girls who complain before the show, I don't remember anyone complaining afterward.

Betsy is one of the dancers who at first was nervous about wearing makeup.

"I never wear makeup," she told me. "But I'll do it for you and for the Tap Pups."

I can still picture Betsy when she first came to class four years ago. She was so timid, with glasses on her nose, and blond hair. Sure enough, Betsy went straight to the back line, and each time I gave her advice on how to improve a step, she would just look at me with her big eyes and not say a word. Then when she'd mastered it, I'd hear her call out from the back row in a breathless, excited voice, "Oh my goodness, I got it! I really got it!"

The majority of my dancers have never taken a single class before joining the Tap Pups, and this was true of Betsy. As a little girl, she used to put on her bathing suit and strike Rockette poses in front of the bedroom mirror, but she never managed to persuade her mother to take her to classes. Her family put such emphasis on academics that dance was considered unimportant.

Betsy was a smart little girl and always did well at school, even though she was painfully shy. After graduating college as a science major, she got a job as a microbiologist in a lab at Cornell University. Soon after, she met her husband and returned to school, getting her certification as a high school teacher. The couple moved to a rural area outside of Harrisburg, where Betsy was put in charge of developing the gifted program at a secondary school, and where she became mother to two boys.

Betsy was fifty-six, with her sons in college, when she happened to be looking for the movie times in the local newspaper one day. That's when she saw an advertisement for my classes.

The dancer inside Betsy finally got her wake-up call.

"When I get back from the movie, I'm enrolling in tap class!" she told her husband.

Betsy started coming to class on Thursday nights, but before long, she was having such a good time that she enrolled in two a week. By her own admission, Betsy has always been a wallflower. She would cross the street rather than say hello to someone. Now Betsy was staying behind after tap class to socialize with the other dancers. She started coming to our "Tap Jams," social gatherings where the dancers can tap together and meet other dancers at all levels. When a group of Tap Pups went to see the musical *Billy Elliot* on Broadway, Betsy joined them.

As I came to know Betsy, I learned that her personality was very different from how she seemed at first. Although she was definitely on the shy side, she was opinionated. She was fun. Betsy was one of those people who smiled with her entire face: eyes sparkling, nose crinkling. After wearing makeup in her first spring show, Betsy started wearing eye shadow on a regular basis.

"I love how it makes me feel!" she told me, as if eye shadow were a special secret that no one had ever shared with her.

The year after she started dancing, Betsy took a trip to visit her husband's aunt in Philadelphia, someone she hadn't seen in about three or four years. When the aunt opened the door, her jaw dropped.

"Oh my goodness, what happened to you?" the woman asked Betsy. "You look fabulous. You look ten years younger!"

Betsy's students at school noticed the difference too. They started calling her "DQ," the Dancing Queen. By the end of her first year, she came to the studio showing off a brand-new pair of reddish-orange patent leather heels.

"I've never worn heels in my life!" she admitted. "It's like there's always been this showman inside me who has been waiting to get out!"

At the age of fifty-six, Betsy had tried something new and succeeded at it. With every step that she conquered, she gained the confidence to try another step and another. She was spending time with a group of people who accepted her and encouraged her newfound style. Hugs and praise are a big part of the Tap Pups' culture and so is the belief that every dancer in the program is capable of fulfilling his or her potential, in whatever form that takes.

Betsy's new outward appearance only hinted at her changed perspective. For some time, she had been considering pursuing a master's degree at a college in downtown Harrisburg.

"I live outside town, and I hate to drive," Betsy explained to me. "I was certain that all the driving was going to be too much for me. I'm fifty-six years old, and I really thought that I was getting too old to do something so far outside of my comfort zone."

After she started tap, Betsy realized that if she could take that step, she was capable of earning her master's. She got into her school of choice, and four years later, Betsy is on the verge of completing her thesis. At the age of sixty, she's even thinking of changing jobs and transitioning into the corporate world as a consultant.

Betsy isn't the only dancer who's taken on a new challenge as a result of coming to classes. Suzi, an attractive, vivacious sixty-year-old, went back to work as a legal secretary after years of staying home due mainly to a lack of self-belief. And Jim, one of the male dancers in today's show—who describes himself as "shy since birth"—credits dance with giving him the confidence to travel to China for work.

For each of these dancers, the biggest step was the first step: coming to a class. In each case, the confidence was there within. It just took a nudge to bring it out.

AFTER my dad died, to a certain extent, day-to-day life resumed. My mom went on with her bowling tours. I was often alone at home. They say time heals, and I was so young that I guess on some level, I just accepted that this had happened to me. I got on with things. I was such a good girl as a teenager. I knew I couldn't let my mom down. But every time I accomplished something, my first thought was: "Oh, I wish my dad could be here to see this!" I learned that you don't miss someone *less* as time goes on. You miss them more, because you have to experience their absence over and over again. Every Father's Day, every Christmas, every birthday since, I've missed my dad. To this day, when I hear his favorite song, "Sentimental Journey," I'm brought to the edge of tears.

At fourteen, my life changed in other ways too. I danced in one more recital with Miss Bette and then stopped going to her classes. Miss Bette and my mother begged me to stay, but I was growing up, and most girls I knew were dropping out of dance class at that age. We had reached the point when our lives revolved around school and socializing with friends. Dance class was for little girls.

We had begun to discover boys. The year before Dad's death, I started dating my high school sweetheart, Bull. I was thirteen years old when I had my first kiss, and Bull was my guy. He was a year ahead of me in school, tall, with dark brown hair like my dad's. Bull was popular, was voted class clown, and was a great dancer. He played football and basketball, but baseball was his real talent. A southpaw, he was scouted by and tried out for the Boston Red Sox. Not too surprising, my dad loved Bull, who represented the athletic son he'd always wanted.

The scene of my first kiss with Bull was an outdoor dance on the tennis courts by our school. The DJ was playing "Goodnight Sweetheart, Goodnight" by the Spaniels, which everyone knew was the last dance of the evening. As the song ended, Bull made his move. He was taller by a foot but just as inexperienced. As he bent down to kiss me, he didn't judge the angle well—his lips bumped into mine, crushing them against my teeth. My new boyfriend was so nervous he immediately pulled away, mumbled good night, and bolted from the dance floor. I was left standing there by myself in the middle of the tennis court, completely starry eyed, convinced that I'd just had the most romantic experience of my life.

From then on, Bull would come to my house, and we would hang out, listening to records while I taught him how to dance. These were the days when almost all boys danced, and Bull turned out to be very good. A few of the guys we knew didn't think it was cool to dance fast (either that, or they were worried they wouldn't be able to do the steps), and so they only wanted to slow dance. I was always proud that my boyfriend could jitterbug and cha-cha with the best of them.

Every week on Friday and Saturday nights, my best friend, Mary, and I would get dressed up in our matching "Ben Casey blouses"—inspired by the scrubs worn by the famous Dr. Casey on TV—and Bandstand skirts (A-line with four buttons down the side) and meet our boyfriends at Progress Firehouse. It was an old two-story fire hall where we all went to dance in high school. As soon as you walked inside, you'd see kids from eight or ten high schools: John Harris, William Penn, Bishop McDevitt, Central Dauphin, CD East, Cedar Cliff, Middletown, and my school, Steel-High—the names still run off my tongue. From week to week, all the high school groups kept to their own "designated" spots around the dance floor. There were two DJs, one for each floor, but Steel-High kids liked the guy downstairs. He was from WKBO, the local radio station, and he played all the new records and made us laugh, cracking jokes between tunes.

This was the early 1960s, and many songs had dances that went along with them: for instance, "The Stroll," "The Twist," "The Jerk," "Bristol Stomp," "Madison Time." Dance was how we expressed ourselves. Out on the dance floor, with everyone doing the same steps, we never wanted it to stop. Each school seemed to have a way of making the steps its own. If you did a triple step and added a small kick before the back step when you jitterbugged, that meant you were probably a Steel-High kid. We had a code about almost everything. If you laced your shoelaces upside down, tied by the toes, you were going steady. One lace tied at the top and one tied at the toes signaled that you were unattached.

My laces were tied upside down throughout my teens. I loved Bull. I loved when we jitterbugged to Frankie Ford's "Sea Cruise" or did the cha-cha to "My Girl" by the Temptations. Our favorite slow dance was "A Million to One" by Jimmy Charles and the Revelettes. The first day I got braces, when I was fifteen, we were slow dancing at a dance in the school gym. Bull said something funny—I can't remember what. Well, he was so tall that my head reached only his chest, and when I laughed, my braces got caught on his sweater. I was so young and nervous that I panicked, and as I tried to disentangle myself, I pulled a few threads out of his sweater. Bull also panicked, since he was wearing his brother's new sweater that night and hadn't asked permission to borrow it. We were so young, and our relationship was so innocent. About the steamiest thing we ever did was go on a hayride together and make out under a blanket, on top of a bale of hay.

When I wasn't with Bull or my friends, I was busy in school. I was a good and enthusiastic student. I joined every club. I was treasurer of the student council. I was in the Future Secretaries and Future Nurses clubs. (Truthfully, I never wanted to be a nurse, but all of my friends were in the club, so I wanted to be in it too.) I was in the Library Club. I became the Youth Festival Committee chair, the Prom Committee chair, and was on the yearbook staff. And, of course, I continued on the majorette squad, choreographing the half-time routines.

I was fourteen when the school band director took me aside one day.

"Vicki," he said, "I know you're good at acrobatics, so I'm pulling you out of the line and making you a solo acrobatic majorette." I have to admit that I wasn't the least bit excited about this idea. For one thing, I worried that the older girls would resent me. This was still so soon after my dad had passed away, and the last thing I needed was social problems.

"Please don't do this to me," I begged him. "The older girls should get the solos, not me."

As it turned out, the band director wasn't giving me a choice.

"This isn't a request, Vicki," he told me. "That is what's going to happen."

For the next year, I performed as a soloist in the squad. Much to my relief, none of the other girls gave me a hard time about it. Although I was no longer taking classes from Miss Bette, everything I'd learned from her helped me so much. Thanks to dance, I had confidence. I was able to carry my head high and strut out in front of large audiences without fear. By my senior year, I was head majorette, marching out at half-time to lead the band, a giant white feather plume in my hat with royal blue on the tips, with a short white skirt with white fringe around the hem and matching royal blue braiding on the bodice. During my solo, I'd twirl two and even three batons—my pièce de résistance was fire twirling, with flaming batons swirling all around me. After the devastation of losing my dad so young, being head majorette was one of the highlights of my teenage life, like getting elected class president and winning homecoming queen all rolled into one.

As graduation approached, I knew I had to decide what came next for me. But I don't remember being particularly concerned. It was 1964. Most young women got married not long after high school, and the ones who didn't get married right away became secretaries while they waited. About the most glamorous career any of us could imagine was being an airline stewardess.

I never seriously considered college. In my town, the girls who went to college trained to be nurses or schoolteachers, and neither of those professions appealed to me. My mother would have loved for me to go; like most parents at that time, she hoped I would meet a nice husband if I went to college, but I didn't feel like that was enough of a reason to apply. After all, I'd already found my nice future husband: Bull. Instead, I planned to get a job as a secretary. Just a few miles from Steelton were the giant municipal buildings of Harrisburg, filled with hundreds of offices and departments relying on thousands of state workers. In an era before computers, every department needed armies of girls who knew how to type, do shorthand, take dictation, transcribe minutes, and do bookkeeping. The men ran the departments, and the women ran around after them. At age seventeen, I loved the idea of wearing smart and glamorous outfits to a busy office every day, and if my boss was handsome, all the better. Like a lot of girls my age, I'd taken classes in shorthand, bookkeeping, and typing at school. My senior year, I took the state department's civil service test, so that as soon as I graduated, I could send in my application for the right entry-level job for my abilities.

I just assumed that I'd work for a while as a secretary, and then Bull and I would get married. Although we weren't officially engaged, Bull gave me a little gold promise ring. I wore it around my neck until he got his senior class ring—I don't think he even wore that class ring one full day before he asked me to wear it for him. I can still remember how proud that made me feel. During our senior year, my friend Mary was already planning her wedding to her high school sweetheart. My other girlfriends were either about to get married or about to be engaged.

I knew I wanted to spend one last summer hanging out with Bull and my friends before I started working. Then, two weeks after graduation, the phone rang. It was the mother of a little girl from Steelton.

"Vicki," she said. "Now that you've graduated, could I pay you to teach my daughter how to twirl a baton?"

The woman must have seen me perform as head majorette and wanted me to teach her daughter to do the same. We arranged for a private session later that week.

Five minutes later, another mother called with the same request. She'd heard from the first mother that I'd started teaching now that I'd graduated high school. Word spread, and within thirty minutes I had seven students.

At that moment, a giant lightbulb went off in my head.

I called my mother at work.

"Mom, I know exactly what I want to do with the rest of my life," I said. "I want to open a dance studio. I want to teach the kids of Steelton how to dance!"

"Let's do it!" was my mom's immediate reply.

If I was going to be an instructor, I knew I wanted to teach more than baton twirling. I wanted to teach tap, jazz, ballet, and acrobatics too. I had studied all these forms of dance with Miss Bette from the age of four until I was fourteen, and although it had been nearly three years since I'd stopped going to dance school, I knew I was so well trained that the steps would immediately come back to me. Mom found a place in Philadelphia—Jay Dash Studios—where I could get certified as a dance instructor, so that's what I did.

I couldn't believe I hadn't thought about doing this before. It was the most natural thing for me to go from dancing to helping others find their dancing feet. Around this time, I remember calling Miss Bette to tell her that I was opening up my own studio, and asking her whether that was okay, since our studios would be only five miles apart. Miss Bette didn't skip a beat. She told me how proud she would be for me to have my own studio and that she thought I was going to be an excellent teacher. She also gave me the best advice I ever got about how to teach:

"Remember, Vicki, never assume your students know what you know."

I knew exactly what she meant. Going forward, I would break down every small detail for my students, explaining it all in clear and simple terms.

Soon after I became certified, I found the perfect location for my studio. Someone told me about a vacant space on Front Street: an old shop where they used to engrave headstones, right next door to a photography studio. Never mind that there was still a big metal hook lodged in the ceiling for hanging the granite while they did the engraving. The space had everything I needed, including a room in the back that I converted into my dressing room. The rent was $50 a month, and I had graduation money to pay for the first month. The landlord waived the deposit because he wanted to send his daughters to my classes. My aunt had her friends at the steel mill make metal ballet barres for me. We gave the walls a fresh coat of white paint and installed mirrors. I decided to name my business Vicki's Studio of Rhythm.

Almost every small town in the area had a dance studio back then, Steelton included. The one studio in Steelton was in the east end of town; mine was right in the middle, so that every child could walk there easily. When my studio was nearly ready, I began my own marketing campaign. I got out the local telephone book and called every family that I knew had small children, letting them know that I was opening my own studio. Meanwhile, my mother made me a black-and-white flier that she had copied. I pinned dozens of them to telephone poles and bulletin boards around town. They read:

Vicki's Studio of Rhythm. Classes in tap, ballet, jazz, baton, and acrobatics. Introductory meeting, please bring your children. August 17, 1964, 6:00 P.M.

Three weeks before I opened my doors, I held my introductory meeting at my new studio. I wanted to reassure parents that they could trust me to look after their children; after all, at the age of eighteen, I was only a few years older than some of their sons and daughters! I borrowed folding chairs from a local social hall, set them up in neat rows, and waited for people to arrive. About fifty parents and their children came to see the studio and hear me speak.

"Welcome to Vicki's Studio of Rhythm," I told the packed room, "where every child in Steelton can now have the opportunity to learn how to dance!"

I explained that I'd been one of the lucky Steelton girls who'd taken dance classes. Not everyone had gotten the same chance, and the idea that some kids couldn't afford to attend dance class bothered me. As a result, my classes were going to be reasonably priced: $3.50 per month, and a reduced rate of $6.00 for two classes a week per month. At the reduced fee, that came out to 75 cents a class.

Almost every one of the parents present signed up at least one child for classes. By evening's end, I had students from all over town, ranging in age from three to fourteen.

Classes would be held on Monday and Wednesday evenings (for older kids), and Saturday mornings (for younger children). Although I was excited about opening my studio, I was also practical. I knew that if I wanted to build this into a viable business, especially while charging so little, then I was going to have to get a day job to help pay my bills and to have health benefits. I got a secretarial position at the local redevelopment authority. After work on Mondays and Wednesdays, I would drive from my office five minutes away to my studio and change into one of my dance outfits. I had a collection of leotards in every color—yellow, red, kelly green, powder blue, black with white trim, and aqua, which has been my favorite color since childhood—with matching tights, and either a little chiffon dancing skirt or a tiny patent leather belt around my waist. Matching dance shoes completed almost every outfit.

Although I taught ballet, twirling, and acrobatics, my favorite classes were jazz and tap. These classes were always the most popular, and no wonder. Tap was loud: you pounded your feet in rhythm. Jazz was exciting: you got to do leaps, splits, and to shake your shoulders. These classes also had the best music. Every month I went out and bought a few albums to play on my record player at the studio—everything from big band classics to the latest movie theme songs from *Goldfinger* and *My Fair Lady*.

I started with seventy-five students. My tiny studio was buzzing with children and their parents on Saturdays. Each one of these little girls had her own personality and quirks, and I loved learning what each child needed from me. Although I was young, I had an instinct for the right way to handle each situation, even telling parents of the three-year-olds in my baby class that they had to come in and learn what had been taught that day so they could practice with their children at home. I remember looking over a group of little girls sitting on the floor in a circle in their leotards, giggling together, and I realized I'd created my very own unique version of what Miss Bette had given me as a child.

Like any teacher, I had my star pupils, the ones who were so naturally talented that they were a dream to teach. LuAnne Sprow was one of those. She was eleven years old, tall and slender, cute as anything, with a dancer's natural grace and rhythm. Smart, with a bubbly personality, she quickly became a leader in her class and at all our recitals. At first she excelled at ballet, but soon enough it became clear that tap and jazz were her true talents.

LuAnne became a permanent fixture at my studio, helping me look after the space and becoming one of my student teachers.

Forry Gehret was the son of the family that owned the photography studio next door. They lived above it, so all he had to do was run downstairs, out the door, and two seconds later, he was at class. He was only five years old when he started coming to me, but I knew from that first class that Forry was gifted. He had such a natural ability to pick up steps, it was astonishing, and when he danced, he never stopped smiling. I started putting him in front of the class so that every little girl would follow his footwork, and by the end of the first year, I'd dubbed my little Forry "the Gene Kelly of Steelton."

Of course, other dancers took a little longer to draw out. One of them was Debbie Cuckovic, who started with me when she was eight years old. Along with several other girls, she always stayed behind to help me clean up the studio. Dark haired and dark eyed, Debbie was the youngest in her family, with three older brothers. She was a happy little girl, but when she danced, she often looked so serious. One day after class, it was obvious that she wanted to share something with me.

"Miss Vicki," she told me, "coming to dance class is the best thing I do all week. It's the only thing I do where my brothers stay home. I feel so pretty, and I just want to get the steps right for you."

"Do you have any idea how much prettier you'd feel inside if you let yourself smile?" I asked her. After that, whenever I looked over at Debbie in class, I would give her a wink, and she always smiled right back.

One day at the end of class, a tiny little nine-year-old dancer named Liz Smith burst into tears. I was so surprised to see her cry. I knew she loved her classes, because she always walked into the studio with a sweet smile that seemed to say, "Look at me! I'm at dance class!" Every time I saw Liz, I always wanted to give her an extra little hug.

"What's wrong?" I asked Liz, with my arm around her shoulder, trying to calm her down.

"My mother says I can't come back to class next week! This is my last class!" She wept.

It turned out that Liz's mother had told her that they couldn't afford to pay for classes anymore.

"You go home and tell your mother that you're coming to class next week," I told Liz. "Everything will be okay."

Liz's face looked like sunshine after a cloudburst. I never sent her mother another bill, and she never missed a single class. The following year, Liz's mother was in the hospital and couldn't attend the recital, but Liz performed anyway. I later found out that she walked a mile and a half across town to get there by herself.

Liz's family wasn't the only one struggling financially. I also helped the Moure sisters, Vicki Lee, Cathy, and Darla. Their mother was a good friend of my mom's, so I knew her story. She was a single mom working two jobs to support her family. I never charged her. At the end of that first year, when we were preparing for the recital, the Moure sisters showed up to rehearsal without their regulation fishnet stockings. I'd decided that black fishnets were going to be part of the Studio of Rhythm's performance costume—all the girls wore them in all of my recitals and for rehearsals too. Their mom didn't have the extra money for the official fishnet stockings.

At the studio, I heard two other students comment about the Moure sisters' bare legs. The girls' cheeks turned bright red, and the eldest, Vicki Lee, had tears in her eyes.

I spun around.

"Not everybody needs the fishnets right now," I said. "These girls will have them when they need them."

After rehearsal, I walked up to the sisters, gave all three a gentle squeeze on the shoulder, and winked. I wanted them to know that everything was going to be okay. At the next rehearsal, I made sure to have three extra pairs of fishnets waiting for them. Those stockings probably cost no more than $3, and it was worth every cent to see the smiles on the girls' faces.

In many ways, these girls were the reason I was running my studio. I wanted everyone to be able to benefit from learning to dance, not just the lucky few. And now that they were dancing with me, it wasn't just about learning the steps. Although Forry could have gone professional, and Lu-Anne definitely had a shot, I knew that most of the children in my classes weren't going to become dancers on Broadway. That wasn't the point. I believed dance would help them to become confident and poised young women and men. Through dance, I was sending them the message that it doesn't matter where you come from, or how much money your family makes; you have a reason to hold your head up, put your shoulders back, and feel good about who you are inside. Every year, we took part in Steelton's Halloween parade. I had everyone dressed in little marching outfits, which were aqua with a big white V on the front. Even back then, I had the dancers wear red lipstick, and a dab of rouge, so they would stand out in the crowd. The girls would march, dance, twirl, and even do acrobatics, which always got the biggest cheers from the people who gathered to watch us go by. My girls loved to get dressed up and strut their stuff in front of their family and friends. It gave them such confidence to have those experiences. I wanted these girls to go on to be their school majorettes and cheerleaders, to be presidents of their classes, to be able to speak in public and to live up to their fullest potential. Performing in the parade was going to help lay the foundation for that.

By the end of that first year, I'd doubled my initial enrollment from seventy-five students to a hundred and fifty. People from the area called the

West Shore, on the other side of the Susquehanna River, were coming to my studio. Classes were so full that already I had to move to a larger location three blocks uptown on Front Street. I found a ballroom-size space on the third floor above the local appliance store. It was beautiful, with a sleek hardwood floor that was ideal for dancing. The entrance led to a narrow fifty-foot-long hallway with hooks for coats and bags. The main dance floor was off the hallway, and then there was a small studio where LuAnne and my other student teachers could give special attention to children who needed a little extra help. On Saturdays I'd teach eight half-hour classes in the morning; then my regulars would hang around to help me clean up. In return, I would give them a few dollars to go two doors down to Ray's Luncheonette to grab us some sandwiches. I'd sit at my desk, and my girls would gather around me as we shared lunch together. Saturdays were when the dancers really bonded with one another and made friendships outside of their school cliques.

The year after I opened my studio, I attended a national dance teachers' conference in Philadelphia, bringing my student teacher LuAnne with me. She won the award for the Best Jazz Dancer in the student teacher category, and I won the Best Jazz Dancer and Most Congenial in the instructor category. I remember looking around and realizing that at the age of nineteen, I was running my own business and already receiving recognition for my teaching. My studio's theme song was the Gershwin classic "I Got Rhythm," and it was appropriate. Right out of high school, I'd found my rhythm in life, and I felt so proud that I was helping others do the same.

Chapter 4

• • •

Sunday, June 12, 2011
9:25 AM

"FIVE MINUTES TO REHEARSALS!" I CALL OUT, AND HEAD BACK
TOWARD STAGE RIGHT AND THE MEN'S LOCKER ROOM, TO CHECK
IN ON THE INTERMEDIATE GROUP. THANKS TO THESE LADIES,
A LOCKER ROOM THAT'S USUALLY HOME TO THE MEN OF THE
HARRISBURG SYMPHONY ORCHESTRA HAS NOW BEEN TRANS-
FORMED INTO A BOUDOIR, WITH MAKEUP, CHIFFON SCARVES,
AND FEATHER HEADDRESSES SPILLING OVER EVERY SURFACE.

All the dancers bring food for the day to share among the group, but
it looks like the Intermediates have brought enough to keep them going
for the next week. The counter in the small dressing room next door is
covered with food in foil trays: cheese and crackers, wraps, veggies, fruit,
chips, and nuts.

"Can I grab a water?" I ask, and a dozen voices call back. "Yes! Look
how much we have!"

I lean on the doorway and take a sip.

"Miss Vicki! You have to see this!" calls out Erica, a gorgeous, long-
haired girl in her early thirties. She points to the men's urinal. Space is so

tight in this makeshift dressing room that Erica is using it to hang up her costumes in suit bags, with her curling iron lying on top of it.

I have several thirtysomethings in the Intermediate class, and two of them, Loni and Erin, have decided to bring along a boom box. Music is blaring, and at nine in the morning, the atmosphere in the crowded locker room is more like a party. These ladies recently told me that they call themselves the VIPs: Vicki's Intermediate Pups.

In the middle of this group are Karen and Laura, both thirty years old. Laura is our Julia Roberts look-alike, with the same wide smile and blonde highlights in her brown hair; Karen has red hair, fair skin, and the brightest blue eyes. Laura and Karen first met when they were waitresses in college, and they've been inseparable ever since. Laura's mom, an Advanced dancer, introduced the two of them to our group. We call these girls "the Twins," because when you see one, you see the other.

. . . .

MEET THE DANCERS OF "BANDSTAND BOOGIE"

(THE THEME FROM AMERICAN BANDSTAND)

WATCH LAURA AND KAREN AND OTHER DANCERS IN THE INTERMEDIATE LEVEL DISCUSS TODAY'S PERFORMANCE.

www.youtube.com/vickistappups

. . . .

As I got to know these girls, I've been so impressed with them. They're smart, funny, and wise. They're managing to smoothly combine their careers and interests with motherhood. Laura works in her family's business and has a young son and a daughter, while Karen works in medical equipment sales and had a baby boy earlier this year. Three weeks after giving birth, she was already back in class dancing again. No one can believe how fast she got back her figure and her energy.

Younger dancers like these girls in the Intermediate group tell me that they learn so much from being around the older Tap Pups. What they don't realize is that we learn so much from them. Laura and Karen are wonderful wives and mothers and have successful careers, but they still manage to carve out time for their own interests. These girls understand that by spending one hour a week at tap class, they're taking care of themselves and that their families will benefit from that.

My generation was so different. When the babies arrived, everything else in our lives took a backseat. Our focus was on raising our children, being the wife, mother, chief cook, and bottle washer. Even after the kids have flown the nest, it's very easy for women like us to find reasons to stay home. We were brought up to put everyone else first—our husbands, our children, our homes—and so we happily deprived ourselves even of one hour of class a week as a result.

We're also very good at justifying our decisions to stay home: "I've been meaning to sign up for classes, but I never have the time." "I have too much going on looking after my husband and my grandchildren." "I don't like to drive at night."

I'll never forget one woman I'll call Eve. I met her two years ago when she came into my office just before the first New Beginners class of the season was about to start. She was an attractive lady in her late fifties, and when she told me that she didn't have tap shoes yet, I loaned her a pair.

That morning, everyone did great in class and had big smiles on their faces after it ended. Eve waited until everyone left, then returned to my office.

"Vicki," she said, "do you remember me? I'm the one who has been emailing you for four years. First I registered for class and then had to postpone because my husband needed back surgery and I was taking care of him for over two years. When he was finally able to take care of himself, I tried to register for class, and again I had to cancel, because I was diagnosed with lung cancer."

"Oh, Eve, I do remember you," I said, pressing my hands on my cheeks in surprise.

"I hadn't planned to come here today," she explained. "I was taking a pot roast to my mother-in-law, who lives near here, and when I was diverted because of construction, I happened to see the sign to your studio, so I instantly parked my car to see if you might be here."

"Are you telling me that you just happened to stop by today, ten minutes before a class that was the perfect level for you?"

"Yes," Eve said, laughing, "and I'm so happy to give you this check to finally start my tap dancing lessons!"

We agreed that this was meant to be. Before Eve left, she also had me order a pair of black-and-white tap shoes for her.

The following week, Eve came back for her second class. Once again she seemed to get a lot out of it, and at the end of the class, I went over to chat with her.

"So what did your husband say when you told him you'd signed up for tap?" I asked.

"Vicki," Eve whispered, "I didn't tell one person in my family that I came here today."

"Why not?" I asked, surprised. She had seemed so excited and happy in class.

"My whole life is about doing things for other people," Eve told me. "My husband, my parents, my mother-in-law, my kids. I'm keeping this quiet. This is for me. Then someday I'll whip out my tap shoes and show them all that I can do."

But Eve never got that chance. After a while, she stopped coming to class. Although I tried to call her, I never learned why she didn't come back.

Maybe I'll never know, but it wouldn't surprise me if Eve simply felt too guilty doing something for herself. If this is true, then I know just how she feels. For so many years, if I wasn't doing something for my family, I allowed myself to feel guilty. I hear many of my tappers still have moments when they feel that way, which is why I have to remind them at times about how much we can learn from younger women like Laura and Karen, who have been brought up with choices and who are unapologetic about who they are and what they want to do.

Not so long ago, I learned that Laura and Karen were training to run a half marathon.

"How do you find the time?" I asked.

"We get up at five o'clock and go running when the kids are still sleeping," Karen replied with a laugh. "Our husbands do breakfast."

The first time I met Karen's husband, he was in the lobby of the theater on show day.

"I'm looking for my wife, Karen," he told me. "I thought she might be hungry, so I brought her lunch."

It was a small gesture but one that spoke volumes about the equality of their relationship.

I love to see these younger dancers getting so much out of their lives. When I was coming of age in Steelton in the early 1960s, it was a completely different universe.

AS happy as I was running my studio and teaching my students at the age of eighteen my dreams for the future were clear. There was never any doubt that marriage was my destiny, and that my husband was going to define the course of my life. We all wanted to marry someone who could take care of us, buy us nice clothes, a nice house, nice furniture. If any of us dreamed of a life beyond that, we never spoke of it.

I was such a little lady back then. I don't remember ever leaving the house without my hair done and a matching outfit on. As a young woman, I wore gloves to match my purse, a purse to match my shoes, and plenty of dress hats too—everything had to coordinate. My hair was always "done." Hair back then was all about volume: the bigger the better. We had perms that turned our hair to frizz. We teased our hair. We ratted it, pushed down the ends until our hair sat on top of our heads in a perfect pouf. My nails were always shaped into perfect almonds and painted a bashful pink. I complemented my nails by wearing a shade of Revlon lipstick called Paint the Town Pink. There was no such thing as casual Fridays. The way we looked said everything about who we were and where we were going.

In some of my earliest memories, I can see myself bouncing on my dad's lap while he told me, "Vicki, someday your prince will come." I always dreamed that my prince would arrive, and when he did, he'd look just like John Wayne and dance like Gene Kelly. The message we got from our fathers, we also got from our mothers and our teachers: you're going to be a wife and a mother. In my case, I didn't think to fight the status quo. I wanted to be a wife. I wanted to be a mother. I used to picture Bull and me in one of those little houses up on Cottage Hill by the Steel-High football field, with our two kids, white picket fence, and roses in the front yard. We'd be happy and grow old together. End of story.

As we got nearer to Bull's graduation, though, I started to worry about what our future held. My boyfriend was a year older than me, and I looked to him to lead the way. But Bull was unsure of himself.

"I'll do anything but work at the steel mill," he told me adamantly. Bull hoped to get a baseball scholarship and go to college, and maybe become a professional ball player someday. When that didn't happen, he signed up for an electronics school in Philadelphia. But he figured out quickly that he didn't want to be an electrician. He didn't know what else he wanted to do in life.

Right around the time I opened my studio, Bull came over to my house to tell me his plans.

"Vicki, I enlisted," he said.

I was in shock. I knew boys from my hometown had signed up to join the military, but I never thought that Bull would be one of them.

"But there's a war going on!" I protested. It was 1965, and the conflict in Vietnam had begun to escalate and claim more and more time on the evening news.

"Vicki, I don't know what else to do," he explained. "I really think this is the best thing for me."

I told Bull that he had to stay, that I loved him and that we would figure it out. But he just kept shaking his head. He had already made up his mind. He enlisted and was sent to Vietnam. I remember going down to Philadelphia with his parents to say good-bye. We were all standing by the window at the airport, tears streaming down our cheeks as we watched him board that plane.

For the next year, Bull wrote to me at least twice a week, and I wrote him right back. His letters arrived a full month after he'd mailed them. I'd race to the mailbox every day, waiting to see his handwriting on the envelope. I knew that Bull had been assigned to the military police in Saigon, and that he was in a relatively safe zone, but when he wrote, he told me very little about his day-to-day life. The history books tell me that six thousand American soldiers died in 1966, and another thirty thousand were wounded, but whatever Bull was going through, he kept it to himself.

Instead his letters were all about us. About how much he missed me. How he was counting the days until he saw me again. I wrote back, telling him the latest gossip from Steelton, letting him know that our friends Mary and John were having a baby, that the basketball team was in the state championships again, and about how all the little girls at my Studio of Rhythm missed him almost as much as I did.

The first Christmas he was away, Bull sent me two long silk cheongsam dresses—one yellow and one red—both with mandarin collars and slits on each side from the hip to the ankle, with white silk pants to wear underneath. That spring, at the end of my dancing school's first recital, Bull's mom brought me a huge bunch of roses that he had asked her to give me. The card said, "Wish I could be there with you tonight. Sent with all my love from Vietnam."

Although we weren't officially engaged, everyone assumed that once Bull got home, we would marry.

We never did.

A little while after Bull went overseas, I'd been asked to teach a dance class at the nearby New Cumberland Army Depot. New Cumberland was a holding base where soldiers were stationed before they were deployed, and where they were debriefed before being sent home from Vietnam. Every Wednesday evening, I taught dance to around thirty GIs who wanted to catch up on all the new dances they'd missed while they'd been away. After a couple of months, the woman who'd organized the classes decided to hold a dance party for the men. She advertised in the local newspaper, inviting any girl who was interested to come along and dance with the GIs stationed at the base.

The night of the dance, I was wearing a tight black pencil skirt that reached my calves, a pink cardigan sweater, a black bangle on my wrist, and T-strap flat shoes (perfect for dancing). I was their instructor, so naturally every man there wanted to dance with me. I went from one dancer to the next, and to the next. It was a warm fall evening, and after two hours of dancing nonstop, I decided to go out on the porch for some air. As I tried to get out the door to the porch, I discovered that the furniture that was usually in the common room had been hauled outside to make space for the party. I wasn't going to let that stop me. I hiked up my skirt so that I could crawl under some tables and a few lamps. Finally I stood up and felt the breeze on my face.

I didn't hear anyone following me. Then, all of a sudden, someone tapped me on the shoulder. When I turned around, there was the best-looking man I'd ever seen. He had glossy dark hair cut short, parted to the side, making his blue eyes seem even brighter. He wore a fitted light blue short-sleeve shirt that helped to accentuate his broad shoulders and chest. He was so clean cut, so debonair—the spitting image of Gregory Peck in *Roman Holiday*.

"I've been watching you all evening," he said. "But you were always dancing with someone else. I thought I'd never get my chance."

"I came out to get some air," I told him.

"I know," he said. "I followed you."

I detected a New York accent. I was so flattered that this handsome New Yorker had followed me through a maze of stacked furniture. When he asked me to dance, of course I said yes.

We climbed back through the furniture and walked hand in hand out onto the dance floor. As we danced, we introduced ourselves. His name was Mike Riordan. He'd been stationed at New Cumberland on his way to Vietnam, but a few weeks ago, he'd been hospitalized with a collapsed lung, and it looked like he was going to be given an administrative position here at the base rather than being sent overseas. I'll admit, he didn't have much rhythm. He stepped on my feet. His head stuck out and bobbed about when he danced. But we laughed a lot, and when they played "Goodnight Sweetheart, Goodnight," I remember thinking what a good night this turned out to be.

Mike asked me for my number.

When he called the next day, I explained that my boyfriend was in Saigon, but Mike persuaded me to go out with him as a friend. I wasn't old enough to go to a bar, so we went to a dance at the YMCA. That evening, I learned that Mike had already been out in the world before he'd gotten drafted, carving out a career for himself as an accountant on the Long Island Railroad. He was charming and had this irresistible charisma. There was something about him that made you want to be near him. He was the biggest personality in the room. He said things to me that the Steelton boys would never say to a girl.

That night marked the beginning of Mike's campaign to win me over. In the coming months, he lavished me with gifts and compliments. On Valentine's Day there were a dozen red roses, a dozen white roses, and one pink rose in the center. The card read, "Love is from the heart, it is pure, only for one." It made me feel so special to know that he had singled me out, but I was clear with him: I was Bull's girlfriend, and I was not going to date someone else.

Even so, I couldn't help but compare Mike with Bull. How was life with Bull going to turn out? I still didn't know. A big question mark hung over our future together. Mike, meanwhile, was a few years older and had so many plans, and I began to let myself imagine that I could be a part of them. Mike knew what he wanted out of life. He was going to be a CEO and run his own business. He was going to make a lot of money and own a beautiful apartment in New York City. He said the words that I longed to hear Bull say:

"Vicki, I'm going to take care of you."

I think that need for a man to take care of me was even more intense because I didn't have my dad anymore. Mike was going to climb the corporate ladder, and I loved the idea of being a supportive corporate wife—a Jackie

Kennedy to his corporate JFK. If we got married, we could move to Manhattan, and New York was my favorite city. Every time my mother went to her bowling tournaments there, I'd go along with her, taking open-air bus tours by myself, walking for blocks and blocks, looking in windows, and watching the world go by. New York was fast. It was stylish. All the beautiful people lived there, and now maybe I could be one of them.

Mike must have seen that longing in me and sensed my doubts about Bull, because whenever he talked about his big plans, he included me in them.

"A girl like you deserves to be taken care of," Mike would say. "I'm going to make sure you have everything you've always wanted."

A year went by. I began seeing Mike more and more often. After two years away, Bull wrote saying he was due to come back home now that his tour of duty was over.

I told Mike that my boyfriend, Bull, was going to be back in town soon and that we were going to have to stop seeing each other.

"Vicki, you have to break up with Bull," Mike insisted. "You have to tell him that you're seeing me, that you're my girl now. I want you to write to him and tell him what's going on. It's only fair."

I protested. I wanted to wait until Bull came home. But Mike kept saying that wasn't fair to Bull.

Reluctantly, I wrote to Bull. I didn't want to hurt him, but I didn't want to deceive him either. It had been two years since we'd seen one another. I no longer had any idea how Bull felt about me, and I certainly had a lot of confusion around my feelings for him. Did I want to be with Bull? Did I want to be with Mike? Did I want to be with either of them? I knew I couldn't make up my mind about anything until I saw Bull again. In the letter, I told him that I'd met a guy from New York stationed at New Cumberland but that I wasn't sure what to do. I promised that we would meet up the second Bull returned from Vietnam, sort out our feelings for each other, and try to decide what was right for both of us.

The evening that Bull finally came home after two years away, he drove over to my house and picked me up. He looked so handsome, but the expression on his face told me that he felt just as confused as I did. He took me to a local pizza place for dinner, and I tried to bring up the subject of my letter and what was happening between us.

Bull shook his head. "No, let's see a movie first. We can talk about it later."

"Bull, I don't want to see a movie," I blurted. "We need to talk."

"I'm not ready to talk yet," he insisted. "After the movie."

It was so hard for me to know where Bull was coming from. Did he assume we were picking up where we'd left off? Or did he think everything was over between us? I had no idea. The movie was James Bond's *You Only Live Twice*, but I couldn't concentrate on the action. We sat in total silence. My head was swirling. I knew in my heart that all Bull had to do was pick me up in his arms and tell me that I was his girl. If he still wanted me, I'd never see Mike again. I wanted him to be like 007 and sweep me off my feet. I wanted him to say, "Vicki, you're my girl. You're never seeing that New Yorker again."

After the movie, we got into Bull's car and, finally, we started to talk.

Before long, Bull was in tears. I was too.

"Vicki," he told me sadly, "you taught me everything I know. How to dance. How to dress. How to treat you like a lady. And now you're leaving me."

As far as Bull was concerned, it was over between us. He didn't fight for me. He thought it was already too late. "I can't believe you're leaving me for a New Yorker" was all he could say, over and over.

Bull was defeated. He just accepted that he'd lost me. I knew in that moment, he wasn't my man anymore.

I expected and wanted Bull to take the lead, the same way I did when we were dancing. And so I didn't fight for our relationship either.

"Vicki, I will always love you," he said before I walked away.

"I will always love you too," I told him.

I quietly stepped out of the car and shut the door, closing that chapter of my life forever. Now that Bull was back in Steelton he went to work at the mill. A few years later, I learned that he had married someone else. He's lived in the Harrisburg area ever since. Many times I've wondered what would have happened if we'd stayed together. Of course, I'll never know.

Breaking up with Bull was so painful for me. For a long time, I'd always thought I'd be his wife. I'd planned our wedding in my head. I'd named our children. Now those dreams would never come to pass and I felt lost. Meanwhile, Mike seemed to have all the answers. Every day, he would come over or call. He told me everything I wanted to hear. "Vicki, it's going to be fine. You're my girl now."

Who could resist that smile and those eyes? We started seeing one another officially. Despite my heartbreak over Bull, we clicked. Mike loved spending time with my family and friends. He couldn't believe how important high school football games were to us here in Steelton; he loved the games, the parades, and the parties afterward. He was so proud of me and the fact that I ran my own business; he even began to get involved in helping me with the dance studio. All my students adored him. When he walked into the room, the children lit up, shouting, "*Miiiike!*" I began to let myself imagine what a great dad he was going to be.

Soon after we started seeing each other, Mike returned to his job at the Long Island Railroad, and we began shuttling back and forth between New York and Steelton to see each other on weekends. I missed my boyfriend, but our long-distance relationship seemed to be working.

Then, one evening, I was in Steelton while Mike was in New York. I'd stayed out late to go polka dancing with my girlfriend Sylvia, while Mike was out drinking with friends. We'd arranged to talk on the phone at about eleven o'clock, but when the hour rolled around, my girlfriend was having so much fun that she didn't want to leave. She was my ride home, so I had to stay too. Mike tried calling me at home, but, of course, I wasn't there. He called every social hall in town until he found me. When the manager told me that I had a phone call, I raced to the phone. It was Mike. He demanded that I get myself home in fifteen minutes. "And you better answer the phone, or there will be hell to pay." I was in shock. I hadn't meant to make him angry. All I'd done was go out to a harmless polka night with a girlfriend.

On the way home, Sylvia turned to me and said, "Vicki, you'd better think long and hard about what you're doing here."

No sooner had I walked in the door than the phone rang. I picked up. Mike was furious.

"I want you home waiting for my call!" he yelled. "Not whoring around with Steelton boys!"

No one had ever spoken to me that way. I protested. I even apologized. But Mike was drunk. He kept on for the next hour, calling me the most terrible names and accusing me of the most horrible things.

Finally, I ended the relationship.

"That's it," I told him. "I don't want to go on. We're finished."

In the days after we broke up, I was devastated. I felt that Mike had behaved completely out of character. I was so young that I actually blamed myself. Maybe if I hadn't stayed out so late, Mike never would have lost his trust in me.

The next day, Mike called, and he called the day after that and the day after that. He apologized over and over again. He wanted me back. He would do anything to make it up to me. My mom kept telling me to let Mike go, that I'd be making a big mistake if I forgave him. I didn't listen. When he came down to Steelton, we got back together. My Mike was a sweet and gentle person. I couldn't imagine that we would fight again. He was going to take care of me.

A few weeks later, Mike took me ring shopping and bought me the biggest diamond solitaire I'd ever seen. We were going to get married the following August. My heartbreak was over, and I was walking on air.

My mother was dead set against the marriage. "Vicki, I think you're opening yourself up for heartache," she said repeatedly in the months leading up to my wedding day. She told me that Mike wasn't everything he seemed. Her father was an alcoholic and she knew the signs.

But I was her daughter, and I didn't listen. I convinced myself that she was just saying this because she didn't want me to leave home and live with Mike in New York. I didn't know any better. I didn't know that when your boyfriend has been drinking and his personality changes, that's a very bad thing, to say the least. I grew up in a house where no one drank alcohol, where we didn't keep as much as a bottle of wine in the back of the cupboard. I just trusted that when Mike and I were married, everything would work out. We were in love. We were going to settle down together. Marriage was going to be so good for Mike. He had grown up in a family without much love. His dad drank, and his mother was worn down and withdrawn. Despite Mike's charisma and confidence, I sensed his vulnerability. I felt I could give him the love and the secure family life that he'd lacked growing up. I thought I could help empower him to make all his many dreams come true. In the movies, the good girls always turned around the bad boys, and everyone lived happily ever after. That's the way it was going to be with us too.

Now that the wedding date was set, I put the wheels in motion to move to New York City with Mike. That meant closing up my Studio of Rhythm. I was sad, but I don't think I ever questioned my decision. I was excited about my new life with my husband-to-be.

I sent all my dancers a letter explaining that I'd tried to find someone to take over the studio, but that it hadn't been possible. At the end of June 1968, Vicki's Studio of Rhythm staged its final recital. That night, I danced to "Me and My Shadow" with my student teacher LuAnne and another one of my older dancers. The girls followed along behind me after I did my steps in the exact same formation. It was my farewell performance. The last number of the show was called "A Traditional Spring Wedding—Steelton-Style." I had my older dancers en pointe, dressed in tutus and veils, dancing a ballet routine to "Get Me to the Church on Time." Then out came my best little boy tap dancer, Forry, and my best little girl tap dancer, Denise, dressed up to look like wedding cake toppers, performing a tap routine to "I Could Have Danced All Night." For the finale, everyone twirled and whirled around to the traditional polka, and did kola dances (the Slavic version of line dancing), customary at every Steelton wedding reception.

Mike was there for the recital, beaming with pride. I remember looking over at that smile, that face, that handsome, ambitious man. I was too young to know the value of everything I was giving up. At that moment, being a wife and mother with Mike in New York was all that I wanted.

The morning of my wedding, August 24, 1968, was one of the hottest and sunniest days of the year, with not a cloud in the sky. That afternoon, we were at my mother's house taking pictures with my bridesmaids. My friends, including LuAnne, all looked so beautiful in their pale aqua dresses, my favorite color. My wedding gown had a high collar at the front and an open back covered in lace, with a cathedral veil trailing behind me. When it came time to leave for the church, I remember stepping carefully down the winding wooden staircase so that I wouldn't trip on my hem.

My mother led the way, with my bridesmaids following. Just as she went to open the front door, at that instant, the loudest thunderclap I've ever heard broke overhead. Everyone stopped.

My mother turned to me.

"Vicki, turn back," she said, her voice as stern as I'd ever heard it. Then she pointed her finger dramatically to the ceiling. "Even He is trying to tell you not to get married!"

"Mother, how could you!" I cried. I couldn't believe she was still trying to talk me out of getting married, on my actual wedding day! I was wearing my dream wedding dress. My six bridesmaids were behind me. My whole future was ahead of me.

"Turn back, Vicki," my mother repeated. By now the rain was pounding on the roof like gunfire. "Let me go over to the church. I'll announce the wedding is off, but there's going to be a heck of a party happening at the reception hall."

"Mother, let's just get umbrellas," I told her. "And I'll try to forget you said that."

My mother took a breath and went back upstairs to fetch umbrellas, leaving me and every one of my bridesmaids standing by the door. No one said a word. In years to come, she was going to remind me of this moment: "Vicki, I tried to help you. You wouldn't listen."

We proceeded to make the short walk to the church under our umbrellas, the rain cascading around us. At that moment, a car passed us, beeping its horn. I looked around, and there was my future husband, waving from the passenger window, looking as handsome as ever. For the first time that day, I remember feeling worried. Mike was over an hour late. He was supposed to have been at the church having photos taken with his groomsmen by now. He'd seen me in my wedding gown, and everyone knows that it's bad luck for the groom to see the bride before the ceremony.

I shook it off and kept walking.

My uncle Frank, my dad's oldest brother, was waiting at the church to walk me down the aisle. Inside, every seat was taken. On the bride's side, my female guests were wearing below-the-knee dresses with Peter Pan collars and matching gloves. In contrast, on the groom's side, the New York ladies were in minidresses and low-cut tops, with fake eyelashes and big hair. Mike's best friend's wife, Jane, was wearing a white minidress that barely covered her backside. All the guests on my side were looking with eyes as wide as saucers at the New Yorkers; I don't think they'd ever seen an actual minidress before, much less one in church. It was like the Steelton crowd had just witnessed an alien invasion. Later Jane told me that when she looked over at my side of the church, she thought she was at "frickin' bingo."

With such a strange mix of guests, the reception could have been a complete disaster, but instead it was probably the highlight of my marriage. Both sides of the aisle mingled surprisingly well. The reception was in traditional Steelton form, complete with a polka band—which I'm guessing was a first for the New Yorkers—but after a few drinks, they got in the spirit and joined in the dancing.

Throughout the evening, Mike took every opportunity to hit the bar for another cocktail. I have a photo of my mom dancing with my new husband that night. She's leaning back, with a pained expression on her face that tells you everything you need to know about how she felt about my marriage. Later I found out that every single one of my uncles threatened Mike that night: "You'd better take care of Vicki."

When it came time for us to leave, my mother was inconsolable. She wasn't alone. Before I left, I went over to say good-bye to my students, including Forry in his little suit, LuAnne in her bridesmaid gown, and Deb and Liz in their best dresses.

"What am I ever going to do without you?" LuAnne asked me.

Forry wrapped his little arms around my waist, clinging onto me. Everyone was in tears.

I was weeping uncontrollably by now, filled with so many emotions: joy, sadness, and excitement.

I turned around and saw Mike. My future.

He took my hand and said, "C'mon, Vicki, it's time to go."

Then he literally swept me up in his arms and carried me out of the reception. I still have the photo. I look at it now and see two young people, completely happy, completely in love, and completely naïve.

I should add, though, that behind my smile, I was also terrified. I deserved to wear that white dress and that like many girls back then, a wedding night was a very big deal. When it came time to undress at our hotel room, I was so overwhelmed that I asked Mike to find Janie, my new sister-in-law, so that she could undo the tiny buttons on the back of my wedding dress. I'm sure my new husband must have wondered what on earth he'd done, marrying a woman who wouldn't even let her husband unfasten her dress. More than the thunder breaking above, this should have been a sign that our marriage was going to be imbalanced, awkward, and just plain wrong.

But it was already too late. The following day, we left for our honeymoon on the Caribbean island of Saint Thomas. I left Steelton, my family, my home, my studio, and my dancing days behind me. From now on, I was going to devote myself to being a wife to my husband and a mother to our children. It was like blowing out a candle. Dance went out of my life for the next seventeen years.

Chapter 5

• • •

Sunday, June 12, 2011

9:35 AM

"ALL-STARS ONSTAGE FOR 'A CAPELLA'! FIVE MINUTES!"

Rehearsals are beginning, and first out onstage is the cream of the crop: the dancers I call my All-Stars.

Every Tap Pup walks out from backstage and takes a seat. Rehearsal is the first time that the ladies can watch all the routines from each level, and they're excited. Everyone is here to root for their fellow dancers—and as much as we're excited to dance for the audience this afternoon, in many ways, this is the most special audience of the day.

Click, click, click! Here they come across the stage to take their places, and the auditorium goes silent. These are the most talented performers in the group: a cross between the Golden Girls and the Jets from *West Side Story*.

I first formed the All-Stars in 2006, at a time when our numbers were growing fast. Back then, I was amazed at how many talented and experienced tap dancers were signing up for my Advanced class. All of them had taken tap as children but had eventually quit because they thought that dance lessons were for little kids. Now that they were older, they finally had time to resume passions they'd had when they were younger. Now that they were back dancing, they couldn't believe how much they'd missed feeling that rhythm. Meanwhile, I couldn't believe how skilled they still were as tap dancers, when many of them hadn't danced in thirty years or more.

My son Brian had the brilliant idea to select a core group of these talented Advanced dancers to represent the Tap Pups in performances and at events. The All-Stars are fourteen incredible tappers, ranging in age from Heather, twenty-nine, to eighty-year-old Joan. Everyone else in the Tap Pups looks up to the All-Stars, hoping that one day she (or he) can join their ranks.

This afternoon, the All-Stars are going to be dancing "A Capella," the show opener. In this routine, the dancers create the rhythm purely with the sound of their feet. No music. It's tap stripped down to its essence, and it's one of the most challenging dances in the show because, unlike with all the other dances, there's no sound track to keep the beat.

Rick starts the routine. He's the one guy in the All-Stars, the easygoing, charming giant of the Tap Pups. Tall and broad shouldered, with a bald head and schoolteacher glasses, Rick always dances in the middle of the line, with the rest of the All-Stars on either side of him. I watch as he thrusts out his right foot and dramatically scrapes a circle on the floor, ending with a loud toe hit. He does this again and again until he moves forward. Then two by two, the other All-Stars begin making the same sound, until all fourteen dancers are moving in perfect unison. They begin to pick up the pace, and soon they are dancing with such grace and speed that it takes your breath away.

· ·

ALL-STARS A CAPELLA

WATCH THE ALL-STARS' SIGNATURE PERFORMANCE.

www.youtube.com/vickistappups

· ·

Although you'd never guess from looking at his moves, Rick is sixty-four years old, and he recently returned to dance after a very long hiatus. Rick grew up in the 1950s and 1960s, at a time when everyone—boys included—learned some form of dance, whether it was tap, jazz, or the jitterbug. Rick was no exception. His mother and grandmother signed him up for tap classes at the age of eight, and he kept dancing into his teens, performing in his school's recitals and onstage in high school plays. One of Rick's biggest regrets is having given up tapping when he was fifteen. Like so many teenagers, he'd decided that it was time to move on. Socializing, dating, joining clubs, and participating in his youth group at church—these were a lot more interesting to Rick then. After he graduated high school, he went to college and then to graduate school to get his master's in French. Rick married his high school sweetheart, Elaine, and for many years, he taught French at a local high school. Dance became just another one of those things that he gave up after becoming an adult, like climbing trees, or riding a bike around the block, or spending all day with your friends.

Rick learned about my studio when he was sixty-two years old and at his retirement party. That evening, the superintendent of his school district mentioned that she was taking a tap class. Rick remembers feeling his heart skip a beat when he heard those words: "tap class." Really? There were adult tap classes in Harrisburg?

After a lifetime of working, it can be hard to imagine your days when you retire. Work is validating. It gives us our identity. As much as Rick was looking forward to being freed up from his job, he was admittedly uncertain of how he was going to stay motivated and engaged. He knew it was going to be a transition.

Rick decided to come to our spring show. This was in 2008. As he watched us perform, the retired teacher couldn't believe how many of the steps he remembered from dancing all those years ago.

"It took everything I had to stop myself from getting up out of my seat and jumping up onto the stage," he told me later.

At his first class in forty-five years, Rick was excited but apprehensive. It had been so long. Would he be able to keep up? As it turned out, Rick was a superb dancer with natural rhythm. I loved watching the look of concentration on his face as the old steps flowed out of his feet. That's the incredible thing about learning something as a child: it doesn't matter how long you've been out of the saddle, you never forget how.

Two weeks after Rick started classes, he persuaded his wife to join too. Elaine had taken one year of tap as a child, but had given it up because her mother wanted her to take piano lessons. Rick started practicing with her outside of class, and she quickly moved up through the program. She was hooked. She enjoyed her first exposure to adult tap classes so much that she giggled through her entire first year. Now the couple are two of my most devoted dancers. Rick is in the Advanced group and is an instructor; Elaine is in the Beginner 3s—the level of class below Intermediate. They have something that they love to do together, and they tell me it's saved their sanity during a potentially difficult time of transitioning into retirement.

"There's something innate in all of us that really loves to move to music," Rick reflected one day. "When you're young, you have all these opportunities to dance. But when you're older, where can you go? That's what's so special about your studio. You've created this unique, nurturing space where older people can express themselves through movement."

Rick is someone who has a great marriage, a nice home, a happy life. And even so, dance has helped him fall in step with himself. It's brought him back to that part of himself that always loved to dance. Do we age because the years pass, or do we age because we stop doing the things that we love? In dance class, Rick was dancing some of the exact same steps he'd learned when he was eight years old. He was acting younger, and, as a result, he began to feel younger. At a point in his life where he felt uncertain and was questioning his self-identity, dance helped him become fit and active. He reconnected with a part of himself he'd almost forgotten—once again, he's a dancer.

THE day Mike and I boarded our honeymoon flight to Saint Thomas was the day I stopped leading with my strengths and began the long process of forgetting I was a dancer.

I was so excited to be flying somewhere so romantic with my new husband. I can still picture my going-away outfit: a white sleeveless linen dress with black patent leather piping around the neckline and bodice, black patent leather sling-back peep-toe high-heeled shoes, and a matching purse. I had on my signature short white gloves and a fresh corsage, my hair coiffed, ready to begin my perfect marriage.

Just a half hour in the air, Mike turned to me, already on his third drink. He announced that he had some rules for the rest of the trip, and he wanted to let me know about them.

"I don't want you speaking to anyone else while we're away, you hear me? You're not in Steelton now, Vicki. You can't go talking to every person you meet."

At first I thought Mike was joking. I laughed. I told him that I loved to talk to people, and I didn't think that it was going to be possible to follow his rule.

But Mike wasn't being funny.

"You're my wife," he insisted. "I don't want you speaking to anyone else the rest of this week but me."

Believe it or not, I actually agreed to my husband's bizarre request, even if I couldn't understand it. Maybe Mike was just being romantic, wanting me all to himself, I hoped.

Of course, by the next morning, I'd already broken the rule. When the woman sitting next to me at breakfast asked how long we were staying at the resort, I went ahead and answered—like anyone would.

"Oh, we're here for a week," I said.

Before I could get out the full sentence, Mike kicked me under the table so hard that I had to stifle a cry. My shin bore a dark blue bruise for the rest of the trip.

We fought three times before the week was over. During the day, we got along just fine. We drove around the island, walked along the beach hand in hand, enjoying this time together. However, in the evening, we couldn't agree. Mike always wanted to stay late at the bar. But I didn't enjoy alcohol quite as much as he did. I have a wedding photo of the best man pouring me a glass of champagne, and I'm making a face because I knew I had to toast, but until then I'd never even tasted as much as a sip of alcohol. Whenever I told Mike that I wanted to go back to our room in the evenings, he accused me of trying to control him. We'd fight, and I'd end the night in tears.

By the end of the trip, all I wanted to do was call my mom and tell her I was getting an annulment, but I knew I couldn't do it. A week before, I'd left Steelton after my big white wedding. I couldn't go home so soon with my tail between my legs. I had to try to make this work. And so, I kept mentally forgiving Mike. This wasn't like him. He was probably feeling unsettled by the new responsibility of being married. I had to be patient. He'd go back to his usual self soon.

We returned from our honeymoon and immediately moved into our new home, a small starter garden apartment in Queens, New York. I was happy that Mike's oldest brother, Ed, and his wife, my new girlfriend Janie, also lived there with their two children. I spent the next few weeks getting things straightened out, cooking dinners, being Mike's wife.

Then an opportunity came my way that could have changed everything for me. One evening soon after we moved to Queens, I was making dinner when I heard an announcement on the local news coming from the TV in the next room. I raced into the living room.

"Dancers needed for a new Broadway production of No, No, Nanette!" said the voice. "Strictly tap dancers. No singing required!"

Until this moment, I'd never thought musical theater was an option for me. But maybe there was a way for me to dance on Broadway after all. It's amazing what you can learn when you leave Steelton!

I felt completely certain that I could get a part if I auditioned. It was only three months since I'd closed my studio, and I was in the best dancing form of my life. I paced between the kitchen and the living room in excitement, waiting for Mike to get home. As soon as he walked in the door, I told him about the auditions.

Mike was excited. In fact, he was too excited.

"Vic, this is our big chance," he said. "You're an incredible dancer. This is going to change everything for us!"

From the moment he learned about the auditions, Mike ran with the idea. I was going to be a big star. I was going to be the toast of Broadway. We were going to be able to afford a big house, a flashy car, and beautiful clothes. We were going to make it big.

The whole time I'd known Mike, "making it big" was his obsession. He was constantly talking about how one day he was going to "win the lottery," "hit the jackpot." But until now when he spoke about making it big, it was always in terms of his *own* career. I'd never heard him pin all his dreams on me before. That evening, he had a look in his eyes that scared me: a mix of craziness and determination.

"Here's what we're going to do," he went on. "I'm going to quit my job tomorrow and become your manager. Now that you're in show business, you'll need someone to look after your interests."

"But I haven't even been on the audition yet," I reminded Mike. "Slow down!"

I couldn't believe that my husband was seriously contemplating quitting his job. I knew that Broadway chorus girls didn't make enough money to support two people. Besides, I didn't want to be the only breadwinner in the family. I wanted Mike to be the one to carve out a career, to support us, to look after us.

I tried to reason with him.

"You are not quitting your job just because I'm going on an audition." But Mike wasn't hearing me. He'd already made up his mind, and as hard as I tried, I couldn't persuade him that his grand notion was completely out of touch with reality. Yes, I wanted him to encourage me to go to the auditions, but why couldn't I make him understand that he needed to stay in his job regardless? Mike was living in a dream world. All I could think was, "Oh no, I've married a crazy man!"

I started to cry. I told Mike I'd changed my mind and wasn't going to audition. "I'm not going to let you ruin both of our lives," I told him.

That night in bed, I remember turning over on my side, switching off the bedside lamp, and lying awake, tears streaming down my cheeks.

The day of the audition came and went. To this day, I still wonder what might have happened if I'd tried out: how many interesting people I might have met; how the course of my life might have been different. But I didn't go. I stayed home. If I'd been older, stronger, more experienced, maybe I could have auditioned secretly, but I never even considered going behind my husband's back. My parents never kept a secret from each other. It just wasn't something I knew how to do.

I was so angry with Mike for putting all that pressure on me to be successful for both of us, for wanting me to fulfill his dreams along with my own. But I was even angrier with myself for not being strong enough to make my own decisions. Only a few weeks into my marriage, where had that confident, determined girl from Steelton gone?

And so instead of dancing on Broadway, with my mom's help, I got a secretarial job with an international union based in Manhattan. My first day on the job, I took the Long Island Railroad to Penn Station and then the subway downtown. It was a gorgeous fall day and I was dressed for the role of "sophisticated working girl" in a charming new pencil dress in burnt orange with a matching jacket, a yellow scarf tied around my neck, my hair in a small flip. Everywhere I looked, there were men in their well-cut suits and coats, carrying briefcases; women dressed in tight-fitting blazers with the latest flared skirts underneath. Everyone was so sleek, so stylish. I'd always wanted to live in New York. I wanted to be here, but all I could think while walking across town to my new job was "I should have come here alone."

I spent more than one night that first year crying myself to sleep. When Mike was in a good mood, nobody was more loving or prouder of me. Out with friends, he couldn't stop talking about how happy we were together. His energy and charm were infectious—and during those times, I hung on to his every word. We talked about his career, how he was going to climb his way up the ladder and eventually start his own business. I'd feel so proud that he was my husband. It was only when Mike had downed a few drinks that I learned anything could happen and that I needed to tread carefully.

Our first Christmas after we were married, I took my husband as my date to my office holiday party at a bar near Union Square. That evening, I was chatting with one of my bosses, a tall, good-looking man with striking black hair. Minutes later, Mike came over, glared at my boss, pretended to trip, and emptied an entire glass of scotch all over the poor man's suit pants. I was mortified. Somehow I managed to hold on to my job, but I learned quickly that if I even looked the wrong way at another guy, Mike would accuse me of flirting and having an affair.

I tried to ignore the evenings when Mike stayed out late with "clients" from work. I tried to ignore the alcohol on his breath when he finally came home. I tried to ignore the gin-filled glasses that he always seemed to have in his hand. This was the era of the three-martini lunch, and Mike could keep up with the best of them. It never occurred to me that my husband's drinking was only going to get worse.

The year after we moved to New York, I became pregnant with our first child. This was the way it was supposed to be, and I was beyond happy. Mike was so excited about becoming a father. I was certain that when we had a family, everything would start to finally fall into place for us. It was going to get better. Mike was doing great at work. When he got promoted, when we had more money, everything was going to change, just as he'd planned.

We named our little boy Michael Joseph Jr., after his dad. He arrived three weeks late—this was in the days before it was common for an expectant mother to be medically induced. He had a full head of hair and shining blue eyes, just like Mike's. Even the nurses on the ward were smitten by him.

"Did you see the Riordan baby?" I overheard one saying to another. "He's beautiful."

"Well, he *should* be," she replied. "Did you see his father?"

I wanted to say, "Hello! I had something to do with that beautiful baby too!" But by now I was used to the effect that Mike had wherever he went. He was so good-looking that he literally stopped women in their tracks.

When we brought home our baby, Mike seemed transformed at first. He doted on Michael Jr. and on me. A week after I got home from the hospital, my husband told me, "Go out, get your hair done; I'll take care of the baby." Amazed, I went to get my hair cut and colored. When I came back, Mike was on the floor with his son, cuddling on a blanket, watching baseball on TV. I thought this was the cutest thing I'd ever seen in my life. "I was right," I thought to myself. "Fatherhood is going to be so good for him."

The moment didn't last long. Mike was soon promoted to another position and often had to stay late at work, or at least that's what he said. When I complained to my mother that he was never home when the baby was awake, she told me to quit crying. For the first time, she backed Mike up: "Vicki, you can't expect Mike to work from nine to five and bring in the salary he's making." Meanwhile, I'd stopped working at the end of my pregnancy, so I was mostly alone with our son, from the moment I woke up until he went to sleep in the evening. Luckily, the brand-new soap opera *All My Children* started that year and I instantly became hooked. I saw the very first episode where I met Erica Kane as a teenager, and watched every episode for the next forty-one years. Another daily highlight for me was waiting to tell Mike when he came home what Paul Lynde said that day on *Hollywood Squares*. I was even more grateful that my sister-in-law was in the same apartment complex if I needed her. In the months after Michael's birth, I fell in love with my son and with being his mother. I remember the first time that he rolled over. The first smile. The first step. The first word (which was "Dada," after much coaching on my part). People often stopped me in the street to compliment me on my beautiful boy. He was such a good baby. He hardly ever cried, and his little blue eyes would follow me everywhere I went, watching my every move. I learned that witnessing your baby develop is one of the most exciting and fulfilling parts of being a parent. I also learned that the man I had married didn't want to share in this happiness with me. Mike told me later that every time there was a Notre Dame football game on TV, he would purposefully pick a fight with me so that he could storm out of the house and go to the local bar to watch the game with his buddies.

When our son was nearly a year old, Mike was offered a new job working for a containerized shipping company in New Jersey. We moved into our first house, in a picture-perfect little town called Fanwood. We bought a split-level with a huge backyard, secluded by a fence, on a tree-lined suburban street. It was a fresh start. On the surface, things didn't look so bad. I had a nice house, a car, a handsome husband, and my son. The American dream. But the reality was that Mike and I were fighting more and more. For the most part, Mike was home only on Saturdays and Sundays now, and on weekends he was always miserable and hung over. Fortunately, I met one of my best friends the day we moved to Fanwood. Our next-door neighbor Ellen was married and had two little boys a few years older than Michael. I don't know what I would have done without her during those years.

Pretty quickly, it became clear that Mike didn't want to share the responsibilities of home ownership with me either. I paid the bills, I cleaned the house, I looked after our baby, but I was hoping that my husband would take care of everything else: the backyard, the car, and general maintenance. But Mike kept finding a million excuses why he couldn't do these tasks. One day I told Mike that he needed to go out and mow the lawn because the grass had grown so tall I'd practically lost our son out in the backyard! Reluctantly, he went outside and found a sickle in the shed. When I looked outside, I saw him hacking at the lawn with the sickle, making very little impact.

I went outside. "Mike, what are you doing?" I asked. "Why don't you use the mower?"

"I don't want the neighbors to know that we didn't mow the lawn," he said. "I want them to think I'm practicing my golf swing."

I pointed out that everyone had already seen that we didn't mow the lawn and that swinging a sickle around wasn't going to fool anyone!

"Mike, we have half an acre," I told him. "I don't think you're going to be able to keep up that swing long enough to cut the entire yard."

After a while, sure enough, Mike lost interest in the grass and went inside to watch a football game. The lawn looked a mess. It was as long as ever, but now with big bare patches.

On Monday I decided to go next door and ask Ellen's husband, Dee, if he would show me how to use the lawn mower. That day I mowed the lawn, and I learned another lesson: if I wanted something done, and done right, it would be best to leave Mike out of it.

From that day on, I took charge of our home. I was determined to make the best of things. I enrolled Michael in nursery school, and, during the day, we were a happy family. We socialized with other mothers and their children. We played in the house and the backyard. It was only after I put my son to bed that I sat, waiting, never sure of what the evening would bring. The more I asked my husband to stay home with us, the more we argued and the more he ran away. What kept me going was that things would always get a little bit better after they got worse, and that would give me the faith that it wasn't too late, that things could always improve.

My brother-in-law Brendan, a Catholic priest, was determined to help us. He arranged for Mike and I to go to a "marriage encounter" weekend at a local convent. This was a new program to help men and women work through their marital difficulties. My mom stayed with the baby while Mike and I participated in group counseling sessions with thirty other couples. I had to write my husband a letter telling him how I felt, and he had to do the same. I wrote about how hard it was for me that he would rather stay out drinking than spend time with his family. He promised he was going to change. We came home fully reconciled. A couple of weeks later, I found out that I was pregnant again. Although I was nervous to bring another child into this marriage, I was also excited. I was an only child, and more than anything, I wanted Michael to have a sibling. The pregnancy was a blessing in disguise in so many ways.

But despite the marriage encounter weekend, the situation with Mike did not improve. I was seven months pregnant and in the middle of one of our fights when Mike threw his full glass of Scotch on the rocks in my face. Until then, I'd been miserable in my marriage, but I'd never felt afraid of my husband. After Mike left for work the next morning, I packed a bag, got little Michael out of his bed, put him in the car, and drove to my mom's house in Pennsylvania. I just knew that I had to get away from Mike for a while to have time to think.

For the next two weeks, my mother fed me, looked after me, comforted me. By now she had remarried. Her new husband, Jim Gustin, also from Steelton, worked with her at the United Steelworkers union. I was very fortunate that my mother married another wonderful man who also offered unconditional love and treated me like his daughter.

"Don't worry, Vicki, we'll take you to the hospital when your little one arrives," she said to me one day.

Her words shook me. Take me to the hospital? What was I doing? I was about to have Mike's baby! I needed to be home with my husband! I didn't want my mother to take me to the hospital. I was a big girl. I could take care of my own life, or so I thought.

And so I went back to Mike. Brian Scott Riordan was born on Valentine's Day 1973, and he was just as handsome as his brother. Although having two children was a big transition, I loved knowing that my boys were going to grow up together. As an only child, I had missed out on having a sibling. My dream was that my sons would always be close and have one another. I put all my focus on the children, trying to relegate my problems with their father to the back of my mind.

It never occurred to me that when Mike stayed out late, he might be with another woman. I still believed he was a troubled man who was good at heart. But then, one morning when Brian was about a year old, I was sorting the clothes Mike had thrown in the laundry. As I reached for his T-shirt, an unfamiliar smell of perfume hit me. I grabbed the shirt, marched over to the bed, and threw it in Mike's face, shouting at him to wake up and explain.

Mike started to make his excuses:

It wasn't the way it looked.

It was a girl he knew from work.

She was upset. He was comforting her. He gave her a little hug. He asked her to dance, just to cheer her up.

"We didn't sleep together, Vicki!" Mike protested. "We were just dancing together!"

I couldn't believe that my husband was actually saying this to me.

"What did you say?" I demanded. "You're using dancing as your excuse? Of all the lies you could have come up with, you're throwing dancing in my face?"

Here I was sitting home every night with our kids, and Mike was telling me he was out dancing? I was mad about the perfume. I was mad about the girl and the betrayal. But what made me even more furious was that Mike didn't realize what he was saying to me.

Five years since our wedding day, and Mike had forgotten he'd married a dancer.

I'd nearly forgotten it myself.

Mike knew he had gone too far. From that moment on, no one could have been more apologetic. He swore he'd never hurt me again. He stayed home all day. We had dinner together. My husband became the Mike I thought I'd married: attentive, romantic, loving. He charmed me back into his heart. Living with Mike all those years was a lot like walking along a gangplank. Every time I reached the end and I was about to jump, he'd reach out and grab me back.

As time went on, I learned never to fight with him after he'd been drinking. So many nights when Mike came home late, I would try to run away and hide. One night when Brian was three and Michael was five, they were upstairs sleeping when Mike came home in one of his rages. I didn't want to fight, and I didn't want the boys to overhear us. I don't remember ever hearing my parents argue when I was a child, and I knew I would have felt so frightened if they did. That evening with Mike, I just wanted to block out everything. But Mike wouldn't let me. He kept coming at me, yelling at me, right in my face. Such terrible names. I remember trying to escape from him, going downstairs to our family room. Mike came after me, cornered me against the wall, by the door out to the yard. He had both legs on either side of me, standing over me like Hercules, pinning me to the wall. I couldn't go left. I couldn't go right. I slid down to the floor and wrapped my arms around my knees, trying to block him out.

"Look at you!" Mike yelled. "You're absolutely pathetic!"

I was sobbing; my eyes and my throat were raw.

Finally he stepped away.

"I don't care if you cry all night!"

My husband left me there huddled on the floor and went upstairs. I remember hearing the crack of the gin bottle opening. I started pulling my hair back from my face over and over, not knowing what else to do. Mike's words rang in my ears. I felt my own hands tugging at my hair, and suddenly I could see myself in this sorry state. "Who am I?" I remember thinking. "Who have I become?"

To this day, I ask myself, Why? Why did I stay as long as I did? Why does anyone stay in an abusive relationship? I think first and foremost you stay because you feel you don't have any other choice. Everything in my life had prepared me for being a wife. Nothing had prepared me for leaving my husband. I didn't even want to contemplate my life on any other terms besides marriage. On the one hand, there was staying with Mike. On the other hand, there was going home to my mom. My life with Mike was miserable, and there were many, many times when I would have given my right arm to leave, but at least if I stayed in the marriage, I had my own home, I had my own life, and, most important, the boys had their father. More than anything, I wanted the boys to grow up with their dad. The thought of being a divorced single mom, living back home with my mother again, left me feeling crushed.

The other thing that kept me going was hope. Despite everything, I still felt in my heart that Mike could mend. I just kept thinking that things would get better, that I was his wife, and it was my job to stand by my man. I stayed with my husband because I was strong enough to stay. I came from a good home, a good family. I felt that I could take whatever he was going to throw at me, and that, somehow, by pure strength of will, I could "fix him." Soon Mike would realize how much he was missing, give up the drink, and begin to put his life back on track. It sounds so naïve in retrospect, but my dad had always been so good to my mom, and I just couldn't give up my dream of Mike turning out to be the man he'd always said he was going to be.

This was the era before support groups were well known, and it took me nearly eight years of marriage before I learned about Al-Anon, the organization for family members and friends of alcoholics. Even after that, it took me awhile to get up the courage to make the appointment. I was so scared of what I might learn there. Ellen, my neighbor, urged me to go, and even offered to watch my boys for me.

When I arrived, the counselor gave me a handful of pamphlets. I started to read. I kept reading. I couldn't stop. Every word rang true. I was reading a perfect description of my husband. How did the author of these pamphlets know so much about Mike? Every trait was there: the drinking, the anger, the disappearances, the other women. Every trait except for one: Mike still had his job. These pamphlets said that every alcoholic is on a downward spiral and that eventually he loses everything, even his employment.

"Okay, there's still hope," I thought. "Mike still has his job."

The counselor thought differently.

"It's only going to get worse," she said. "Leave now before it's too late."

People say that the truth can set you free, but it can also scare the hell out of you. That visit to Al-Anon only reinforced my denial. I didn't want Mike to have this label on him. I didn't want to be the wife of an alcoholic. I just wanted him to get better. Yes, he had this terrible disease but I had to believe that he could heal. When I got home, I dropped the pamphlets in a shoebox and hid it in the back of my closet, where Mike would never find it. I told myself that I'd give Mike one last chance to prove to me that all the years I'd invested in this marriage had been worth it. At least now that I understood his problem, things were going to get easier. I could work around it, or so I thought.

Around that time, Mike was offered a promotion to a new position in New Orleans. It was a chance for all of us to start again. Maybe things would be different down there.

My husband went ahead of us to begin his new job, leaving me behind in New Jersey to sell the house and pack up our belongings. Down South, the weather was so warm that Mike forgot to pay our heating bill. It was the middle of winter, and the house got so cold that the pipes in our basement froze and cracked. By the time I realized what was going on, the basement was flooded with three and a half feet of water. That was where I kept all of my things from my Steelton days: my costumes from the Studio of Rhythm, my custom shoes and dance wear, my record player and records, the large acrobatic mat that my boys loved to play on—even my wedding gown. I stood there with water up to my knees, looking at all of my most prized possessions. Soaked and ruined.

And so this is how the first act of my life played out. I was so strong, so happy, so directed at age eighteen. I had my own business. I knew what I wanted from life. And then eight years after my wedding day, I was standing in a basement looking at what was left of my studio. I was devastated, but I was so deep into my marriage that I didn't make the obvious connection. Mike had wrecked everything I valued the most, through sheer wanton carelessness. Worst of all, I'd allowed him to do it.

Chapter 6

• • •

Sunday, June 12, 2011

10:15 AM

NEXT UP ONSTAGE ARE MY NEW BEGINNERS, REHEARSING THEIR ROUTINE TO THE SONG "CHICAGO." THIS IS THE MOST CHALLENGING DANCE FOR THIS GROUP. IT'S BEEN NINE SHORT MONTHS SINCE THEY MADE THEIR FIRST TAP SOUND AND ALTHOUGH THEY'VE COME A LONG WAY, THIS IS THE FIRST TIME ANY OF THEM HAVE PERFORMED ONSTAGE. HALFWAY THROUGH, THE DANCERS STEP OUT OF THEIR ROWS TO FORM SHORT LINES, LINKING ARMS TO CREATE THREE REVOLVING PINWHEELS. THEN THEY TURN AROUND AND REVOLVE IN THE OTHER DIRECTION. IT'S NOT EASY TO EXECUTE, AND THE GROUP HAS BEEN STRUGGLING IN REHEARSAL. WE GET TO WORK, FINESSING THEIR POSITIONS ONSTAGE, MAKING SURE THAT EVERY DANCER KNOWS WHERE SHE'S GOING TO BE DANCING AND HOW TO GET FROM POINT A TO POINT B.

"It's going to be worth it, ladies," I tell them. "The pinwheel is iconic, and the audience is going to love it. This is the moment when you're going to look and feel like real tap dancers!"

MEET THE DANCERS OF "CHICAGO"

WATCH THE NEW BEGINNERS DISCUSS THEIR

FIRST PERFORMANCE.

www.youtube.com/vickistappups

While I'm concentrating on the rehearsal, I can relax knowing that my right-hand man—my son Brian—is taking care of everything behind the scenes. Brian is thirty-eight years old now and has been working with me for the past five years. He's dark-haired with blue eyes like his father: my dancers think he looks like a young John Travolta. He wears many hats on the day of the show. He's making sure that the music and lighting are ready to go. He's working with the camera crew that is filming the big event. He's handling the local newspaper reporters and TV crews who are here to cover the performance. On show day and throughout the year, Brian is my advisor, my confidant, my *rock*. My son, who was born during such a troubled time, has turned out to be one of the greatest blessings in my life.

Today Brian has his two nieces working alongside him: my granddaughters, Olivia and Savanah. Olivia, who just finished her freshman year at Temple University, is helping with the press; Savanah, who is going into her senior year of high school, is our photographer, capturing the scenes backstage and the dancers in rehearsals. The girls are my son Michael's daughters, and he'll be here later too to help Brian set up for when the audience arrives. My mom, who is now nearly ninety, has also played her part, spending the past three months sewing all the accessories for the dancers: pinning feathers and sequins to hair clips, headbands, and gloves.

We're four generations working together to create this show.

Without Brian and the rest of my family, a show on this scale just wouldn't be possible. Since Brian came on board with the Tap Pups, our annual performances have gotten bigger and better every year. It was Brian's vision that took us to the next level, and every member of the Tap Pups knows that he's the secret glue holding this production together.

I'm a very fortunate mother in that I'm extremely close to both of my boys. Our bond goes back to all those years we spent as just the three of us. When Brian was a toddler, he would follow me around the house; he hated to let me out of his sight. Anytime I walked out of the bathroom and into the hallway, I'd invariably trip over him waiting for me outside the door.

Of my two boys, Brian was the inquisitive one. From a young age, he wanted to know everything.

"Mommy, when you were little, what was your daddy like?"

"What was your favorite color?"

"What were your favorite subjects in school?"

"Who were your best friends?"

Over the years, our conversations became more sophisticated, but the questions kept coming. Whether Brian was at college or working in advertising and branding in New York City, we would talk on the phone every day. At a certain point, Brian offered to help me take my dance program to the next level, and to my surprise, I learned that he already knew a huge amount about my approach and how I was running things. I had no idea that all these years, my son was listening just as closely as he'd followed me when he was a little boy. He had banked all our conversations in his memory.

Since 2006, Brian has devoted countless hours every week to helping me expand the Tap Pups program from a brand and marketing perspective. I've come to understand so much about Brian's world and what he does for a living. And through working with me, Brian has been able to give back, not only to his mother but also to so many others in his hometown.

"Mom," Brian said to me one day, "I've been thinking for a while that we need to clearly define your philosophy for the program, so we can effectively communicate to other people about what you're doing and how you're doing it. And I think I've managed to boil it down to three words."

"Tell me, Brian," I said, laughing, because I never thought about having a philosophy. I just do what I do.

"It's so obvious. Look at how every one of your dancers lights up when they see you or while they are dancing with you. I'm sure there are many more things that your dancers get from your program, but at the core, it's happiness that keeps them coming to classes. You can sum it up in three words: 'happiness through tap.'"

Brian had hit on the essence of the program. It was so simple and so true; the same feeling that had inspired me ever since my days teaching at the Studio of Rhythm in Steelton. Since then, those three words—"happiness through tap"—have appeared on our T-shirts, our website, and our advertisements.

In the past few years, I've been asked the same question so many times: "Vicki, how did you do this? How did all of this happen, and happen so fast?" At first I had to scramble for the right words, because there were so many things I wanted to say. Now I just get to the bottom line:

"Everyone needs a Brian!" I reply.

I'D decided to give Mike one last chance and move down South with him, hoping that life in New Orleans would be different from life in New Jersey. And it was different, just not in a good way. Mike was like a fish that had gone from an aquarium to an ocean. In New Orleans, there was a bar on every corner, and he had a standing reservation at a bar stool in each one of them. From the outside, I had the life I'd always wanted. We lived in an even bigger house, with a housekeeper, and we were members of the country club. The problem was that my sons and I saw Mike even less than we had before. Years later, my son Michael told me that he could still remember lying awake each night when we were living in New Orleans, waiting for his dad to come home, then listening to the sound of us fighting when he finally did. I just assumed that the boys were asleep by that hour. I was devastated to learn that my son had heard all those arguments. It's something I'll never be able to undo.

In the end, it wasn't Mike that wore me down. It was the realization that what was happening between us wasn't affecting just me, it was affecting my boys.

When we arrived in New Orleans, Michael started second grade, and Brian went to nursery school. The boys were happy in their classes, and I knew that, whatever else happened in their lives, they had somewhere fun and stimulating to be during the day. Although I was at home on my own in the mornings now, I tried to be as involved as I could in the boys' schools and to participate whenever needed. I think I probably overcompensated, knowing that Mike rarely stepped up to the plate.

The fall after we arrived in New Orleans, there was a parents' night at Brian's nursery school. He was so excited. All the kids were going to choose an activity for their moms and dads to try out. Brian decided that he liked playing in the sandbox best, so that's what his dad was going to do, and he assigned me to sit at his desk and draw a picture. Brian couldn't stop talking about parents' night. He was such a happy, clever little boy, always chatting away, telling us about his day and what he was going to do tomorrow.

The day before parents' night, Brian took me by the hand up to my bedroom to help me pick out my outfit for the big night. It was a black sleeveless scoop-neck dress, with a high waist, ruffles around the bodice and hem, and a little rosebud print, creating vertical stripes. That evening at dinner, Brian mapped out the entire event, telling us everything that was going to happen and how he couldn't wait to hear about how Mommy liked his desk and how Daddy played in the sandbox.

When the evening of parents' night came around, I was terrified that Mike would forget to show up or would deliberately find a reason to stay out late. But instead he actually came home on time. I couldn't believe it!

I called out to him from the kitchen, "Welcome home! Now hurry up and get ready; the babysitter will be here in a few minutes."

Mike walked into the family room. He cracked open the gin bottle, poured himself a drink, and dropped into his chair.

"Nah, I decided not to go," he said as casually as if he were turning down a ham sandwich. "Call the sitter and tell her not to come. I'm staying home tonight."

Brian was playing with his toys, right there in front of his dad. His face crumbled. He began to cry, as any four-year-old would. He jumped up onto his dad's lap, threw his arms around his neck, and began begging him to go to parents' night.

"Daddy, you have to go! You have to sit in the sandbox. Who's going to sit in the sandbox if you don't go? I'll be the only one without a daddy there if you don't go!"

By now I had learned to expect the worst from Mike, but it was beyond my wildest imagination that he would do this to his little boy.

"C'mon," I pleaded with Mike. "Don't do this to Brian! You know how excited he's been. The babysitter is booked. Just come with me!"

Mike didn't answer. He reached for his newspaper and held it up in front of his face, pushing Brian away.

Brian slid to the floor until he was lying facedown. He began pounding his fists, tears streaming down his cheeks.

Mike hiked the paper up higher, as if nothing was happening.

By now Brian was inconsolable. He could barely breathe. I went into full damage control mode. I grabbed my coat and my purse, scooped up my son, and hugged him close. I told him it was going to be okay, that I would go to the parents' night on my own.

"I will do my task, *and* I will sit in the sandbox too, Brian," I promised him.

I told Brian that I loved him and that I would be back soon. And then I got in the car and drove to the school alone.

My heart was breaking. I remember thinking, "Mike Riordan, you can hurt me, but you are not going to hurt my boys ever again."

For so long, I'd justified staying because the boys needed their father. Now it was finally clear that the longer I stayed, the more it was going to damage my beloved sons in the long run.

It didn't happen right away. I had to plan, to work up the courage and the momentum. But six months later, finally, I said the words:

"It's over, Mike. I'm not doing this anymore. I want out."

For my entire marriage, I'd essentially been on my own. I'd taken care of our boys, cooked, shopped, and looked after the house. I'd paid the bills. I'd cut the grass. I'd taken the cars in for service. I'd hauled out the garbage. I'd taken care of everything because Mike was never there to help me.

"You taught me to leave you," I told Mike. "Thanks to you, I don't need a husband anymore."

To his credit, Mike agreed to move out of our family home, and I put the wheels in motion to sell our house. I didn't have to wait long after that before I could leave: the first couple that looked at our house decided to buy it. On the day that we said good-bye, I realized that Mike actually had a look of relief on his face. I'd been holding on and holding on thinking that he needed me, never understanding that he felt just as miserable and trapped as I did. So in the early summer of 1978, I moved back home to central

Pennsylvania to be close to my mom, almost ten years to the day that I'd left on my honeymoon.

At the age of thirty-two, I was a single mom with two young boys. We had the money from my share of the sale of our house in New Orleans, but not a penny more. We needed a place to live. I needed a job. The boys needed a school. Even so, I knew that this wasn't the toughest thing I'd done. Staying with Mike would have been a whole lot harder.

My boys were my priority, and I found that I could make the right decisions quickly because everything was for their benefit. It's amazing what a mother can achieve when she's motivated by the love for her children. Two weeks after I returned to Pennsylvania, someone told me about a secretarial position that was open at the American Federation of State County and Municipal Employees (AFSCME), a local union. I hadn't worked as a secretary in more than eight years, but I knew I was qualified. I went to the interview, and I got the job.

On the way home that day, I happened to see a FOR SALE sign outside a little brick ranch house with green shutters on Jefferson Street, in a convenient neighborhood halfway between my new job and my mom's house. I went in, looked around. It was the right size and definitely the right price. When I was assured that the owners could move out in a month so that we could live there before school started, I made an offer, and it was accepted on the spot.

When I got home, Mom asked me, "How did you do on your interview today?"

"I got the job," I told her, "and I just bought a house on my way home."

"You did *what?*"

Just a few weeks back in Pennsylvania, and I already had a paycheck and a mortgage. Despite a modest salary, the job gave the boys and me the security we desperately needed to survive. I knew that our health benefits were covered. I knew that there was money going into a retirement account every month. Most important, the position had some flexibility. If Michael or Brian was sick, my bosses let me go home to look after him. I knew I was lucky. I was lucky to have my mom nearby and to have gotten settled so quickly. Best of all, the boys didn't have to wait for their dad to come home anymore, and they didn't have to fall asleep listening to their parents fighting.

Some of my favorite and happiest times with my boys occurred immediately after I purchased our little house on Jefferson Street. Every Saturday and Sunday morning, Michael and Brian would hop in my bed to watch cartoons or old movies. We spent hours in that bed just laughing, talking, and roughhousing—all before breakfast. We were truly a tight unit, just the three of us.

Even though money was always a problem during those first few years when I started to work full time, spending quality time with my boys was imperative. I was able to negotiate using my vacation time to take off every Friday during the summer months when the boys were off from school. I wouldn't have traded those extra Fridays I had with the kids for anything.

Since I didn't have enough money to take Michael and Brian on an actual vacation, I used our three-day weekends to take the boys to amusement parks, on day trips, picnics, and to the community pool. We would also visit our family and friends who lived out of state.

Even so, there were days when I wavered. Had I done the right thing? Were my sons going to be okay? In the weeks after we left New Orleans, I watched Michael and Brian like a hawk. I was so worried that they were going to suffer as a result of being separated from their dad. There were some rough moments. Brian had nightmares at times. Michael, as the oldest, wanted to overcompensate for his dad's absence by being the "little man of the house." He wanted to help with the lawn, and take out the garbage, and look after his little brother. I had to explain to him that those were *my* jobs, and it was okay to let me do them. Meanwhile, I was dealing with my own sense of failure: that I'd made the wrong choices, that our family was incomplete, that I was on my own.

There was so much stigma surrounding divorced families back then. I enrolled my boys in a parochial school, thinking it was for the best, but it turned out that my sons were the only kids in school with divorced parents. Meanwhile, Mike was under the impression that our situation was temporary. He moved back to Pennsylvania to be nearer to us. As far as Mike was concerned, he and I were going through a rough patch and would eventually reconcile. There were days when I wondered if I *should* take him back. Maybe it would be better for everyone that way.

Then came my wake-up call.

Throughout our marriage, Mike had been physically threatening, but he'd never made me feel like I was in serious danger. Then, eight months after we left New Orleans, my lawyer finished preparing the divorce papers and had them served. That evening, the boys and I were just getting home from midget football practice. Michael had made quarterback his first year playing (his team went to play-offs and won the league that year), so we went to practice four times a week. Just as we were walking in the door, we saw Mike's car swerve into our driveway, tires screeching and brakes squealing.

Right away, I knew we were in for a rough night.

I opened the front door and called to the boys.

"Go in and start your bath right now. Your dad isn't feeling well."

Michael, eight, and Brian, five, no longer took baths together, but they knew by the tone of my voice not to question what I was telling them.

At that moment, Mike barreled through the front door. His eyes were wild and intense, his pupils enormous. I'd never seen him like this before. He looked frightening.

Then he came toward me.

"How dare you! How *dare* you!" he shouted, shaking the divorce papers that he clutched in his fist.

I backed into the dining room and tried to get to the other side of the dining table, but Mike was too quick for me. In a flash, he had his hands around my neck. I was up against the wall, my feet barely touching the floor. I tried to shout, but nothing came out. I remember thinking, "I can't breathe; I'm going to pass out."

Michael and Brian jumped out of the bath and ran naked into the dining room. They were wet and screaming, trying to pull their dad off me. Michael jumped on Mike's back and wrapped his little arms around his throat.

"Get off my mommy!" he was screaming.

Brian was on the floor and wrapped both of his legs around his dad's ankles while desperately trying to bite Mike's calf.

Mike released his hands from around my throat.

"Now, guys," Mike said, reaching to hug them. "Don't get too upset. You know how your mother overreacts."

I staggered forward, wheezing, trying to catch my breath. The boys were crying. Mike ushered them back into the bathroom, reassuring them that everything was okay.

But the moment he stepped back into the dining room, he lunged at me again, his hands back around my throat. Again I tried to inhale but couldn't. My eyes began to swim; my brain fogged. I remember thinking, "I'm going to die."

And just then the doorbell rang.

Mike, startled, loosened his grip just long enough for me to get free. He ducked into my bedroom for cover. I ran for the front door.

Standing there was the person I wanted to see most at that moment: my aunt Dutch. She has always been a strong, athletic woman. Right then and there, I knew there had to be a God, because Dutch never popped in unannounced. But that night, she happened to be passing by and spotted Mike's car in the driveway.

"What's going on here?" she wanted to know. "Where is he?"

"Don't leave us," I pleaded. Dutch nodded and came inside.

My aunt waited in the living room while I walked into my bedroom to tell Mike that he had to leave immediately. As I turned the corner to go in, he lunged at me for the third time and threw me on my bed.

"Aunt Dutch is here, Mike," I told him. "And one scream from me, and you're dead!"

Mike looked over my shoulder, and there stood Dutch. He bolted out of the room.

"Hey, Dutch, how ya' doing?" he muttered cowardly as he raced toward the front door.

After Mike left, I was still trembling, but I knew I couldn't let the boys see that I was afraid. I cleaned up the living room, where the remains of knocked-over plants were scattered on the floor. Dutch helped calm down the boys and get them ready for bed. Then the four of us gathered downstairs, and Dutch got out a pack of cards.

"Let's play a round," said my aunt.

I made popcorn. We played a game that my mom and Dutch had taught me when I was a little girl. I always called her "crazy Aunt Dutch" because she was so good at making everyone laugh. That night, Dutch joked around while we played. Her complete calm was exactly what the boys needed. I needed it too. My aunt stayed with us that night and every night for the rest of the week to make sure we were safe.

We needn't have worried. In the weeks and years to come, Mike pretty much vanished from our lives. He unraveled. He became increasingly lost, not just personally but professionally too. He was fired from his job because of his excessive drinking. The Christmas after we separated, Mike came to see his boys for the first time since that terrible night. It was snowing outside, but for some inexplicable reason, Mike wasn't wearing a coat; he had on nothing but shorts, a T-shirt, and sandals with no socks. I remember looking at him and thinking, "There's the man I used to love." He handed each of the boys a Christmas card. Inside were the words "IOU one Christmas gift. Love, Dad." My sons never did get those gifts promised to them.

In the years to come, despite everything that had happened between us, I used to call Mike and beg him to contact the kids. He would say that unless he had money and a job, he didn't want to see them. "But, Mike," I'd reply, "the boys don't care about money; they just want to spend time with their dad." Sadly, Mike was the same stubborn Mike. He was impossible to convince. He didn't want to see the boys until he had his life "back on track." Mike kept trying to chase the "big time" careerwise and ended up focusing his energies in all the wrong directions. I'm certain that if he'd stuck with one thing, he would have succeeded. He was such a smart man. But instead he pretty much squandered his talents. In all the years I was bringing up our boys alone, Mike never contributed in any way: no child support, birthday gifts, or school clothes, and certainly no moral support—not even a simple phone call to say, "Hi, how are you? How are the boys?" Or, more important, "Can I talk to the boys?" Michael and Brian kept up a close connection with their dad's brother, Uncle Brendan, but over the years, they had minimal contact with their father.

Money was tight, to say the least. No sooner had I gone to work for the union than it underwent a staff reshuffling and I had to accept a job as a receptionist, reducing my already small salary.

I remember my mom asking me one day, "Vicki, how are you doing financially?"

"I'm doing fine, Mom," I told her. "I can afford everything except for groceries."

For the first two years after we left New Orleans—until I was promoted to the secretarial position I'd originally been promised—my mother gave me $50 a week so that I could put food on the table.

It was my brilliant mom who suggested that I take the New Year's Eve shift as a coat check girl at the steelworkers union social hall.

"Mom," I told her, "I am not working as a coat-check girl! I already have a job!"

But my mother insisted that the tips were good and that I should give it a try.

The night of New Year's Eve 1979, driving to the party, I was so upset that I had to stop the car. I'm a pretty humble person, but even so. Last New Year's Eve in New Orleans, I'd celebrated at the country club with champagne, and now I was on my way to check coats at my mother's office for someone else's party. But I knew I didn't have a choice. I wiped away my tears and took my place next to the coat rack. As it turned out, the evening wasn't so bad after all. The tips kept coming, and a few older gentlemen even brought me glasses of champagne. For some reason, that French wine tasted even better sitting in a tiny room full of coats. Happy New Year to me!

The next morning, I went to my mom's to pick up the boys, and I told her the good news: I'd made more in tips in one evening than I earned in an entire month as a secretary.

"Mom, I have enough money in tips to pay all my bills for the month, money for food, and I even have one hundred dollars extra to start a savings account!"

That week, I opened my first-ever savings account as a single mom. I made sure to tell my mom that I was happy to be the steelworkers union coat check girl at every future function. I was having so much fun that it didn't hit me until spring that the coat check business would soon come to an end. I remember laughing out loud and saying, "Oh no, people don't wear coats in the warmer weather!" But by now at least I had enough money in my savings account to keep us going until fall.

In the coming years, I worked nine to five and kept up my coat checking on the side. After I started working, however, I became a different kind of mother. I changed from being strong and focused to someone who avoided the word "no" because I felt guilty about the time I spent away from the boys. It wasn't easy. I hated leaving my sons all day. I knew how lonely it could be for a child who comes home after school to an empty house. I always envied my friends whose mothers were there to greet them at the end of the day with fresh cookies and a hug. What saved me was that I knew I didn't have any choice. I couldn't afford to stay home. It wasn't a debate for me. I was the mother, but I was also the sole provider.

After about five years of working full time and saving my coat-checking tips, we were actually able to move to a bigger house in a better neighborhood. This was a top priority for me—I was determined that my boys would have a nice house to grow up in, whether or not they had a dad to help take care of them. The house was a white-brick, L-shaped ranch-style home with black double French doors set in a cutout alcove. I fell in love with that house the moment I laid eyes on it. I made an offer far below asking price, and by some miracle, it was accepted.

This new house had a huge, unfinished basement, and that became the boys' indoor playground. It was big enough for them to ride bikes, rollerskate, and play hockey with their friends. By now Michael was thirteen, and Brian was eleven. Michael was an excellent basketball player, and the basement was where he practiced his drills. Brian liked to practice his tennis game against the farthest wall. In order to brighten up the basement a little, I hung my old dance studio banner in the middle of the sidewall, up against the stone-gray cement blocks. The banner was handmade in aqua and white felt, my signature colors, with white fringe along the bottom. It read:

Vicki's Studio of Rhythm
Steelton

The banner had survived all the many moves from house to house. It had come with me to New York when I was twenty-two and newly married. Somehow it had survived the basement flood in our home in New Jersey. It traveled to New Orleans. And the banner was still in one piece, all these years later, now that my boys and I were living alone.

My boys grew up under that banner in the basement. It was a reminder to us all that I had been a dance teacher once upon a time. But it was also a reminder that dance was something I had left behind because I was "too old and busy for that." Dance was something I did before I left home and got married, when I was younger, before the cares and worries of adult life took over.

I was a single mom now, and my entire focus was my boys. Of course, I worried about them growing up without a father. Sometimes I wonder how different things would have been if I'd had daughters and didn't have the additional pressure of being a mom and a substitute male role model rolled into one. I remember when Michael was thirteen, he decided he had to shave. It was his first time, and he was getting ready for a dance. He ran into the kitchen and asked me if I had an electric razor, since he was too nervous to use a real one. In a panic, I searched for a tiny woman's electric razor I'd purchased years ago. I was so happy for him when I found it in the back of my closet that I rushed it to his room.

"Aw, Mom!" Michael said with a sigh. "The first time I need to shave, and you give me a *pink* electric razor!"

I assured him that tomorrow we could go shopping for his very own razor, but to this day, I don't think he's ever forgiven me for that pink razor!

Michael has always been the quieter of my two boys. He had his grandfather's talent for athletics. And he was such a source of strength, always looking out for his little brother. Brian, by contrast, was the comedian, talkative and outgoing. One day when Brian was in eighth grade, he told me he was going to run for student council president, which didn't surprise me in the least. Later that evening, we started to plan his campaign. At the time, Brian was obsessed with GQ magazine and could often be seen walking around with the latest issue tucked under his arm. He called the magazine his bible, so I decided to design his campaign poster to look like the cover of GQ. I cut out the magazine logo and headlines that read, "Introducing the Unbelievable American" and "New Style: Natural Confidence." I glued these onto his school picture and made a hundred copies. Brian went to school the next day to kick off his weeklong campaign, proudly carrying his posters.

Then, on the morning he was giving his election speech, I handed him a small cardboard box and said, "Knock 'em dead, Brian!" Inside were 350 royal blue satin ribbons with gold lettering, his school's colors, that read, "Brian S. Riordan for President, Swatara Junior High, 1987–1988."

Brian was ecstatic. When he left for school that morning, he raced out of the house to the bus stop, and for once, he wasn't running because he was late for the bus, he was running because he was flying high.

I had to call in quite a few favors at work to get those ribbons made. I didn't have the extra money to pay for something that wasn't an "essential," but I wanted Michael and Brian always to have the opportunities I felt they deserved.

Later that day, he called me from the school's pay phone after his speech. He was breathless.

"Mom, I just gave my speech! I was the last candidate to speak. When it was finally my turn, I stood up at the podium and saw hundreds of kids staring back at me. I couldn't believe it."

"Brian, were you scared?"

"No, Mom," he said excitedly, "I loved it."

The next day, my son became the new student council president of Swatara Junior High. Later that summer, at the Pennsylvania Association of Student Councils' weeklong leadership camp, attended by the student council officers of every school in the state, he won the award for top student leader in Pennsylvania. In the years to come, Brian was president of his class every year until he graduated college. My boys didn't have their dad. We didn't have a lot of money. But that didn't mean they couldn't succeed. That was my philosophy as a single mom.

I kept hoping that I'd meet a new man. When I first separated from Mike, I remember thinking that I probably wouldn't be single for long. Someone was certain to come along. I dated, and there were a few short-term relationships, but nobody worth mentioning in a book. At a certain point, I realized that I wasn't looking just for a partner, I was searching for someone who could become part of my family—who could be a father to my sons—and that person proved hard to find.

As both boys moved into their teens, my longing for someone only intensified. To be honest, I would have loved a man to help share the responsibility of bringing up two teenagers. Michael and Brian's needs were becoming more and more expensive. They wanted sports equipment, the latest sneakers, they were already asking for money to take girlfriends on dates. Meanwhile, college was looming, and our new house was costing a lot more to run than I'd expected.

Until now we'd always managed. After we moved into the new house, though, I found myself lying awake nights trying to make the figures add up. In the back of my mind, I knew how important it was to save for college for my sons, but to be honest, I was so concerned with our day-to-day survival that if I dwelt on our long-term financial situation for more than a second or two, I'd probably start crying. My priority was always to make the mortgage payments, so that we could keep our home and the boys would have a nice place to grow up in. I used credit cards to live, but I knew I had to be very careful. I paid everything on time, even if it was just the minimum payment due. My mom hand-made all of my work clothes, since I couldn't afford to purchase them. (This was the time when *Dynasty* was on TV and she made five suits for me using sewing patterns modeled after the big-shoulder-pad style of Alexis and Crystal.) If we took vacations, we'd stay with a friend in another state, and I would have to save for months beforehand to pay for tickets to amusement parks and meals at restaurants.

Despite my best efforts, after six years of single-handedly trying to stretch my modest income, I realized we were starting to sink financially. My knight in shining armor was nowhere in sight. This was all on me. It was no one else's problem.

I did the math, scratching out the figures in pencil in my notebook. I realized that I had two options if I didn't want to fall behind.

1. Make the extra money I needed to get ahead again.
2. Start thinking about selling our house and moving some-where smaller.

I knew that option two wasn't practical; the last thing I wanted to do was to sell the house and uproot the boys again. But where was I going to find any extra money when I was already spending every cent that I earned?

Then, one night as I was trying to fall asleep, it came to me. It was so obvious that I couldn't understand why I hadn't thought of it before. I already knew how to earn the extra money.

I was a certified dance instructor, wasn't I? I could go back to teaching dance.

Chapter 7

• • •

Sunday, June 12, 2011

10:40 AM

BY MIDMORNING, WE'RE DONE REHEARSING THE SHOW'S FIRST FOUR DANCES. TIME FOR A SHORT BREAK. THE DANCERS ARE GATHERED IN THE AUDITORIUM, SITTING IN SEATS OR CONGREGATING ON THE MEZZANINE, WHERE THEY'VE BEEN WATCHING AND SUPPORTING THEIR FELLOW TAP PUPS ALL MORNING.

I pick up the microphone.

"Okay, everyone. Before we go any further, we're going to watch the videos that the audience is going to see this afternoon."

A huge white screen descends from the back of the stage.

There's an "Oooooh" from the dancers, and the theater goes quiet.

Every year during the show, it's our tradition to have the dancers step onstage between the numbers and introduce themselves to the audience.

"Hi, my name is Cindy Kuentzler, I'm fifty-five years old, and I'm the owner of a hair salon."

This year we're doing things a little differently. During last week's rehearsals, Brian filmed the dancers and their introductions, so that we could project them onto the big screen during showtime.

"Let it roll, Brian," I say.

One by one, the dancers appear on the huge screen.

"I'm Mary Elizabeth Shettel, and my age is seventy. I'm a happily retired great-grandmother."

"I'm Lynne Ritter, and I'm fifty-five, and I work as a legal secretary."

"I'm Jim Fisher, I'm thirty-one, and I'm a manager at the GAP."

"I'm Sue Hamilton-James. I'm fifty-six and a nurse practitioner."

We started the tradition of these introductions from my very first show. Over the years, these introductions have provided an opportunity for groups of supporters to cheer for their favorite dancer: "Go, Mom!" "I love you, Grandma!"

But these introductions aren't only for the audience's benefit, they're for my dancers too. When I was young, it was very common to hear people say, "Don't ever ask a lady her age." The message was always that you should be ashamed of growing older. But why? I want my dancers to feel proud of how far they've come and how much they've achieved.

The majority of Tap Pups performing today are in their fifties and sixties. It's a time of major transition for women, when it's hard not to lose confidence in yourself as you grow older and your appearance inevitably changes. All those years of caring for children can leave you feeling depleted and unsure of your role after they leave home. It's also a time when many women fall out of step with themselves. Meanwhile, we live in a youth-obsessed culture where all our older movie stars are getting nipped and tucked to stay in the game.

Every year, I have new dancers who are nervous about stepping out into the spotlight.

"Oh no, you aren't going to make me talk too?"

"I hate that part of the show!"

"Why can't we just dance?"

As it turns out, when these women do get up and state their name and age, they realize that it feels a lot better than they'd expected. In fact, it gives them a giant boost of self-confidence.

"I'm Susan Cunningham, I'm sixty years old and a retired lieutenant colonel from the United States Marine Corps."

"I'm Deb Shellenberger, I'm fifty-six years old. I'm a happy housewife and horse lover!"

Instead of hiding their ages, the dancers realize that they actually want people to know that they're fifty, or sixty, or seventy. Suddenly those numbers have a positive shock value to them: Hey, here I am. I'm old enough to claim Social Security, and I can dance, and keep up with the best of them!

It becomes all about owning your age.

After each dancer appears on-screen, there are loud cheers and applause from their fellow Tap Pups sitting in the audience. I turn around to watch the dancers watching themselves on a twenty-foot screen, like movie stars at their own premiere.

THE truth is, I didn't go back to teaching dance because I wanted to write a book, or create America's largest *anything*, or change anyone's life except my own. I started teaching dance again because I needed to make ends meet and survive at a time when I was very low. Dance was the one thing I knew. My dancing had already helped me when I was graduating high school and didn't know what to do next. Now dance was going to save me all over again—only it wasn't just me this time, it was my boys too.

That night in 1986, lying in bed, trying to figure out how to make up the shortfall on my mortgage payments, I already knew the type of classes I wanted to teach. I didn't even consider going back to teaching children. I knew that there were adults out there who wanted to learn to dance.

For the past year or so, I'd been going out dancing at a local 1950s-themed bar called Rod's Road House Cafe. This was the mideighties, and there was a retro revival going on around town. *Happy Days* was still on TV in reruns, *Peggy Sue Got Married* was a hit at the movies, and bar owners all over Harrisburg were jumping on the nostalgia bandwagon, hosting fifties-and-sixties nights.

It was a girlfriend from work, Dagmar, who first asked me if I wanted to go out dancing at Rod's with her. At the time, Michael had just turned sixteen, and he was actually responsible enough to stay home and look after his younger brother. If I wanted to go out in the evening, I didn't have to pay for a babysitter or ask my mom to come over. That Friday night, I drove over to Rod's Road House to meet Dagmar.

Rod's is still a fixture in Harrisburg. It's a 1950s-style diner with shiny blue booths and a giant jukebox in one corner. Right next to the bar is a huge vintage pink Cadillac with the trunk cut out where they set out hors d'oeuvres for happy hour. The décor is a lot of fun, but even so, my first night there, my eyes were magnetically drawn to the back of the restaurant and the dance floor.

It was packed. The DJ was playing "Rock Around the Clock," and everyone was jitterbugging. My eyes went from face to face, and I realized that I actually recognized some of the dancers. Some I knew from high school. Others I'd met through work or were parents I knew through my boys.

I didn't wait for someone to ask me to dance. I grabbed Dagmar.

"Hey, let's jitterbug!"

The next second, I was snapping my fingers, moving my feet to the all-too-familiar steps: one, two, three . . . four, five, six, back step. Just like I'd learned from my mom and my aunt. Just like I used to dance with Bull.

Out on that dance floor, I wasn't at Rod's Road House anymore. I was back at Progress Firehouse, the place where we all used to go to dance when we were teenagers. With my eyes closed, listening to that music, moving in the old sequences of steps I knew so well, there was no difference between now and twenty-five years ago. "Nostalgia" isn't a big enough word to describe it. What I was experiencing was more like time travel. Where had I been all those years?

That night at Rod's, I barely stopped dancing. At one point, I did go back to our table to reach for my drink. I was thirsty and breathless. I'd been dancing so hard, my hair looked like I'd just stepped out of the shower. A guy tapped me on the shoulder. I thought he was going to ask me to dance.

Instead he pleaded, "Please don't go back out there; I'm exhausted just watching you."

"Shame on you, you should be out there dancing too!"

And off I went back to the dance floor.

By the end of the evening, I was exhausted and energized at the same time. I hadn't felt this way in years, not since the days before my marriage. I didn't want the feeling to end. I left Rod's that night walking on air.

Dancing at Rod's brought out the teenager in me, the girl who loved to dance each week at Progress. On Friday nights, I would put on something simple, like jeans and a T-shirt, and head out to my new favorite bar. I wasn't going out to meet a man, I was going out to dance.

Then, while I was out on the dance floor one Friday night, a woman dancing next to me stopped and asked me to show her my steps. I ended up giving a dance lesson right there in the middle of the dance floor.

"That's it, step backward, and then forward again. Follow my feet. You've got it!"

It seemed like every time I went to Rod's, the person dancing next to me would ask, "Hey lady, teach me how to do that step!" and I would show him.

Now that I needed the extra money to provide for my boys, my brilliant idea was to teach adults the social dances of the fifties and sixties: the jitterbug, the cha-cha, the Bristol stomp. I saw a niche for myself. A generation was shifting. All of us who'd been teenagers in the 1950s and 1960s were in our thirties and forties now. We had teenagers of our own, and for the first time in a long time, we were looking for ways to go out and have fun. We were ready to dance again, and we wanted to dance to the music we knew and loved from the old days, using the steps that we remembered from back when we were young.

I called our local recreational center to see if it had any interest in a 1950s–1960s dance program. The director said yes immediately, explaining that the center paid by the hour.

I was never going to make the extra money I needed earning just $5 or $6 an hour. This was a make-or-break situation for me.

Without skipping a beat, I told him bluntly, "That's not going to work. I need to get paid for every person who attends."

"I'm a certified dance instructor," I continued. "I know I can teach. I also know that through word of mouth I can pull in a lot of people for you."

The director paused. I thought I'd lost him.

To my surprise, he said, "Okay, I'll make an exception. And, I'm also joining your class."

At my first class, there were fifty people waiting, and everyone paid for the entire session, mostly in cash. That night, when I came home, Michael and Brian were waiting up for me. I told my boys to put out their hands. Then I dealt them each ten $5 bills.

"We love you being a dance instructor!" they shouted, leaping up and down.

"Okay, boys, calm down," I told them. "Don't expect this every time Mom gets paid."

But I was so proud of myself I could have burst.

Money aside, I discovered that I loved being around dance and students again. Everyone in my class was similar in age to me, and we all enjoyed hearing the old songs and doing the steps we'd first learned when we were teenagers. The experience was a pure confidence boost. When I was teaching, I was more than a mom, more than a secretary. I was an instructor again. I knew what I had to do. I was connecting with people, communicating with them, making them smile. When friends asked me what I was up to, I didn't have to say, "Oh, you know, the usual." I told them, "I'm teaching these fifties and sixties dance classes, my students are fabulous, and you wouldn't believe how many people showed up last Wednesday!"

The reactions I got from my students reinforced that teaching came naturally to me. The pleasure I felt out on the dance floor at Rod's translated directly to the smiles I saw on my students' faces. One couple I taught brought me a bouquet of flowers at the end of the six-week session. They wanted to thank me for saving their marriage.

"Vicki," they told me. "Lately we had nothing that we liked to do together. And now we have the jitterbug!"

A brother and sister took the class together, and at the end of the six weeks, they came up to me to thank me for the session.

"Vicki, after taking your class and enjoying it so much," the man said, "I finally got up the confidence to ask my wife for a divorce."

"Oh no, that's not good!" was my immediate reaction.

"Vicki," his sister chimed in, "if you knew his wife, you'd realize it's a very good thing indeed!"

Many students told me they wished they could watch my classes on a video. This was right around the time that Jane Fonda and Richard Simmons came out with their exercise videos. As far as I knew, no one had thought to do an instructional video for social dances. What if I could make my own videos?

One evening, I happened to mention my big idea to Brian. I thought he'd appreciate it. At the tender age of thirteen, he was already the budding entrepreneur in our family. His dream was to move to New York City and become a success in business just like his then-idol Donald Trump. He'd already read Trump's book *The Art of the Deal* a dozen times.

"I'm positive that if I could make instructional videos based on my fifties and sixties dance program, I just know people would buy them. I really think this could be a success."

"Mom," Brian said, looking me straight in the eye, "don't just sit there and tell me about it. People don't become successful just by sitting around talking about their ideas. You actually have to make it happen. Let's do it!"

I laughed at his words, but at the same time, I knew he was right.

"You know what?" I said to Brian. "I think I will."

Over the next few weeks, I figured out which dancers I was going to use for the demonstrations, and I asked the owners of Rod's for permission to use the bar for the shoot. The problem was, I didn't know the first thing about how to produce a video. All I knew was that I was going to have to invest money up front—money that I just didn't have. In the end, the project was too overwhelming for someone who was working full-time, bringing up two kids, and teaching on the side, so the videos never moved beyond the conceptual stage.

Nevertheless, I kept expanding the instruction. A little while later, when country line dancing became popular, I went to the local country-and-western music bars and watched the steps, learning all the routines so that I'd be able to teach classes in country line. Although this was never going to be my favorite type of dance, my classes were popular, and so I kept it up. By now I was teaching three evenings a week.

Thanks to my sideline of teaching dance, we stayed afloat financially. We didn't have to give up our house. I could safely make the mortgage payments, and I could pay for extras for the boys. I even put money aside for college and for the future. All thanks to dance.

Michael and Brian continued to do well at school, both academically and athletically. In their senior years, Michael was made captain of his school's basketball team, and Brian became the Pennsylvania State high jump champion. My boys started dating, and I taught them how to be gentlemen: for instance, always opening doors for a girl or lady. They've always had excellent manners. Although the teenage years aren't always easy, I think both boys sensed that I had high expectations for them, and they didn't want to fall into anyone's stereotype of "children of divorced parents."

When it came time for Michael to graduate high school, he decided to go to Harrisburg Area Community College until he figured out what he wanted to do with his life. Two years later, he came to tell me that he'd met my future daughter-in-law, Jen. Six months after that, they had a beautiful wedding. Mike was going to become an air traffic controller in the US Air Force. Soon after, he enlisted.

Right around the same time, Brian was graduating high school. I always thought my empty nest phase would happen gradually. Instead, both my sons were going to leave me within a month of each other. Michael was going to start air force basic training in July. A month later, Brian was beginning his freshman year at Ursinus College, a small private school near Philadelphia.

"You two are almost three years apart in age," I told the boys. "This is not the way it's supposed to happen!"

After both my sons had gone, the sense of loss was overwhelming. I'd devoted so much of my life to raising them that I really didn't know what to do with myself now that I didn't have to make them dinner, or pick up after them, or do their laundry. I felt like I'd lost them. In fact, the only thing I'd lost was a sense of perspective.

About two weeks into his freshman semester, Brian called.

"Mom, I'm so sick, I'm so sick," he croaked into the phone.

"Oh no, Brian! What's wrong?" I went into instant Mom mode. "Are you okay? Do you have a fever? Do you have a sore throat? Are you coughing?"

"I don't know," he replied. "I guess I have a fever. I don't know. Mom, I don't know how to be sick without you!"

I was already running around searching for my keys so that I could drive the two hours to Brian's college. Brian had to persuade me that he didn't need me to come take care of him, that he was okay. He just needed to hear my voice. Even if Brian didn't want me to race to his rescue, the call made me realize that on some level, my boys still needed me and always would. That Thanksgiving, Michael and Brian both came home, and I realized that one of the biggest joys of being a parent is that your grown-up children come back to visit you. Yes, my boys were living away from me—Michael was at boot camp now—but in some respects, that was a good thing. Their world had broadened, but they always included me in it.

I was lucky in that another big change was happening in our family during this time. The same year the boys left home, Michael and Jen announced they were going to have a baby. Later that year, I became a grandmother, at the age of forty-five. Michael was only twenty when Jen got pregnant, and although I had my reservations at the start, my son was so happy and so much in love that I had to trust that whatever happened, he'd find a way to work it out.

As Jen's due date drew nearer, I went to the toy store and bought the largest teddy bear I could find—it was literally more than half my size. I walked through the store, carrying my bear and *dying* for someone to ask me why I was buying it. No one did, but as I was standing at the checkout, I made sure to tell the clerk that it was for my first grandchild.

When Michael called me from the hospital to tell me Olivia had arrived, I was floored. After all these years, we had a girl in the family. We finally had a girl.

I grabbed my car keys and the giant bear and practically broke the speed limit to get to the hospital, stopping on the way to buy the biggest pink bow I could find to tie around the bear's neck.

When I met my little granddaughter for the first time, she was as tiny as a bean, with gorgeous crystal-blue eyes, peach-white skin, and hints of blonde hair on her head. The prettiest little girl I've ever seen. Holding her in my arms for the first time, I was overwhelmed. We had a little girl. Michael was a dad. I was a grandmother.

Olivia's arrival lifted my spirits like nothing else could. In those early weeks, I got to babysit her and spend time with her on a regular basis. A few months later, Mike and his family moved to the air force base at Melbourne, Florida. Now that they were gone, I remember thinking to myself, "Well, wait a minute; this empty nest thing isn't so bad. Both my boys are doing fine. I have a beautiful granddaughter. I'm finally free to do whatever I want. I don't have to run home at five o'clock sharp. I don't have to shop for all those groceries or cook big dinners. I don't have to do anything I don't want to do anymore. I can watch whatever TV show I want to watch without anyone fighting me for the remote. When I come home at night, everything is just the way I left it when I walked out the door in the morning."

There was just one thing missing: I still didn't have that special someone in my life. And then, a year after the boys left home, all that changed.

I was with a friend at a dance club in a nearby town when we ran into an old high school buddy of mine, Pete. That night he happened to be out with his friend Larry.

"Larry, remember Vicki, my high school friend that I talk about?" Pete asked his friend.

Larry just nodded and smiled in my direction. I smiled back. He was tall, with broad shoulders and a smile to match, dressed smartly in a sports jacket and jeans. I always say that you can tell a lot about a man by looking at his shoes, so I snuck a look at Larry's footwear. He passed my test: he was wearing a pair of black leather tasseled loafers.

There was a fifties-and-sixties band playing at the club that night, so, of course, Pete asked me to dance. Whenever I looked over my shoulder, I saw Larry looking right at me. After a few songs, Larry finally held out his hand.

"Vicki, would you dance with me?"

I took Larry's hand with my right and let go of Pete's with my left, stepping into Larry's arms. I felt nervous, not because I didn't want to dance with Larry, but because the song was a jitterbug, and I was praying that this good-looking man was a good dancer too.

Larry twisted me around, keeping perfectly in step. "Are you kidding me?" I thought to myself. "Larry is better than good. He's a fabulous dancer."

That evening, we danced to every song that followed.

At the end of the night, Larry walked me to my car. I think we both knew that something was happening between us. As he closed my car door, I remember wishing that he kissed me good night. Instead, he was a perfect gentleman. He waved as I pulled out of my parking spot.

The next day Larry called simply to wish me a good morning.

My fiftieth birthday was around the corner, and Larry offered to take me out to dinner to celebrate. This was our first date. We went to an Italian restaurant in Baltimore, about an hour from my house. I'd been on enough bad dates by now to know that a very good thing was happening that night. Once we started talking, the conversation continued all evening.

Larry ordered red sangria, and as the waiter poured my drink, I commented on how pretty I thought the pitcher was. Larry quietly asked the waiter to go and ask the manager if the pitcher was for sale.

"Not the drink," he specified. "The actual pitcher."

Somehow Larry managed to persuade the restaurant to sell it to him. Then he handed it to me.

"When I come over, and I bring you flowers, you can put them in this, and it will remind us of our first date together," he said.

In the weeks to come, that pitcher was always filled with flowers. More importantly, I learned that Larry and I had so much in common. He loved to dance. He was a great golfer, and I was beginning to enjoy the game. He was fun and sociable, but I noted with relief that when he was out for dinner or at a bar, he never drank too much. Larry was thoughtful. He always booked a favorite restaurant of mine, or he would order in food from the same place, and we would have a romantic night at home, with candles out on the deck at the back of his house, and the two of us dancing after dinner under the stars.

Whenever I was around Larry, I could relax. I felt secure and happy, something I hadn't experienced with a man in my entire adult life.

My fiftieth birthday turned out to be a happy time for me. Turning forty had been a lot harder by comparison. At forty, I was a single mom, supporting my two boys, worrying about my mortgage payments. At fifty, I allowed myself to enjoy this new freedom that came with the boys leaving home and this love that was blossoming at the exact same time. I moved into my own "bachelorette" condo, decorating it just the way I wanted to, with white furniture and peach carpeting, and pale peach–colored walls. I was living on my own terms. For the first time in a long time, it felt like my life was under my control.

There were more positive changes ahead. Brian graduated college and moved to Philadelphia and then to Manhattan, to work in advertising. Michael and Jen had another little girl, Savanah, who was just as beautiful as her sister. I was so proud of our expanding family, and of Michael and Brian and the lives they were creating for themselves. Suddenly all those years of working and striving for them turned out to be more than worthwhile.

And then something truly unexpected happened.

Carmen Williams was the director of a local recreation department and a student in one of my fifties-and-sixties dance classes. It was the last week of the six-week session when she ran up to me after class. Like everyone else in the room, she was pink cheeked and out of breath from dancing so hard.

"Hey, Vicki, didn't you tell me you also used to teach tap dancing?" Carmen asked.

"I sure did," I told her. "But that was a long time ago!"

"How about it, Vicki?" Carmen asked. "Why don't you think about starting an adult tap class? I've wanted to be a tap dancer my whole life!"

Carmen was around the same age as me; I'd never heard a grown woman express interest in tap dancing before.

"Really?" I asked.

"Really!"

My first reaction was that it seemed like a long shot. How many adults were actually going to sign up for a tap class? It wasn't as if tap was having a comeback like the jitterbug. I had my hands full with my day job and teaching. My first inclination was to say no. It just didn't feel like a smart thing to focus on right now. But at the same time, something in my heart told me that maybe I should give it a chance. Tap had always been my favorite kind of dance.

"Okay," I told Carmen hesitantly. "But I'll need at least eleven other students to make it worth my while. And I'll have to charge you more for these classes because tap is a lot harder to teach than the jitterbug."

"Great!" Carmen replied.

After I left that day, I honestly thought that no one would sign up for class, and we could forget ever having had this conversation.

I couldn't imagine where Carmen was going to find eleven adults who wanted to tap-dance.

Chapter 8

• • •

Sunday, June 12, 2011
11:00 AM

THE LAST CLIP FADES FROM THE BIG SCREEN ABOVE THE STAGE. THE DANCERS IN THE AUDITORIUM ARE APPLAUDING, TURNING TO ONE ANOTHER, AND LAUGHING BECAUSE THEY KNOW THAT BY THIS AFTERNOON, THEIR FAMILY MEMBERS AND FRIENDS ARE GOING TO BE SITTING IN THESE SAME SEATS, WATCHING THE EXACT SAME SHOW. "WHO WOULD HAVE THOUGHT I'D END UP A MOVIE STAR?" THEY'RE JOKING TO ONE ANOTHER. "WHERE'S THE POPCORN?"

As the applause dies down, I grab the mic again. "Okay, back to rehearsals!" I tell the dancers. "It's time for 'Shake, Rattle and Roll'!"

This year, I've choreographed a new routine for the Beginner 3s. They're going to be dancing to the classic tune made famous by Bill Haley, the same song that I danced to as a nine-year-old at the drive-in with the car headlights as my spotlights.

The dancers line up, and the music begins.

Dancing in the third row today is Alberta. At sixty-four, she's petite and attractive, with short hair and a low voice that always sounds surprising coming from someone so small. As we begin rehearsing "Shake, Rattle and Roll," I see that Alberta has the biggest grin on her face of any of the dancers in her group.

This is not the Alberta I first met four years ago.

When Alberta began coming to my classes, she was better known for her frowns than her smiles. She arrived with her two good friends Linda and Deb—and I quickly started calling these ladies the Three Musketeers because they always stood together in the back row, rarely chatting to anyone else. At that point, it was unusual for me to have ladies signing up in a trio. Most dancers came alone, and so they naturally reached out and made friends with the other dancers. The Three Musketeers, however, were a clique. Even though Deb could have taken a class at another location nearer to her home, she drove to my studio each week so that she could dance with her friends.

Alberta was a beginner dancer when she came to me, and like any beginner, she needed a lot of individual instruction. But whenever I went over to show her how to shift her weight or move her foot, she'd cross her arms and practically scowl at me; or hold out her hand, as if to say, "No thanks, I don't need help." Her two friends were a little more responsive, but overall, these ladies preferred to keep to themselves.

I was determined to connect with them. I knew that the Three Musketeers weren't going to like it, but after a few weeks, I decided to separate them. I told them that I needed them to dance next to different dancers, since I noticed they were following one another's footwork and kept making the same mistakes. I moved Alberta over to one side of the room, put Deb in the middle, and Linda on the other side. Although the ladies weren't happy about this initially, after another week or two, they were already starting to become better dancers. They were even starting to chat and make friends with the other dancers in the class.

When that year's spring show came around, we had our usual preshow rehearsal. As the beginners walked out onstage to run through their routine, I decided to surprise the Three Musketeers.

"Alberta, Deb, Linda: You ladies have improved so much, I want you dancing together in the same line during the show. Move back to your original places, please!"

The three friends practically skipped into their former positions, while the rest of the class gave them a big round of applause.

Later that afternoon, after the show was over and we'd taken our last curtain call, I saw someone running toward me. It was Alberta. She was yelling out my name and literally pushing the other dancers out of the way.

Before I could speak, Alberta had wrapped me in a giant bear hug.

"Vicki, I loved it out there!" she exclaimed. "I absolutely loved it. I want to do it again—right now!"

"Don't worry, Alberta, there's always next year," I told her, hugging right back.

When the Three Musketeers returned to class the following fall, they no longer hung out in a corner together. They were friends with the rest of the ladies, and they even joined the groups of dancers who went out for drinks after class.

The next year, Alberta's mother got sick. Alberta told her husband that she would quit tapping in order to have more time to take care of her. But he said he wouldn't hear of it, telling Alberta, "Vicki's taken you so far out of your box, this is wonderful. You can quit anything else, but you're not quitting tap class."

WHEN Carmen, the director of the rec center, first asked me to teach a tap class for adults, I'd been convinced that the class would be canceled due to lack of interest. She proved me wrong. A week before the new session, she called to tell me that seventeen students had signed up for tap class. Seventeen!

I was due to teach my first class in January 1997. The evening before, I dug around in the back of the closet in my spare room, looking for my little dance bag from my Studio of Rhythm days. A small tote bag made of dark denim. Wherever I went in my life, I always tucked that bag away for safekeeping in a closet or high on a shelf somewhere. Inside it, I found my old shoes: the pair of black high-heeled tap shoes with straps across the top and small squares of metal on the soles.

Would the shoe still fit? It had been thirty years since I'd last slipped a tap shoe onto my foot. I cautiously stretched out the back of the heel to squeeze my foot inside. The leather felt stiff, and when I went to fasten the buckle, I felt a twinge of arthritis in my hands—something that certainly hadn't been a problem the last time I put these on at the age of twenty-two!

Even so, there was no doubt about it: the shoes still fit.

I went out into my vestibule, with its ceramic tile floor, to try out a few steps. I knew it wasn't the best surface because it was so slippery, but I had carpet everywhere else in my home, and I needed to make sure that the old leather shoes weren't going to hurt my feet.

Shuffle, hop step, slap step.

The metal on the tile made a crisp, sharp *click*, and my feet felt fine in the old shoes.

Now for my favorite heel time step:

Stamp, pull hop, slap, slap, toe heel stamp.

Yep, it felt as good as ever.

By now I was starting to bounce on the balls of my feet, just like I used to do in my Studio of Rhythm days.

I tried a few more combinations.

Shuffle, hop, shuffle, step, slap, ball change.

After so many years, I still knew exactly how to do those steps. Done and done. They were locked in my memory, just waiting for me to find them again. I took off the shoes.

The next day I got in my car. Off to class. I went through the lesson plan in my head: I knew I was going to start with the basics. It was a no-brainer; keep it simple. Slap, shuffle, shuffle series, ball change, and if I needed a bit more material to fill in the hour, slap heel, double heels, and stamps.

My first tap class was being held in the cafeteria of a local elementary school. As soon as I walked in, I realized that tapping in a space like this was going to be a challenge. The walls were painted with murals of cartoon animals and bugs, and there was one very short, child-sized water fountain in the corner of the room. Half the vinyl floor tiles had been replaced with mismatched squares that stuck up at odd angles. Some were cracked and even missing altogether. All of them were dirty. I found an extralarge mop in the janitor's closet and ran it over the floor, sweeping aside crayons, cookie crumbs, and even an entire chocolate chip cookie, feeling quite sure that Gene Kelly never had to deal with this!

My new students started arriving. Carmen was the first. She was beaming; clutching the box containing her new tap shoes. At her side was her friend and coworker Andrea, a petite woman with big blond curls, smiling just as widely as Carmen. The two of them sat down and started comparing their new shoes, putting them on their feet excitedly. Soon the other students started arriving. I met Judy and her friend Tanya; then Terese, Korry, Aggie, Gloria, Brenda, Sherry, Debbie, Virginia, Jean, and Joanie. Everyone looked nervously excited. Then there was my old friend Linda. We'd first met when our sons played baseball together, and I'd invited her along because I knew she had loved to tap when she was a child.

A mutual friend named Nancy, who'd also tapped before, also walked in the door.

There was one man in the class. His name was Bert. I recognized him right away. By coincidence, he was Dr. Zumoff, my former allergist. I had visited him for my asthma about twenty years ago.

"Well, Dr. Zumoff," I said, "I never would have guessed you had aspirations to tap!"

"Oh, Vicki," he told me, "you have no idea. I've wanted to dance like Gene Kelly my entire life!"

Dr. Zumoff had arrived at class in perfectly tailored black pants and a black V-neck sweater. He was doing his best impersonation of my idol.

I calculated that the ages in the class ranged from around forty-five to the eldest, Aggie, who was seventy-six.

Then it finally hit me. This was really happening—all these adults were so serious about taking this class that they had actually gone to a store before class and bought themselves new tap shoes.

Nancy was the exception.

"Vicki, see these?" she asked, holding up a pair of black high-heeled shoes with straps across the top, very similar to my own. "My old tap shoes! I haven't worn them in nearly thirty years."

"Same here," I said, showing her mine.

"I can't believe I'm getting to put them on again!" she said.

"Trust me, I know exactly how you feel."

When everyone was ready—shoes on feet—they stood up and walked to the center of the room. People were giggling because they already were making "that noise." There's just something inherently fun about walking and hearing your feet go *click, click, click.*

I lined up the class in three rows in front of me. Linda and Nancy hadn't tapped for years, and the rest were absolute beginners, so obviously we needed to focus on the basics as I'd planned. I started with a warm-up routine to "Green Onions" by Booker T. and the MG's, the same warm-up I'd always used at Vicki's Studio of Rhythm. I just deleted a few jazz moves to make it more age appropriate for an older crowd. I knew that we weren't able—or, quite frankly, interested—in doing splits on the floor to stretch out our legs and hips.

By the end of the class, we'd done slaps, shuffles, slap heel, slap double heel, and my signature three and twos (three slaps followed by two stamps). To my surprise, my students were already beginning to put together the steps. They were actually dancing. Everyone was pink in the face, hair wet around the neck, but everyone was smiling.

When we were finished, my students came up to me one by one and thanked me for such a great lesson. Carmen had the biggest smile of anyone in the group. I gave her a giant hug.

"Thank you," I told her. "Thank you for making me put my tap shoes back on. I'd forgotten how much I love teaching people how to tap-dance!"

In the coming weeks, I realized that teaching tap again was so different from teaching social dances. Of course, I enjoyed those classes, but for me, a country line routine or even the jitterbug can't ever compare. Tap is an art form, and like all true art forms, it's extremely hard to master and wonderfully challenging to teach.

After that first week, the class grew to twenty-two, as five students each brought a friend. The students who had tapped before felt the same way as the students who were trying the steps for the first time. Tapping made all of us wrinkle our brows in concentration, but at the same time it also made us smile. We were moving in complex sequences of rhythm, and we didn't need to explain to one another why it had this effect on us, because everyone in class agreed: it just felt good.

As the session progressed, I did run into some interesting new challenges, however. When I taught tap before, it had always been to young children. Whereas kids have such a natural ability to learn, adults take longer to pick up the steps. As the weeks went on, I realized that I had to adjust my expectations.

Aggie always liked dancing in the third line. At seventy-six, she was hard of hearing, and after I gave each instruction, she would squint, cup a hand to her good ear, and yell, "What'd she say?" Someone in the second row would yell out, "Aggie wants to know what you said!" By then, someone in the front row was already yelling back to Aggie, "She said, 'Slap, heel'!"

Then there was Virginia, always wanting to be precise, raising her hand and asking questions: "Is my foot pointing to the right?" "Where should my left hand be when I do that shuffle?"

Joanie was one of the older dancers, and as hard as I tried, I couldn't seem to get her to loosen up. She was so stiff.

"You have to relax a bit more," I kept telling her. "You have to get off your feet more. Hop after you do that shuffle."

As much as I kept encouraging her, I just didn't know how to get Joanie to move.

It was only many weeks later that she lifted up her T-shirt and showed me what was underneath: a full back brace.

"Oh my gosh," I said. "No wonder you couldn't hop! Why didn't you tell me?"

"I didn't want it to hold me back!" Joanie explained.

After that, I would start each class by asking everyone to tell me their ailments and health issues up front, so I could be better at helping them during class. As dancers started lifting up a pant leg to reveal a knee brace, or showing me an arm that wouldn't lift higher than a sprained shoulder, we'd all have a good laugh about who had the most aches and pains that week—myself included.

As the weeks went by, the class was getting better and better at mastering the basic tap steps. Now it was time for me to introduce hand, arm, and head movements.

I quickly noticed that when my students used their hands and arms, they weren't at all graceful. They needed to use "ballet hands," with their fingers extended, middle fingers curving toward thumbs, and pinkies out. The little girls I'd taught at the Studio of Rhythm knew just what I meant when I said ballet hands, because they were taking ballet and tap at the same time. But what about my adults? I'd lay money on Dr. Bert Zumoff's never having taken a ballet class in his life.

"I want you to hold up an imaginary full-stemmed glass of champagne in your hand," I told them instead. "Pointer finger up, holding that glass ever so lightly with your fingers relaxed. . . . Now transfer that full glass with an ease in your arm so as not to spill it . . . and hand it to the person next to you."

We practiced several times, and it worked beautifully. They got it. I watched each student staring intently at his or her full glass of champagne while passing it gracefully from hand to hand.

Wait a minute. Aggie was passing her glass too quickly.

"Slow down," I told her. "You're spilling your champagne!"

"No, I'm not," she yelled. "I already drank it!"

I left each tap class on a high. It didn't matter that so much time had passed since I'd last put on my tap shoes. Teaching tap took me back to Steelton and my Studio of Rhythm on Front Street—that time before marriage, working, motherhood, and all the responsibilities of life.

Those old black, scuffed tap shoes turned out to be my version of Dorothy's ruby slippers in *The Wizard of Oz*:

They carried me home.

The September after I first returned to teaching tap, I learned that I had enough students for two classes a week. I was now teaching fifty dancers in total. In a single year, we'd more than doubled in size. The new Tuesday night class was the bigger of the two, with thirty dancers, all of them women. I remember feeling happy to see that Carmen and her friend and colleague Andrea had both returned to their Wednesday night class.

By now I had gotten to know Andrea better. I'd learned that she had two boys a few years younger than mine and that she lived about a ten-minute drive from class. She was in her midforties, and because she had spent so much time performing as an actress in local theater, there was a boldness and confidence about her that just drew me in her direction. I loved that when Andrea wanted to emphasize what she was saying, she would take her hand and flip her hair back away from her shoulder. She always seemed to say what was on her mind, yet at the same time, Andrea had such a tender side; she watched out for others in the group, making sure that everyone felt included.

Although Andrea was a familiar face, some of the other students I'd never met before, so at the beginning of the first class, I thought I had better get everyone to introduce themselves.

Everyone took turns and said her name—"Andrea Catlin," "Jenna Di-shong," "Susan Croushore"—until we got to a lady with short brown hair and a big grin in the second row.

"*Annette!*" she shouted out.

This lady knew we were all old enough to get the joke. She was imitating the roll call from the original *Mickey Mouse Club* TV show circa 1955. Growing up, all of us had wanted to be Annette Funicello, the prettiest Mousketeer in the clubhouse (and the only one who wasn't flat chested!).

It was clear from the beginning that "Annette"—otherwise known as Kay—was one of the most vocal and engaging members of the group. She was no more than five foot two, but what she lacked in height, she made up for in personality. She was always the first to crack a joke, encourage another dancer, or flash me a smile to let me know she was enjoying class.

After a few weeks, I noticed that Andrea and Kay would always run off together at the end of class. One evening I overheard them making plans to go to a local bar for dinner and drinks.

"Are you girls going out?" I asked.

"Yes, would you like to join us?" Andrea replied immediately.

That evening, we went to the local Knights of Columbus.

Andrea explained that they came here because it was quiet and they could always get a table.

"Plus, the beers are cheap!" Kay said with a laugh.

Inside was a dark bar with a formal dining room next door. A group of men were playing darts in the back. As we walked in we found seats at a high, round table near the bar.

The girls ordered a pitcher of beer and hot wings. I asked for wine.

"So how long have you ladies known each other?" I wanted to know.

It turned out that Andrea and Kay had been friends for about ten years. After Andrea had such a good time in the first session of tap, she recommended the class to Kay.

That evening, I learned that Andrea had always wanted to tap-dance as a child. Her mom had tapped when she was a little girl—and even won a Shirley Temple look-alike contest—but for some reason, she'd never taken Andrea to classes.

"I was one of three sisters," Andrea pointed out. "I guess there wasn't money to spare."

MEET THE DANCERS OF "42ND STREET"

WATCH ANDREA AND SOME OF THE ADVANCED DANCERS

DISCUSS THE FINAL ROUTINE IN TODAY'S PERFORMANCE.

www.youtube.com/vickistappups

Andrea was about four years younger than me. She grew up in Harrisburg, on the other side of town. We joked that maybe if she'd lived closer, I could have taught her in my dancing school.

Kay told us about her teenage years, during which her entire social life had revolved around a local barbecue joint with a jukebox.

"That's where we went every Friday and Saturday," she remembered. "It was like our *Happy Days*: we danced until our parents came to drag us home to bed." Like so many dancers I was meeting at this time, dance had always been a huge part of Kay's life, but she had no formal training, and she'd certainly never tried to tap-dance until now.

Before long, our trips to the Knights of Columbus became a Wednesday night fixture. Soon Jenna and Susan, two other members of the class, were joining us. Every time we gathered there, the ladies would want me to show them the latest step we'd learned in class that night. We'd jump down off our stools, and I'd start putting them through their paces. The grizzled old-timers propping up the bar looked at us like we'd lost our minds. Of course, that didn't stop us from coming back week after week. And soon, those old-timers would start greeting us with a loud cheer, "Here come the tap ladies!"

We were a varied group. Andrea, Kay, and Jenna were married. Susan was single with no children. I had my boyfriend, Larry. Andrea and I had sons. Jenna had daughters. Kay had a son. We came from very different professions. Andrea worked for the rec center, Susan was in health care, Jenna had her own business, and Kay was a teacher's aide. But even so, my new friends had one thing in common besides tap class: they weren't afraid to speak their minds, and I loved that.

At times I felt like goody-two-shoes Sandra Dee with the Pink Ladies, in *Grease*. The girls all smoked, while I didn't. They were outspoken and loved shock value, while I tend to be more reserved. When they would drop the F-bomb after having a few beers, I would clasp a hand to my chest and gasp that they would use this word so liberally. This would always make them fall over laughing.

"Are you for real, Vicki?" Susan asked me on more than one occasion. She was convinced that I was putting her on.

"I can't believe you think I'm pretending!" I kept telling her. Finally, I managed to convince her that this was just the way I was raised. "My mom always told me that if you resort to swearing, it shows you have a lack of vocabulary."

Of course, the girls thought this was hilarious.

We quickly figured out that of everyone in the group, I was the oldest by about three or four years. Even though we were all baby boomers, in many ways it felt like we came from different generations. I'd grown up with Elvis and Fabian; the others were teenagers around the same time that the Beatles and the Rolling Stones were on the scene. While I was worrying about my "reputation," being ladylike, and wearing gloves with pretty dresses, my new friends were rebelling against the status quo and wearing bell-bottoms and turtlenecks. In 1969, the year of Woodstock, I'd been married for a year and was pregnant with my first child. Meanwhile, they'd been at college, protesting against the Vietnam War, and catching the wave of the women's liberation movement.

One time Andrea summed it up like this: "Vicki, it's like we're blue jeans, and you're a lace dress."

Our similarities, though, always outweighed our differences. We met at the right place at the right time. Everyone in the group was at a point in her life when she needed girlfriends to listen and share.

Jenna was tall and blonde, with a quiet but direct way about her that I always enjoyed. Married with daughters in college, she'd signed up for tap class hoping it would distract her and keep her busy during a rough transition time. With her girls away and her sister recently having moved back to Pittsburgh, she missed having family close by. Over drinks one Wednesday, Jenna confided that tap class was the first time she had ever signed up for something on her own, without a friend.

"I'm not an outgoing person," she said, then laughed. "I still can't believe I did it!"

"Most women I know don't even want to go to the ladies' room alone, let alone to a tap class!" I pointed out.

Susan, my other new friend, had never tap-danced before. She was a general's daughter. Dark haired, with bangs and big blue eyes, she too had decided that she needed to do something to help her through a tough time. Both her parents had just died within the same month, and to make life more complicated, she'd ended a very difficult relationship. Tap was her way of doing something positive for herself.

Those evenings at the Knights of Columbus, we'd talk about the things that mattered to us right now. We'd laugh and complain about the hot flashes, the gray hairs, and the bad knees that we'd never had to worry about in the past. One night Andrea had us howling as she described the day that she realized it was possible to have "back fat."

"I mean, I understand flab around your middle, but how is it possible to have fat on your *back*?"

We'd have big round-table discussions about our jobs, our families, the men in our lives, our children. From the beginning, we understood that unsolicited advice about our kids was a no-no. But when it came to our relationships, men were fair game. We'd pull apart every situation piece by piece, trying to figure out how to put it back together to make a better picture.

It had taken me until my fifties to realize how essential it is to have time with girlfriends. These evenings with my new friends were a surprise for me. Of course, I'd had girlfriends in the past, but I'd never been part of a big group like this before. My mother was the same way. I don't ever remember my mother having a "girls' night out." When she went out to dinner or to a party, she went with her husband. She raised me to focus on my family, and girlfriends were sort of beside the point. Now that I had my new group from tap class, I even remember feeling almost a little guilty that I was putting so much emphasis on people who weren't family. It actually felt "wrong." My entire life, I'd been taught that my happiness depended on my family's happiness. That's how deeply it was ingrained in me.

"I never realized how important it is for me to be able to talk about everything I'm going through with women my age who get where I'm coming from!" I explained to Larry one day.

Meanwhile, my boyfriend was clear that spending time with friends was fine with him. For Larry, his friends were his family, and he valued his time with them as much as he did time with me. He would often go on golfing trips with his buddies. At first I remember feeling a little hurt and left out. Then I realized that when Larry was away, I got to spend more time with my new tap friends, and that was a good thing.

I began arranging other opportunities for the Tap Pups to socialize: We took trips to New York to see shows on Broadway. We went on golf outings. I even had T-shirts made with "Vicki's Tap Pups" across the front for classes and performances. I've always known that I could teach dance and inspire others to become better dancers, but this sense of community was something that I hadn't expected. Over time, the program began to take on a momentum of its own. We were starting to form a sisterhood of tappers.

Then we got some terrible news. We had been dancing together each week for about a year and a half when our friend Kay learned she had developed a rare form of cancer and was going to have to begin chemo right away. Kay kept coming to class for as long as she could until she didn't feel strong enough to continue. Various members of the Tap Pups took turns spending time with her at her home, making sure she had everything she needed. Bald from the chemo, but still as upbeat as ever, she managed to join the Tap Pups on a trip to see the musical *Chicago* on Broadway. That day, she considered getting a henna tattoo on her head. That was Kay. Though her sickness was taking away her physical energy, it was strengthening her incredible spirit. As the days wound down, Kay wrote her own obituary in which she listed her loves, her favorite activities, and her affiliations. "Member of Vicki's Tap Pups" was high on the list.

She died a year after her diagnosis, at only fifty-two years old. Her viewing was held on a Wednesday night. Tap night. After class, sixteen Tap Pups, dressed in our matching Tap Pups T-shirts, went to say good-bye to Kay. On a table by the casket, at Kay's request, her husband had displayed Tap Pups shirts and her tap shoes.

The next Wednesday, my girlfriends and I went to the Knights of Columbus, as we always did. We sat at our usual table. It was glaringly obvious that someone was missing. As we raised our glasses to our friend, we all had tears in our eyes.

Our conversations about life continued, but with a new appreciation of the preciousness of time and of friendship. Since then, our Wednesday night group has been through a lot. In the ten years since Kay passed, we've stuck together through breakups, illness, and loss; we've celebrated engagements and our children's marriages. But one thing remains constant: every Wednesday night, we still make time to go for dinner together after tap class.

Chapter 9

• • •

Sunday, June 12, 2011

11:35 AM

• •

"SHAKE, RATTLE AND ROLL"

WATCH THE BEGINNER 3s IN ACTION.

www.youtube.com/vickistappups

• •

AS WE FINISH UP THE REHEARSAL FOR "SHAKE, RATTLE AND ROLL," THE BEGINNER 3S CATCH THEIR BREATH BEFORE HEADING BACKSTAGE TO GRAB SOME LUNCH AND TO START GETTING READY FOR SHOWTIME.

Right in the thick of this group—as she always is—I notice Anni. She has been coming to class for four years now, and during that time, she's probably taken more classes than any other dancer in the program. Right now, she comes twice a week, but in the past, she's been known to attend as many as four classes each week.

Anni is a successful businesswoman working for a local publishing house. She's fifty-eight, with short, straight dark hair, shining brown eyes, and a smile that she flashes easily and often. You'd never guess it to look at her, but the dancer in the gaggle of women heading backstage is happier, more content, and forty pounds lighter since the breakup of her marriage two years ago.

It's been an eventful couple of years for Anni, as it would be for anyone coming out of a long relationship. On nights when she wasn't coming to class, Anni spent a lot of time reflecting on her new life. One thing was certain, she was going to make it her own, and tap was going to be a big part of that.

I remember reading an article that said the first step to feeling happier is to act happier. It doesn't matter if you feel miserable, put a smile on your face, and before long, you'll actually feel like smiling, because when you give off positive energy, it comes back to you. This was true of Anni. I noticed that Anni would often stay behind to chat with other dancers under the chandelier that hangs over the lounge at the front of my studio. One of the first women that Anni befriended was Betsy: the schoolteacher with the students who call her Dancing Queen. The two of them started standing next to each other in class, and I'd often see them joking and helping each other out with the steps.

Soon Anni and Betsy started getting together with some of the other ladies in that class: Sue, Nancy, Joyce, and Sheri. They developed a significant bond. These women were close in age but had very different careers—they worked in publishing, medicine, administration, and education. Like many of the friendship groups in the Tap Pups, they might never have found one another if it weren't for dance.

I'm a big believer in the power of new friendship. That's not to take anything away from old friendships—our old friendships are irreplaceable— but new friends can bring something really valuable to the table. Because they're not bound by the past, new friends are great at shifting us forward.

Mr. and Mrs. Victor Grubic,
Steelton, 1945.

Me at age three in 1949,
at my parents' softball practice.

Me at age five in 1951,
performing "Rhythm in
My Nursery Rhymes."
This was one of the many
costumes I wore while
performing on a local
talent show, *TV Teen Time*,
hosted by Ron Drake.

My mother, Charlotte "Rusty" Grubic,
world champion bowler, 1959.

In my Steel-High head majorette outfit, 1964.

"Miss Vicki," Studio of Rhythm, 1965.

My two star dancers, Forry Gehret and LuAnne Sprow, 1967.

Steelton's Memorial Day Parade, 1968.

Introducing Mr. and Mrs. Michael Riordan, Steelton, 1968.

With Aunt Dutch and my mom,
doing our signature jitterbug, 1968.

With my boys, Michael and Brian, on a family cruise, 1976.

Our new house in Chambers Hill, Harrisburg, PA, with our dog Jazz, 1983.

Brian's campaign poster for student council president, Swatara Junior High, 1987.

Michael's return from air force basic training, 1991.

The original Vicki's Tap Pups, 1997.

One of our first performances at a local nursing home, 1999.

The last spring show "before Brian" at Good Hope Middle School, 2006. (*Left to right*): Andrea Catlin, Jenna Dishong, Linda Beaver, and Barb Warfel.

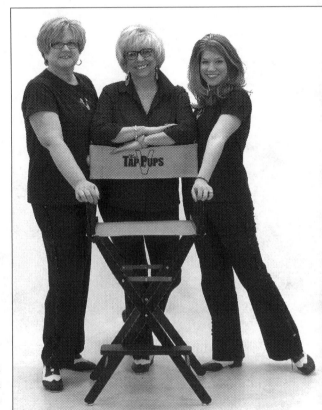

"My Girls": LuAnne and Jessica became instructors in September 2007.

Vicki's Tap Pups Studio & Cultural Center grand opening with my family:
Michael, Savanah, Olivia, and Brian, August 2008.

The Harrisburg Saint Patrick's Day Parade, 2009.
The Tap Pups walk past the Forum, where they perform their annual spring shows.

Vicki's Tap Pups open for Joan Rivers at the Whitaker Center for Science and the Arts in Harrisburg, March 2009. (*Left to right*): Tiny Burns, Sandi Komaromy, Lynne Ritter, Joan Rivers, LuAnne Davis, Vicki, and Jessica Simmons.

New Beginners rehearse in the studio for the twelfth annual spring show, May 2009.

Preparing "comfort bundles" for the spring show to support the YWCA of Greater Harrisburg's Domestic Violence Shelter, June 2009. (*Left to right*): Sharon Caba, Dianne Tiboni, Linda Beaver, Vicki, and Brian.

Five, six, seven, eight . . . TAP PUPS! Final bow at the twelfth annual spring show at the Forum, June 2009.

Rain delay, waiting to open for Chubby Checker and Patti LaBelle,
Philadelphia Museum of Art, July 2009.

For "our Jeanne": the amazing quilt that Deb Pitzer (Beginner 3) created while
Jeanne Schmedlen was fighting breast cancer, February 2010.

New York City bus trip to see *Memphis* on Broadway, October 2010.

Everyone needs a Brian! Preparing for rehearsals to begin for "Let Me Dance," our fourteenth annual spring show at the Forum, June 12, 2011.

Rehearsals begin. "Big smiles, big arms!" (*Left to right*): Carol Kennedy, Cindy Kuentzler, Terrie Davis, Ellen Spaulding, Deb Shellenberger, Peg Biasucci, Lana Meidinger, Deb Minner, and Margie Adelmann.

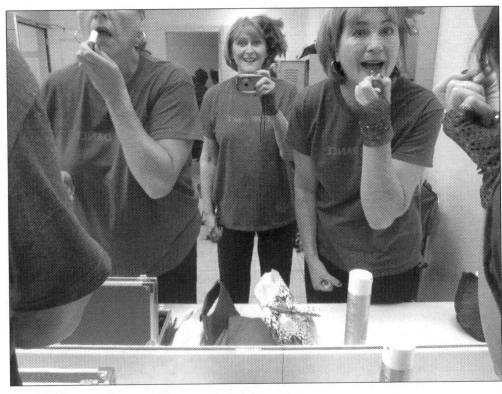

A few Beginner 3s primping for "Shake, Rattle and Roll." (*Left to right*): Vicki Clark, Susan Cohen, and Diane Markley.

Some Beginner 3s dressed for "Shake, Rattle and Roll." (*Left to right, back row*): Sheri Virnig, Beth Hess, Margie Adelmann, Kathryn King-Solon, Diane Markley, Terrie Davis, and Beth Goldstein. (*Front row*): Denise Kennedy, Anni Lodge, Betsy Riter, Jackie Doyle, Carol Tyndale, Nancy Pavelic, and Claudine Battisti.

New Beginners perform Bobby Darin's "Queen of the Hop" in front of the big aqua V. (*First row*): Vonnie Cressler, Jana Poole. (*Second row*): Donna Benson, Mardi Sawyer. (*Third row*): Jeanne Wagner, Karen Storm, Jennifer Skoff. (*Fourth row*): Cheryl Brubaker, Gretchen Petri. (Photo credit: Savanah Riordan)

New Beginners onstage for the second time, looking like real pros as they perform "Chicago." (Photo credit: Savanah Riordan)

Advanced and Intermediate levels performing "Jump Jivin'" and bringing down the house. (Photo credit: Savanah Riordan)

They don't pigeonhole you as "the shy one," "the funny one," "the one who always got the guys." New friends can't dwell on yesterday, and so they let you become the woman you want to be today.

At every key transition point in a woman's life, she makes new friends: in high school, in college, when she has babies. But what happens when the kids leave home, and she's dealing with an empty nest? What happens if she ends up separated from her husband—a very common experience for women at this point in their lives? This is a time when most women would love to meet a new group of friends, but there's not always an obvious way or place for us to connect like we used to do.

Thanks to tap, Anni had a great reason to get out of the house, to be around like-minded women each week. She didn't have to call or email to make plans for dinner or drinks. She knew that as long as she kept coming to class, she would always be in the company of friends.

I imagined that Anni was someone who always drew people to her in this way. In fact, that wasn't the case. Anni could remember times when she would go out for dinner in the past, and she'd look across the room and see a big group of women together. They'd be laughing, and Anni could tell from their body language that there was a closeness and comfort between the women, and she'd think, "Wouldn't it be great to have a group of friends like that?"

One night at the end of our summer session, Anni and her tap friends went out for dinner to say good-bye before the break. This time of year, the dancers are always sad that classes are ending, even though they'll be back in three weeks for the fall session. They miss the lessons and one another. Anni's farewell dinner with her friends was a lot of fun, filled with conversation and laughter. Then, as the evening wound down, Anni realized she'd become part of a group of women friends just like she used to watch from the other side of a restaurant. As she sat back she envisioned herself as others must see her, and in that moment, Anni realized what a wonderful journey she had made since taking that first step onto the dance floor four years ago.

AT the age of fifty-five, I was so proud of my sideline of teaching dance and what I'd created in this new tap program. Meanwhile, my boys were grown and doing so well with their lives, and my little granddaughters, Olivia and Savanah, were bringing me so much happiness. And, for the first time in my life, I felt that I was in a happy and healthy relationship with a guy. I honestly thought the hard times were behind me.

Then, of course, just when I thought I was coasting, I hit another bump in the road.

It was 2002 and I'd been dating Larry for five years when we started talking more seriously about our future together. We were more or less the same age, and retirement was around the corner for both of us. For Larry, retirement meant more golf, his passion. For me, it meant finally giving up my day job working for the union that had been my employer for close to twenty-five years. Like Larry, golf had become one of my favorite pastimes, and I was looking forward to playing the game on a regular basis. Larry wanted to move to Florida. I wanted to stay closer to home to be near my family, but we both agreed that we'd always need a base in Pennsylvania. So on weekends, we began to drive around the area together, looking for "our house." It felt so exciting to be able to say those words, like I was twenty-two again. Except that this time I was going to get this one right.

Our house.

However, nothing that we saw felt just right. Then in August of that year, Larry announced that he'd found it.

"Vic, let's go see our new house" were his words.

We drove over. It was a four-bedroom contemporary in a new development outside of town. The day we visited, there were blue skies above and the gentlest breeze rustling the trees—the perfect summer day. The house was beautiful and spacious, featuring big picture windows, stunning large rooms with ornate pillars framing the dining room, and a landscaped yard. Larry took one look at its huge, unfinished basement and said exactly what I was thinking:

"Vicki, this would make the most perfect studio for you."

I grabbed his hand, we hugged, and he gave me a kiss. I was excited but also nervous. It was a lot of house, and I was concerned that we couldn't afford it. When we got into his car, Larry just put his hand on my arm and squeezed gently.

"It's fine," he reassured me. "We can afford to do this."

On the drive home, we started talking about making an offer.

Then, just as we were about to pull into my driveway, Larry said something to me that stopped me in my tracks.

"Vicki, before we buy the house, I have something to ask you."

"Oh my word," I thought. Was Larry finally going to pop the question, sitting in his car in my driveway?

And then he paused.

"It's about your kids."

"My kids? You mean my grown-up sons?"

"Yeah, I mean, how often do you need to see your kids every year?"

"Larry," I said, "that is the dumbest question anyone ever asked me."

"No, I'm serious. I'm thinking, maybe birthdays and Christmas?"

I caught my breath. Ever since Larry and I had known each other, he'd always made it clear that he wasn't interested in spending a huge amount of time with my family. If Michael or Brian came to visit for the weekend, Larry usually made other plans so that I could spend "one-on-one" time with my sons. Initially, this was very hard for me to accept. My family means the world to me and always will. But as time went on, I'd reconciled myself to the fact that family time wasn't Larry's idea of a good time. Although he loved his family, he just wasn't a family-oriented type of guy.

"Larry, the way you feel about family is so foreign to me," I used to say to him. "I love my mom, my sons, and my granddaughters so much. I really enjoy spending as much time with them as possible. I would love it if my partner felt the same way."

"Well, the way you're so close to your family is foreign to me," he would simply reply.

Of course, conversations like these always worried me, but I tried to put them in the back of my mind. Everything else about our relationship was so great. We had so much in common. We truly enjoyed the time we spent together. Maybe I had to stop expecting my partner to be everything and a cherry on top. And so for the five years of our relationship, we just danced around the family issue.

But now we were sitting in his car, about to make an offer on a house. We couldn't skirt the issue anymore.

"So what do you think, Vicki? How often do you need to see your kids each year?" Larry asked again.

"Can you say that one more time please, Larry?" I asked, my heart pounding now, my blood pressure rising. "Because I don't think I just heard you right."

"Vicki, your boys are grown men," he told me. "You should have clipped their wings at eighteen."

I felt my eyes fill with tears.

We kept talking, but Larry wasn't prepared to budge. Everything he was saying sounded perfectly logical to him. But I was never, *ever* going to tell my sons that they could visit me only twice a year. That was nonnegotiable.

Larry and I were deadlocked. By the end of the day, I knew in my heart that there wasn't going to be a house with Larry. There wasn't going to be a future. How could I live with someone who wasn't going to make my boys feel welcome in my own home?

From that point on, the cracks in our relationship began to widen. The house was never discussed again. All we did was argue. I became obsessed with the fact that Larry didn't want to spend time with my family and, to be honest, began reading too much into everything he said.

"Where do you want to eat tonight?" he'd ask.

And I'd hear, "You do know the boys are not invited to eat with us tonight, right?"

I felt like Larry was making me choose between him and my family. At the end of the day, there was no contest.

Breaking up with Larry was like ripping off a Band-Aid. I thought it would be less painful to slowly, slowly peel it away, but I was wrong. It took me the next six months to get up the courage to actually end the relationship with Larry. Despite our relationship's stalemate, I loved him so much.

It was New Year's Day 2003 that I finally did it. I woke up lying next to Larry at his house. He was still sleeping and hung over from the night before. I climbed out of bed and left without waking him. Larry had a little too much to drink during the New Year's Eve party. For the first time, I no longer felt proud to be his lady.

For months now, I'd known things weren't right, but I hadn't been ready to let go. Driving home that day, I started thinking about my goals for the new year, what I wanted for my life and what I hoped to achieve, but all I felt was confusion and uncertainty. I'd been in this limbo for too long. I couldn't go on like this. The last thing I wanted was to face another year with this man who was so completely misaligned with me on such a core issue. Enough was enough. Time to stop crying.

That morning Larry called from the golf course. He was looking forward to eating our traditional New Year's Day meal of pork and sauerkraut.

Pennsylvania Dutch superstition says that this meal brings good luck for the year ahead.

"So what time is dinner, Vicki?"

"Larry, I have to tell you," I said, taking the deepest breath of my life, "you're not invited."

Larry must have thought I was joking, because he laughed.

"I'm serious," I said. "You're not coming."

"What do you mean I'm not coming?"

"I mean we're done! It's a new year. It's a new me. I'm moving on."

On the other end of the line, Larry was silent. Despite our problems, I don't think he thought it would ever come to this. Especially not this afternoon and over the telephone.

"Larry, I love you, and I never thought we'd ever break up. But I just can't do this anymore."

In the coming days, I was able to keep strong and stick to my decision. Larry called me more than once.

"Are we okay now?" he asked.

"No, we're not okay."

"Vicki, you're really serious about this breakup."

"Yes, unfortunately, I'm completely serious."

And then, after a week, Larry stopped calling.

"I'm fine," I told myself.

I said the same thing to my family and friends: "I'm fine."

But the truth was, I didn't feel fine. In fact, I felt really, really sad. I'd just broken up with the man I loved. I'd literally chosen to be alone.

I was fifty-six years old and on my own. My worst fear had come true.

The same questions kept going around and around in my head: What in the world have I done? Why did I just break up with the man that I love?

During the day, I went to work. Three evenings a week, I taught my dance classes. The rest of the time, I hibernated at home, curled up on the couch, wearing my favorite comfy red robe, watching my shows. Oprah Winfrey and Dr. Phil were my gurus, and TiVo became one of my best friends. I remember Dr. Phil turning to the cameras, looking straight into my eyes, and saying, "Those of you that are sitting at home pining away on the couch because of a broken relationship, don't forget the reason you left him in the first place. You're not pining away for the man he was. You're pining away for the man you wish he would have been."

"Oh, Dr. Phil," I thought, "you really are speaking to me!"

I became addicted to pretty much every reality show on television: *Survivor*, *The Apprentice*, *Big Brother*, *Dancing with the Stars*, *The Bachelor*, *The Amazing Race*, and my favorite, *So You Think You Can Dance*. I'd get into imaginary conversations with the shows' producers: "I could have totally won that challenge if I were younger!" I'd tell them. "If only I'd met you when I was twenty-three!"

Then *Sex and the City* would come on, and I'd listen to those women debating their "issues" and think, "Where was *Sex and the City* when I was thirty? Back then, all we had was *Laverne and Shirley*!"

Many nights, I fell asleep right there on the couch, the television humming, so that I didn't have to lie awake listening to the thoughts buzzing around and around in my head. What had gone wrong? Why was I in this situation? Why me? Why this again?

Yes, I'd experienced breakups in the past. But I always bounced back. I knew that if I started going out again, chances were that I would find someone new. Whether or not he was the *right* person was another story, but I always felt confident there would be someone out there. This breakup, on the other hand, felt very different. Now that I was fifty-six, I felt I just couldn't assume that I was going to meet someone the way I had when I was thirty-six or even forty-six. What type of guy was I going to meet? And how was I going to meet him? So many of the single men I knew who were my age were interested in younger women. And the older men were, well, how can I put this? Older. The real truth was that I was having serious doubts whether I even wanted to meet someone else and have to start all over again. Relationships are a lot of work, and I wasn't sure I had the energy anymore.

There was another big difference this time around. I was living alone. My boys had grown up and left home, and that meant there were no longer any daily "mom duties" to distract me. In the past, if I was feeling low, I knew that at some point in the evening, one of my sons would come charging through the door wanting dinner, or to talk, or to sit on the couch with me. The house felt so lonely and quiet without them. I knew I had too much time on my hands, but for the first time in my life, I didn't feel like getting up and finding any type of distraction other than the TV set in front of me.

There was something else preying on my mind that had never been an issue before. For the past six months now, I'd been eligible to retire and receive benefits through my job. I should have felt happy about this, but, in fact, just knowing that I could retire made me feel like time was running out. I was waking up to the fact that I was probably going to be retiring and growing old on my own. The words kept going around and around in my head: "This wasn't the way I planned it would be. This wasn't how I planned it at all!"

Every Wednesday night when I taught my tap classes, no matter how low I may have felt before class, my dancer's confidence came back to me. "Head up!" I used to tell my little girls in the Studio of Rhythm. "Shoulders back. The show must go on! And don't forget to smile." The rest of the week, I pretty much stopped going out. My Wednesday night girls wouldn't take no for an answer, and so I soon gave up trying to make excuses to go home and curl up on the couch.

Jenna would come over, bringing Chinese food and a bottle of wine. Susan was more determined. She'd call and say, "Look, Vicki, let's go out together Saturday night. We'll take it slow. Just dinner and a drink."

After the breakup with Larry, I was so relieved that the girls never said "I told you so." I could remember back to when I'd been seeing him for a couple of years, and Andrea suggested that maybe, just maybe, Larry wasn't "the one." "Vicki," she observed, "for someone who loves her family as much as you do, it just seems really strange that you've chosen a guy who doesn't enjoy being around family." Now that the relationship was over, Andrea didn't say I told you so. She just listened. She hugged me and was simply there for me when I needed her.

It was a new experience to have my tap friends rally around me like this. In the past, I'd always kept my sorrows to myself. Believe it or not, I'd never thought of relying on a group of girlfriends to help me through. My dance class and students gave rhythm to my week, in every sense of the word.

After only a few weeks on the couch, even my sons started to figure out that I wasn't bouncing back the way I should have. The problem was, it was hard for me to talk to either of my boys about what I was going through. Brian, in particular, always had reservations about my relationship with Larry. The first time he'd met Larry, we'd gone out for dinner, and on the ride home, my son turned to me and said, "Mom, really? He seems like a nice guy, but I get the impression that he's not really a family man. He reminds me of a lot of the other guys you've dated, even down to the tasseled loafers."

Knowing that Brian had always felt this way about Larry, it was very hard for me to discuss with him the failure of the relationship, about my disappointment that I hadn't been able to make it work, and the sense of defeat I felt about my future. I loved to hear about what he was up to in Manhattan, but lately I didn't feel that I had much to bring to the conversation. I think we both sensed the imbalance. I just kept asking Brian questions about what he was doing, and he would follow my lead for a bit. But he'd then throw the dreaded question at me:

"Mom, how are you?"

"I'm fine," I tried to convince him. "Really, I'm fine."

I really didn't have any energy to say anything more about Larry to anyone. I know that time heals all wounds, but I was taking my time and I was okay with that.

"You still staying in so much? Are you sure there isn't something fun you want to do this weekend?"

Fun? I thought to myself. Does anyone really have fun? I tried to remember the last time I felt that way, and I drew a blank.

"Brian," I told him, "I know this is hard for you to understand, but I'm getting older, and people my age just don't care so much about going out and having fun all the time."

But Brian didn't buy it. He told me it was just my funk that was talking.

"Mom, you have to listen to me," he said. "I know you, and this isn't you. Stop using that *old* word. You're not old, and even if you were, the mother I know wouldn't be acting like this!"

Unlike Brian, my older son had never been one for chatting on the phone or offering advice, so I knew things were really bad when even Michael started telling me the exact same thing and urging me to get back up on my feet. "Mom, you have to get out more. You shouldn't be staying at home all the time like this!"

I knew that my sons both meant well. Even so, while their concern and kindness made me feel loved, it also made me feel even older. Of course, they didn't realize it, but by telling me to change, they were inadvertently sending me the message that I wasn't strong enough to manage on my own anymore. What had happened? It seemed like five minutes ago that my boys were babies, still living at home, relying on me for everything they needed. How was it possible that my little ones were now giving me advice? I just kept thinking, "How could two men in their thirties possibly know what their fifty-six-year-old mother needs?"

"You have to focus on yourself and do things that are healthy distractions, Mom." Brian thoughtfully booked me massage appointments and sent me several unexpected gifts to cheer me up.

He sent me ABBA's greatest hits and told me it was my "breakup CD." He knew that I'd been too busy raising my kids to know about ABBA during their 1970s heyday, but he was certain that I was going to love their music as much as I loved my other oldies. Sure enough, "Dancing Queen" became my anthem. The next CD to arrive was a compilation Brian put together called *Go Baby Go*, and it was full of high-energy dance songs with lyrics that my son said were going to help "motivate" me during my daily drive to and from work.

"Mom, why don't we get you a gym membership?" Brian asked me cautiously. That always helps to motivate me.

"Brian, you know I hate the gym," I told him. "I'm never going to feel comfortable there. And anyway, I don't want to look muscular."

One day the phone rang. "Vicki Riordan? This is Chad from Gold's Gym, calling to confirm your first personal training appointment."

"I'm sorry," I told the voice on the other end of the line, "but you must have the wrong person. I didn't book an appointment with you."

"No, you didn't," he replied. "But your son Brian did. We had a long conversation about what you're looking for in a trainer, and he wanted me to give you a call before your sessions begin. He's giving you ten personal training sessions as a gift."

Of course, I thanked Chad, hung up, and immediately called Brian.

"Brian Riordan, how dare you!" I told him. "You know I don't want to go to a gym!"

"But, Mom," Brian said, "you need to do something. It's just not like you to sit there and feel defeated. I want you to start feeling like yourself again. If you don't like Chad, then you don't have to go back. Just give it a try!"

"Brian," I repeated, "I am *not* going to a gym. I get plenty of exercise at dance class."

"Too late," my son told me. "I already paid for the sessions."

In other words, my son knew I wouldn't let his money go to waste. I begrudgingly thanked Brian and hung up. Despite my resistance, I ended up going to the gym. Like most people of my generation, I didn't grow up around gyms—in my day, only men went to gyms. I just didn't think I could feel comfortable there. But it turned out that my trainer was a charming young man who made me feel at ease doing something that was completely out of my comfort zone. After a few sessions, I bought my first official gym membership. I knew I was never going to enjoy working out in the same way that I loved to dance, but I realized that Brian was right: if I really wanted to do something about my lack of energy, I was going to have to make this extra effort.

Knowing my son as well as I did, I probably should have guessed that this was only the beginning of interesting things to come.

After a few weeks into my gym membership, Brian and I would often talk about what I would do if I actually did retire from my job, since he knew that this was my ultimate goal.

"Can you believe it?" I asked Brian. "How is it possible that I'm old enough to retire already?"

I didn't know exactly what I wanted to do with my time after I retired from my day job, but I knew I wanted to do something. I was concerned that despite years of hard work, I wouldn't be able to give up my job and be comfortable financially. I was fortunate enough to have saved a modest but respectable 401(k), my pension would afford me the basics, and my health benefits and life insurance would be covered. I would be fine. I wouldn't be able to travel, or have extra money to splurge on dresses for my granddaughters, or go out with my friends for fun dinners whenever I liked. Could I start a business for myself, or work part-time to help get the extra money I was going to need? This would also give my days focus. I was never the type to just sit around.

My first thought was that maybe I could work in a pro shop at a country club. I knew I wanted to keep golf in my life. Only a year ago, I'd founded the central Pennsylvania chapter of the Executive Women's Golf Association, because we didn't have a local women's chapter, and I knew that there were women throughout the area who would want to join. Since then, it had become one of the fastest-growing chapters in the association's history. Maybe if I got a job at a country club, at least I would be able to play golf free of charge!

Then, out of the blue, it came to me. I knew exactly what I could do: open a golf boutique for women! There was definitely a niche. I knew from personal experience that it was very difficult to find feminine and pretty golf accessories around town. In my travels, I'd collected about a dozen pairs of unique and stylish golf shoes—everything from pink wingtips to zebra-print saddle shoes—but I could never find any shirts or accessories to match. Women golfers just weren't well catered to in the Harrisburg area.

"What do you think?" I asked Brian one day. "Can't you see me with a little boutique of my own?"

"Mom, that's a great idea, but to be honest, I don't think it's your answer," he replied. "To me it's obvious," he said intently. "You already have something really cool in your life, and you know it works. That's what you need to focus on. You need to focus on your dance business and keep golf as your hobby."

When he said this, I think I actually laughed. I explained to Brian that, yes, my tap classes were great, but they didn't have the potential to be turned into a business that was going to answer all of my retirement dilemmas. Tap was my sideline. I certainly never imagined that at my age it could be my main focus, especially not in this small town. Harrisburg has a population of four hundred thousand. Realistically, how many of those people were going to want to sign up for an adult tap class?

I just didn't see it happening. That evening, I hung up the phone still feeling convinced that golf was going to be my answer. Of course, when I looked into it some more, I realized that Brian was right. How was I going to come up with enough money to buy inventory to stock my boutique? What if the boutique wasn't a success, and I found myself old enough to be a member of AARP—and seriously in debt? I put the golf idea on the back burner, where it belonged.

As time went on, I started to notice that whenever my younger son and I talked, his questions turned more and more to my dance classes.

"How do you find new students?" Brian wanted to know.

"I don't," I told him. "They come through the rec centers. That's what's so great about this. All I have to do is show up and teach."

"You mean you don't promote the classes yourself?"

"No, I don't do anything—it's word of mouth!" I laughed. "The rec centers have their newsletters, people see them, then they sign up for class."

"I can't believe your classes are so popular and you never did any of your own promotion," Brian told me. "Imagine what could happen if we actually got the word out."

"Mom," Brian said at last, "let me help you with this. With a few smart tweaks, I think we could take what you're already doing well and bring it to a different level. Where it belongs. Then you wouldn't have to worry about your retirement anymore, because by the time you retire, you'll already have something set up that's your passion."

For Brian, teaching tap dancing was the answer to all my troubles. Meanwhile, I thought his idea was the most unrealistic thing imaginable. As for retiring, maybe it was too soon to start planning for the future. I could stay at my job a few more years and figure something out down the line.

The problem was, Brian wasn't listening to me.

"Mom, I know you. If you want to truly be happy, you need to be able to retire comfortably and on your own terms. And if you can bring your classes to more people while you do that, what could be better?"

Brian was still so young. His life was ahead of him. I didn't know how to explain this to my son. "How can I move forward," I wanted to ask him, "when it seems like all the good opportunities are in the past?" I wanted to tell him, "Brian, it's just too late."

Larry and I had made so many plans. We were supposed to move in together. Grow old together. Spend our golden years sitting on the porch in rocking chairs together. But now there was no house. No porch. No rocking chairs. When I thought about the future without a partner, I felt like I was staring at the tail end of a dream—a dream that had first brightened my life more than fifty years ago, when I was a little girl.

All these years, I kept waiting for my dream, my prince, my house up on Cottage Hill. Even after my divorce from Mike—when it was obvious that my life was going to be more complicated than I ever could have expected—I kept waiting. I think that's why retiring and being single hit me so hard. I was running out of time to meet that soul mate, a man who would love and support me the same way that my dad did for my mom.

It can be very hard to watch dreams like that slip away.

Chapter 10

• • •

Sunday, June 12, 2011

11:45 AM

NOW THAT MORNING REHEARSAL IS OVER, THE DANCERS ARE
STARTING TO HEAD BACKSTAGE TO EAT LUNCH AND GET READY
FOR SHOWTIME.

"Before you go, I want to tell you something," I tell the ladies gathered in the auditorium.

I remind the dancers the true reason why we're performing today. Since 2006, our spring shows have raised money and awareness for the YWCA of Greater Harrisburg's Domestic Violence Shelter. Over the past five years, the Tap Pups have raised a combined total of $30,000 for the shelter, which provides a safe haven and support for women victims of domestic abuse.

When we started to support the YWCA, we wanted to do something that would have a direct impact on these women and their children. Through our work with the shelter, we learned that many times these women flee their homes in life-threatening situations. Most arrive at the shelter with only the clothes on their backs. A couple of years ago, we created a program where we donate "comfort bundles" to the shelter. These consist of new sheets, towels, a pillow, pillowcase, and blanket. The women and their families entering the shelter can use the comfort bundles during their stay, but they can also keep them when they leave. It's a small reminder that people in their community care about them and support them. Last year alone, the donations of Tap Pups and friends of Tap Pups produced 110 comfort bundles. This year we're hoping to put together even more.

The dancers tell me how much they appreciate being able to support the comfort bundle program. It's such a direct and easy way to help other women in our community. Our bundles are tangible. You can truly see how these will help someone who is emotionally and physically bruised. So many of us are mothers and grandmothers, and our hearts go out to these women who have to run to the shelter, especially when they arrive with their children. We all can appreciate how something as basic as a blanket can be a very big deal, and how easy it is to take a clean, fresh towel for granted.

Recently, the YWCA forwarded me a letter. It was from a woman who received one of the bundles after spending time at the shelter with her young daughter. Up onstage, I want to read it to the Tap Pups so that they can remember why they're dancing, and why the bundles are so important.

"Dear Vicki and the Tap Pups," I read aloud. "I just want to thank you and let you know how much I appreciate the bed packets your organization has donated. I came here with nothing, so for my daughter and me to have such new stuff was wonderful. My daughter was so excited as we smelled the new sheets. It's been a real long time since I had anything new. Thanks again! I don't know who you are, but Tap Pups ROCK!"

I realize I'm welling up as I finish reading. It's a wonderful thing to be able to express yourself through your passion. It's incredible to be able to do that alongside so many people who feel the same way. But it's even better when you know that simply by doing something you love, you're helping others. That's the true bigger picture here.

"Mom, you've always told me stories about how important dance was to your generation," Brian pointed out to me on the phone one day. "I grew up knowing that. There must be a lot more people in Harrisburg who miss having dance in their lives."

Brian hadn't given up on his idea to help expand my dance program, but he knew he needed to draw up a few new scenarios and approaches for me to be on board. Based on his experience in building brands and marketing, he knew that seeing is believing.

In May 2004, Brian came home for the Memorial Day weekend to help celebrate Michael's thirty-fourth birthday and to take Olivia and Savanah to Hersheypark. On his train ride down, he wrote a quick five-page outline of a three-year plan to show me how easily I could grow and expand my business. Later that weekend, we sat down together with Michael—just the three of us at the kitchen table—and looked over the detailed outline Brian had typed up.

He then started to read:

"Welcome to Vicki's Studio of Rhythm. A return to a simpler time when dance was coordinated and fun. When it seemed you had to learn a new dance every week. A time when you would meet up with your friends at the local fire hall for dances. When you developed new friendships through dance. Lace up those shoes, feel the rhythm, and come on in to find happiness through dance, once again."

"How do you know all this?" I asked Brian.

"Mom, are you kidding? I grew up around you. When you tell me stuff, I listen!"

Following the introduction came Brian's three-year plan for my "business."

As I started to read, my eyes began to swim.

According to Brian, I needed to:

- Create a new logo, a website, business cards, stickers, and car magnets.
- Increase my class sizes to maximize my teaching time.
- Reintroduce my fifties and sixties social dance programs.
- Develop new business opportunities by offering my services at private parties, weddings, conferences, and conventions.
- Develop an instructional video/DVD.

I was going to launch this reinvented version of my Studio of Rhythm in September. Four months from now! And press and marketing were going to start even sooner.

Brian seemed quite confident in his plan, but to be honest, even reading it made me feel anxious and totally exhausted.

"Brian," I told him, "you have to realize that you're speaking a foreign language. I don't know anything about press and marketing! Also, this seems like a lot of work. I don't think I have time for this!"

"That's where I come in, Mom," Brian insisted. "I'm going to help you."

I heard what he was saying, but my son worked full-time and had his own life in Manhattan.

"You're too busy to help me with this," I told him. "And it's just completely unrealistic to think I can pull this off on my own."

I explained to him that I was quite sure I already taught every adult in the Harrisburg area who wants to learn to tap dance.

"Let's just see," he said.

"Mom, I know it looks like a lot," Michael said, "but if you let Brian help you, he can break it down for you. The whole idea of the plan is that you do this piece by piece, not everything all at once."

"Just wait," Brian persisted. "You'll see. It's not as hard as it looks!"

"Okay, Brian, we'll see," I said. But in my heart, I knew that I wasn't going to change my mind. Eventually Brian would tire of this idea and give up—or so I thought.

For the time being, though, my son took me at my word. He still called me every day as he'd always done. He still came to visit. But he took a break from trying to persuade me to "change my life."

Recently, I'd been given a new job in the same union, as an office manager, working in a new office for a boss that I knew and respected, and for the first time in a long time, I was challenged and extremely busy at work. I was feeling pretty good about my current situation and no longer felt panicked about making a change.

A year and a half went by. Then just before Christmas 2005, Brian called me with some very upsetting news. He had been forced to leave his job. For the past three years, he'd been running a start-up operation in an entrepreneurial job that he truly loved and for which he'd helped grow a small local business into a global success. He put his heart and soul into this company and thought of the owner almost as family. Unfortunately, when the time came for a real contract and profit sharing to happen, he got cut out. He knew this day would eventually come, but the experience had been so fulfilling, he never wanted it to end. For the first time in his life, Brian—upbeat Brian—seemed genuinely crushed.

"This is the toughest breakup I will ever go through," he told me on the phone.

Over the next few months, I visited him in New York as often as possible. I immediately put on my "mom hat," trying to give him good advice and emotional support, no longer worrying about myself. We talked a lot about what he wanted to do next. We both knew he needed to do something more entrepreneurial, something that he believed in and that he could throw himself into 100 percent. The jobs he was being offered didn't come close to that.

Over the next few months, our conversations about my dance classes became more detailed too. Brian now had time on his hands to really think things through for me. Whenever we discussed my program, I saw how excited he became and how interested he was in everything to do with my classes. It helped me to be strong for Brian. I knew how to do that. And as a result, I realized that I was becoming more open to his ideas for my future.

One day the following spring, we were talking on the phone about my program.

"Brian, if you are really serious about helping me to build a larger program," I told him, "then you need to see my classes. Until you see me teach, you won't truly know what I do."

Tap had come into my life after he'd left home. Even though we'd had so many conversations about my classes, Brian had never seen a single class.

"Sure, I'll come home this week in time to watch your Wednesday night classes," Brian replied without hesitation.

"No, Brian," I insisted. "If we are doing this, you need to observe all three levels of classes. You need to stay for Thursday night too. Each one is unique in its own right, and there is a lot for you to absorb."

He quickly agreed and was in Harrisburg the next week.

The first class was my Wednesday night Advanced class with the girls I'd been teaching for nearly ten years. The venue was still the old school cafeteria, with its chairs and tables pushed up against the walls.

After my ladies laced up their shoes, they took their places and started to dance. Within five minutes, Brian was on his feet, giving the class a standing ovation.

"Oh, please, Brian, sit down! You haven't seen anything yet!" my old friend Andrea told him, flicking her hair from her shoulder. "That was just our warm-up!"

Then the class did its routine to "Rockin' Robin," the Bobby Day song we all loved to dance to back in the fifties. The moves were fast. They didn't "slush" their feet: the sound of their taps were clean. Everything was precise. My Advanced dancers were at the point where their legs and feet were so relaxed that the steps just flowed. I knew how hard they were working, but Brian wouldn't be able to tell from looking at them. This is the beauty of tapping: making something incredibly difficult look completely casual and effortless.

Glancing over at my son, I saw my class through Brian's eyes, and it felt really, really good.

After we were finished, Brian came toward me with his arms stretched out.

"Mom, who are you?" he asked. "I feel like I don't even know you! You were awesome out there! And these ladies are incredible!"

Brian hugged every woman in my class, congratulating them all on their moves.

"Whoa! I knew you would be good. But come on!" he exclaimed.

After class that night, Brian and I drove home together.

"Mom, look what you've created here! Your Tap Pups program is genius! Those dancers are really good. And their energy! Mom, their energy is contagious! They love dancing, and they love you. This Tap Pups thing is actually even better than I thought!"

"Well, Brian." I smiled at my younger son. "What did you think I was doing all these years?"

Yes, I was flattered by his comments, but it was more than that. Until that moment, I don't think I'd ever been able to look at my classes from an outside perspective. Of course, I loved teaching my tap dancers, but I didn't spend much time thinking or talking about expanding my program because I loved what I was doing and was proud of it. It was a true wake-up call to see Brian's reaction to my program. It was as if he were holding up a mirror and showing me exactly what he saw: the person I was and who I became when I was teaching.

"Mom, you are really good at what you do. Look at all those women in your classes. They are such a wide range of ages and backgrounds. Dance seems to be a complete equalizer for them. There are women in this town who need you. I think you could turn this sideline into a business and finally have the life you deserve when you retire."

For the first time, when Brian talked about my program and attracting more students, I actually listened.

That night we went to a restaurant overlooking the river. We sat in a booth with the best view and ordered dinner. Brian pulled out a notebook, and we started the beginning of a conversation that continues to this day. In many ways, it was the same conversation we've been having since he was a little boy; it was just that, after that night, it became more focused, more energized. It became real.

Brian wanted to know about every dancer in the program. He couldn't believe that one of my oldest dancers, Millie Hitz, was still tapping away in her seventies.

"Mom, when she got to that stack of chairs in the cafeteria that was in her way, she just tapped around them. She didn't skip a beat! I love that lady!"

I told him about Andrea, who had never taken dance classes as a child but always wanted to be a dancer. I told him about all the other women who said the exact same thing: "I've been wanting to do this my whole life!"

I told him about Deborah, who was, by her own admission, overweight when she started lessons. After only a few weeks, she realized that she was getting out of breath, and she wanted to be lighter on her feet. The exercise that she was already getting gave her the incentive to start dieting and eventually hire a trainer. In the three years she'd been dancing with me, Deborah had lost four dress sizes, ran her first 5K race, and looked fabulous.

I explained to Brian that tap is such a great form of exercise that anyone could enjoy it at any age.

"When you tap-dance, you keep your legs loose and your knees flexed," I explained. "It's really a perfect way to move."

Although a lot of women in my class needed a lot of encouragement before they could feel confident in their movements, if I stuck with them, eventually they started to feel the positive impact.

For so many of the dancers, this was the first time they had joined something that had nothing to do with their husband or children. They weren't used to doing something for themselves. But now that they were, I was amazed to see how quickly they embraced their classes. It was almost like they'd been waiting for something like this to come along. You could still see it in the glow they exuded at the end of the class. For one hour, they'd been so focused on getting the steps right that they didn't think of anything else. For that one hour, it was like the rest of the world just went away.

I told Brian about how that feeling of camaraderie continued after we finished dancing too, and what it had meant to me to have Andrea, Jenna, and Susan in my life.

Brian listened intently. I could see that he was taking in everything. For the first time, I allowed myself to believe that Brian was serious about his commitment to helping me. Looking over at my son, I realized he wasn't a little boy anymore. He was an adult, with experience, talent, and a lot to offer. Why wouldn't I let my son encourage me the way I'd encouraged him all these years?

When we arrived home, Brian said something to me that took my breath away.

"What you have created is so inspirational and amazing for these women, Mom. What do you think about leveraging what you've built with the Tap Pups to raise money for some kind of women's initiative?"

Of course, I told him I would love that.

"What if we could help a single mom and her family who are struggling financially?" Brian suggested. His idea was that we could start with something small like raising money to buy them groceries, just like my own mom had helped me all those years ago. He knew that nothing could be closer to my heart. I suggested that we call the YWCA of Greater Harrisburg to see whether someone there knew of a single mom with two boys we could help. Until then, I'd never thought of my classes as a means to help anyone besides my dancers and me. Who would have imagined that something I'd created could help others? But maybe Brian was right. Maybe I could start giving back.

I called the YWCA and talked to the person in charge of its donations. She explained that although she respected our idea, it was hard for her to allocate money to an individual family. She suggested that instead we donate to the YWCA's Domestic Violence Shelter.

I didn't need to stop to think. Of course I said yes. As I listened to the director describe some of the emotional and mental abuse experienced by these women, it hit very close to home. My situation had never reached the point where I had to live in a shelter with my boys, but if I hadn't had such a strong family to lean on, who knows how my story could have ended?

It was decided. The last class of the year was coming up, and as usual, I was going to invite friends and family to watch the dancers. At the end of the class, we'd ask for donations on behalf of the shelter. I was excited about what we were about to do, and I felt extremely proud that I was at a point in my life where helping others was a possibility. I also didn't realize that by agreeing to Brian's idea, I'd opened a door. He was now involved in Vicki's Tap Pups, and he made an immediate impact on me and my ladies.

From that point on, my youngest son kept calling and emailing me with all kinds of new twists on the usual way that I did things. First of all, he kept referring to my last class of the year as a "recital." I explained to Brian that I didn't use that term for good reasons. It was just a small get-together so that friends and family could see what we had been doing every week for the past year. I needed to keep this event low-key because I knew that my dancers were doing something far out of their comfort zone, and I didn't want to intimidate them by calling it a recital.

"It's a get-together," I explained to Brian. "Just our last class of the season, except that people can invite family and friends, and we get a little dressed up."

"Okay," Brian said. "That makes perfect sense. The word 'recital' really does make it sound like a kids' show, and your ladies are hardly kids."

Then he wanted to know how many years we'd been doing these "get-togethers."

I quickly did the math and said, "Well, I guess this is our tenth year."

"Interesting" was all that he said.

Then, a couple of weeks before the last class, I asked Brian if he could help me by putting together the program: a simple printed list with the names of the routines and the dancers. Brian agreed. And so when my son started asking me questions about specific steps and music, I just assumed that he was putting more information on the program. I educated him about slaps, shuffles, and time steps—the different types of steps that we did—and the ages of the women performing. I still had no idea why he was spending so much time on his write-up. I knew my ladies were going to love it, but it seemed way too much effort for such a small gathering.

After about twenty minutes, Brian called me back.

"Hey, Mom," he said. "So I just sent out a press release to the *Harrisburg Patriot-News* and three local TV stations. Here we go! Let's see what happens!"

"You did what!" I yelled so loudly that my boss, Mike Fox, actually poked his head around his office door and asked if I was okay. "What on earth did you do that for? My ladies are going to kill me! What if camera crews actually show up?"

"Then that would be good," Brian replied. "Make sure your ladies look fabulous. I know you will!"

"But Brian," I protested, "it's just a last class! You can't send out a press release!"

"It's already done, Mom. The Tap Pups are amazing, and I think people would care about what is going on here. This is going to help raise awareness for the YWCA too. What you're doing actually is newsworthy. And anyway, if I'd waited for your green light on this, we'd never get the press release out."

I hung up the phone in disbelief. Brian knew I wasn't going to be comfortable with a press release, which was why he hadn't told me he was sending it out. Yes, I'd had the occasional write-up in local newspapers over the years, but the reporters had always initiated the story. It would never cross my mind to go to them. Sending out a press release seemed like blowing my own horn, and since when did I do that? I also felt very protective of my Tap Pups and never wanted them to feel like I was exploiting them in any way.

The next week, I knew I had to tell everyone in my classes about Brian's press release and that there was a *slight* chance that our little show might receive some news coverage.

I really didn't want the dancers to feel uncomfortable, but their response was the complete opposite of what I'd been expecting.

"Bring it on!"

"Who do you think will be there?"

"TV cameras?!"

"Will there be photographers?!"

As it turned out, the press release caught the attention of the *Patriot-News*, the main newspaper in Harrisburg. It wasn't going to cover the show, but the editors there did love the idea of the Tap Pups and the fact that we would take time to help support other women in the community. They asked if they could do an article on us later in the summer.

So for the time being, I put Brian's press release in the back of my mind. The last class of the year was on the horizon, and since we were going to be raising money for the YWCA, I wanted it to be the best one yet. For the past few years, we'd always held our get-togethers at Good Hope Middle School auditorium, one of the locations where I taught my tap classes. When the big night rolled around, we had an audience of about one hundred family members and friends, our largest gathering to date. For the first time, Brian was there to see my dancers, and he made sure that his brother, my grand-daughters, and a few of his friends from high school were all in the audience, as well as my mom and Aunt Dutch. In nine years of teaching tap, I'd never had so many members of my own family attend.

That night, I was waiting in the wings, just like I always did, while my dancers took the stage. There were about thirty of us performing that night, and we were a diverse group. There was Deanna, our youngest dancer at twenty-nine, and eighty-year-old Dot, our oldest. There were also my good friends Andrea and Jenna, now two of the best dancers in the group. Everyone was wearing a black Tap Pups T-shirt, black high-heeled tap shoes, and black pants, with a signature aqua scarf tied around their necks. Simple but chic.

The auditorium held about forty rows of seats. It wasn't the biggest performance space, but nothing to sneeze at either. Behind the curtain, my ladies were getting in some last-minute practice and reviewing their hand movements. Even though this was a small show, everyone wanted to be perfect.

Millie, the dancer that Brian had singled out in my classes, was especially nervous.

"I can't believe that I'm dancing onstage at my age," she said. "I know that I have family out there, and I'm terrified. I'm thinking I never should have invited them."

I told Millie what I tell all my dancers: "Remember to smile and let everyone know how much you love tap dancing. They won't even notice if you make a mistake!"

That night at Good Hope, my dancers performed eight numbers and received one roaring round of applause after another. Before the end of the show, I presented Millie with an award for Most Improved Dancer of the Year, by which point the audience was on its feet, and Millie was grinning from ear to ear. "Sign me up for next year, Vicki," she said.

Then I thanked the audience for attending our last class and all the dancers for working so hard. Brian then introduced a representative from the YWCA of Greater Harrisburg's Domestic Violence Shelter, who spoke about how much it meant to the organization that the Tap Pups had chosen to help women who came to its shelter, having no other place to turn. We told everyone that on the way out, there would be a chance to make a donation. My granddaughters, Olivia and Savanah, then stood by the door holding collection baskets.

When we tallied up the donations later that evening, we found that we had raised $340 for the YWCA. I was pretty impressed, but Brian just shrugged.

"Not bad for our first time around," he said. "But wait until you see what we're going to do next year!"

"Oh, Brian," I sighed.

That fall, inspired by that initial contribution, Brian and I decided to see the YWCA shelter for ourselves, to find out more about the organization and what we could do to help.

The shelter was at the very back of the YWCA building, heavily guarded, with locks on every door. The director, a British woman named Sally, showed us around. We saw four small rooms containing a total of sixteen single beds and a few cots for babies and children. The facilities were extremely basic, with cinder-block walls and industrial tiles on the floor—like a college dorm inside a fortress. Sally explained that many of the women who arrived here were fleeing for their lives. When we asked why the shelter was empty, she told us that she had invited us to visit at a time of the day when she knew the women were involved in a program elsewhere, so that there wouldn't be any chance that we could reveal anyone's identity and possibly endanger her life.

"What kinds of women come here?" I asked.

"You would be surprised," Sally replied. "We have women from all walks of life. All ages. From every social class. Domestic violence is a problem that touches the lives of one in four women in America. Many, many women in this community and across the country don't feel safe in their own homes, and if they have to run, they need to know that they can come to a safe shelter like this one."

Yes, I had lived through my own experiences of abuse, but it wasn't until I visited the shelter and heard the stories of these women that I began to understand that my story was far from unique and that this issue was much more widespread than I'd ever imagined.

Sally took us along a corridor to the family room, with connecting kitchens and a big family-style dining table. At the end of the corridor stood life-size wooden cutouts of women's silhouettes, all painted bright red and each bearing a victim's name.

"We made the cutouts for a benefit we had last year," Sally explained. "Each one of these represents a woman who was killed as a result of domestic violence. We tell people that these are the women who didn't make it to the shelter, or who we had to turn away because we didn't have enough beds that night."

Sally wanted to know more about the Tap Pups and the mission of our group to help the YWCA.

"We meet so many women who are literally just trying to survive, they would never have the luxury of even considering the possibility of taking one hour a week to do anything just for themselves," she told me. "But the Tap Pups are such a fun and impactful group of ordinary women doing something extraordinary, it would surely help to raise awareness in the audience and our community to understand what is truly happening right in their own backyard and offer support."

After Brian and I left, I knew what he was thinking. I was in tears before we even spoke.

"A few of those stories really got to me, Brian."

"I know, Mom, I know," he said. "I was there."

Chapter 11

• • •

Sunday, June 12, 2011
12:45 PM

LESS THAN TWO HOURS UNTIL SHOW TIME: THE NERVOUS ENERGY BACKSTAGE IS BUILDING, AND SO IS THE UNMISTAKABLE SMELL OF HAIR SPRAY. ALMOST EVERY LADY IN THE GROUP IS IN FRONT OF A MIRROR, CURLING IRONS AND MAKEUP BRUSHES IN HAND. ONE OF THE NEW BEGINNER DANCERS, KAITLIN, A FORMER MODEL, HAS BROUGHT A PROFESSIONAL MAKEUP KIT AND IS MAKING UP THE LADIES IN HER CLASS ONE BY ONE. THERE ARE NEW DANCERS HERE WHO TELL ME THAT THEY HAVEN'T WORN FULL MAKEUP IN TWENTY-FIVE YEARS, AND NOW KAITLIN HAS THEM IN FOUR SHADES OF EYE SHADOW. BLAINE, ONE OF THE GUYS IN THE SHOW, OWNS A HAIR SALON AND HAS WOMEN LINING UP TO GET THEIR HAIR DONE.

I head over to the ladies' room stage left, where the Advanced dancers are putting on their costumes. Later this afternoon, I'm going to be performing to the song "Me and My Shadow" with this group, and I need to get my own accessories and makeup ready for showtime.

The routine for "Me and My Shadow" was choreographed with one very special dancer in mind: my friend LuAnne.

At the age of fifty-eight, LuAnne has been dancing with me longer than anyone else in the Tap Pups. She first came to my Studio of Rhythm when she was eleven years old. Back then, she was one of my star girls and my student teacher. Today she's one of my instructors with the Tap Pups. LuAnne, a tall woman, has short brown hair with blonde highlights, deep brown eyes behind her glasses, and exudes a warmth that draws her students in and brings out the best in them.

As I walk into the Advanced dressing room, LuAnne is heading out. She grabs my arm and gives it a squeeze.

"We've come a long way from Steelton," she says, smiling.

"About three miles, to be exact!" I laugh.

LuAnne and I have so much shared history that many times we don't have to finish our sentences. We know exactly what the other one means.

When I first told LuAnne that I was going to be performing "Me and My Shadow" at the show this year, she shrieked.

"Don't tell me you're leaving us again!"

LuAnne can remember precisely the last time I danced this routine. It was at my final recital at the Studio of Rhythm in 1968, before I left to get married and move to New York with Mike. During "Me and My Shadow," I danced in front, tapping each sequence on my own, and then LuAnne and my cousin Linda danced behind me, imitating my steps as I went along.

"Don't worry," I told LuAnne. "I'm not going anywhere this time."

OVER the years, I'd lost touch with many of my students from the Studio of Rhythm, but I always kept in contact with two of them: LuAnne and Forry. When I first left Steelton, Forry was nine years old. He would send me long letters that reeked of cologne. When I asked him why he did this, he told me that since my studio always smelled of *my* perfume, he wanted to have his own signature scent too. After he graduated high school, Forry thought about moving to New York and dancing on Broadway. He was so talented that there is no doubt in my mind that he would have been a star. But his mother had other ideas. By now she knew that Forry was gay, and she feared that New York would expose him to a lifestyle that terrified her. So Forry stayed in Steelton and opened up his own dance studio in the same small, one-room studio that had been my first Studio of Rhythm, right next door to his parents' photography studio. It was no surprise to me that he became one of the most sought-after dance instructors in the area. When I was living in New Orleans, Forry invited me back to Harrisburg to attend his school's first recital. The show was superb, and at the end, he invited me onstage and presented me with a bouquet of flowers.

"This is Miss Vicki," he announced, "the person who taught me everything I know."

"Thank you, Forry," I whispered in his ear. "It's a good thing your show was so good, especially since you gave me all the credit!"

LuAnne had opened her own dance studio in Steelton for a time as well, teaching alongside my cousin Linda. Then, when she met and married her husband, she gave up teaching, just like I did. She had two daughters, and family life became her focus. When I moved back to Harrisburg after my divorce, I'd go over to LuAnne's home on a regular basis. Her husband, Ronnie, was a high school football coach, and my boys adored him. The minute we arrived, they'd run to Ron, and he'd roughhouse with them and play ball with them in the backyard—the kind of things that they would have loved to have done with their dad.

When I returned to teaching tap in 1997, I invited LuAnne to watch our year-end class. Afterward, she came up to me and gave me a giant hug.

"Your dancers were great, and I wouldn't expect anything else."

"Hopefully, before long, they'll be advanced enough so that you'll want to join the class."

LuAnne just laughed.

It was the following summer after I started teaching tap again that I learned the very sad news about Forry. I knew he had been diagnosed with HIV about ten years before, but now his doctors had told him he had full-blown AIDS and that he didn't have much longer to live. At that time, the antiretroviral drugs that could have saved Forry's life were only just becoming available. Forry's doctors knew that he was losing his battle against the virus and that there was nothing they could do to save him.

"You have to go and see Forry," said our mutual friend Susie, who had once danced alongside him at the Studio of Rhythm. "He hasn't got much longer. He wants to see you before he goes. He keeps saying he's said goodbye to everyone except Miss Vicki."

I knew that Forry was in bad shape; I just didn't realize how bad things were until Susie called. I was so naïve about the disease and believed, as many people did at the time, that I might be at risk if I visited him. But as I listened to Susie tell me that she went to see him every day, I felt deeply ashamed that it had taken me so long. I was his dance instructor, and I loved him. I should have been there for him.

When I arrived at his house, both Forry's partner and Susie were there to greet me. Forry was lying on his couch, his head propped on pillows. He was so pale, with big gray half circles beneath his eyes. The skin on his handsome face was stretched tight across his cheekbones, leaving deep hollows below.

"Miss Vicki!" he said.

Forry always called me Miss Vicki. He could never break the habit.

"Forry," I said, holding his hand. "I'm so sorry it took me so long to get here."

We hugged, and he reassured me it was okay. I was finding it hard to keep from bursting into tears as I held the little boy who had been my most talented student. I was a dozen years older than Forry, but he was the one going first.

"Miss Vicki," he said, "I have something to show you. I want you to see videos of my favorite dances I've choreographed over the years."

He started searching for the routines he wanted me to see.

"Watch this one. Wait: it's coming right up! Look how he lifts her! And watch this move as she comes out of the lift! That was one of my favorites."

Every routine was more polished, professional, and creative than the last.

"I knew from the first moment you entered my studio that you were a star, Forry," I said.

Forry squeezed my hand and looked me straight in the eye. "Miss Vicki," he said. "I need to ask you something."

"Of course, Forry."

"Will you dance with me?"

"Oh, Forry," I replied, "it would be my honor."

"Just about everything I ever wanted to do in dance, I've already done. But that's my last wish. From the time I was a kid, I always wanted to dance with you. Just you and me."

Although I'd danced with the older girls like LuAnne during our recitals, Forry was always too young to dance a duet with me. As a little boy, he'd beg to dance with me in our recital. "We will someday," I'd assure him, "but you need to be a little older." I just assumed that we'd have plenty of time to dance together when he was older.

Now Forry sat up, swung his skinny legs off the couch, and with just a little effort put on his slippers and stood up. He was so tall, about six foot two. Although I could tell he was sick, I was so happy to see that he didn't seem as bad as everyone had been telling me.

Forry was wearing his pajamas, bathrobe, and slippers.

"Let's go out on my patio," Forry said. "I'm not dancing on this carpet."

I took Forry's hand, and we walked outside. The patio faced a beautiful garden with latticework covered in roses. Outside in the backyard, we held hands and faced each other. It was evening, and although it was warm, a light breeze cooled the air.

Forry looked at me and smiled.

"Well, what would you like to do?" I asked.

"I've known for years, Miss Vicki. We are going to do some time steps."

I was surprised because time steps can be physically challenging, but I tried not to show it.

"Well, okay," I replied. "Let's do it."

Susie and Forry's partner were on the patio with us, and we faced them, with the roses as our backdrop and the porch lights as our spotlight.

I let go of Forry's hand and said, "Five, six, seven, eight." And with that, we started to dance without missing a beat. We did all eight time steps in the exact order that I used to teach him as a child. Even in his slippers, Forry had rhythm. You never would have guessed that he was so ill. As we danced, we kept glancing at each other, grinning like fools. And when we finished, we hugged tightly.

Forry whispered in my ear, "I always loved you, Miss Vicki. I'm so happy we finally got to have our dance."

"I know, Forry," I said. "I love you too. Always have. Always will."

Hand in hand, we walked back inside. We said our good-byes and Forry lay down on his couch.

As I walked to the door, I turned around one last time and waved. Forry waved back.

Two days later, Forry's partner called to tell me that he had died.

"Miss Vicki," he said. "I just want to thank you. Thank you for coming and dancing with Forry."

"Please, there's no need to thank me," I told him. "It was an honor to dance with Forry."

"But Miss Vicki," he said, "you don't understand. Forry's been so sick. Until you came to visit, he hadn't gotten up from the couch in six weeks. He couldn't move. He couldn't walk. Then you arrived, and all of a sudden he could do time steps with you out in the backyard."

Forry had stood up from that couch like it was the easiest and most natural thing in the world. I had no idea.

"You gave him his last wish, Miss Vicki, to dance with you, and I'll always be so grateful to you for that."

At Forry's funeral, the church was packed with his former students. I looked around, and I felt extremely proud of everything he'd accomplished.

A few of his students and their mothers stood up to say a few words about him.

"I can tell you for sure," one mother said, pointing up to the sky, "Saint Peter already knows his first time step."

I was the last to speak. I told everyone about how Forry had come to me at the age of five. How his parents lived right next door to my studio. How all he had to do was run down the stairs to get to dance class.

"I have to tell you, I have never, ever seen another dancer who was as talented as Forry," I said. "When I demonstrated new choreography to my other students, I would have to break it down for them. I'd have to show them the same moves over and over before they could learn the steps. But when it was Forry's turn to learn a solo, I could choreograph it right in front of him, and by the time I turned around, he was already doing the steps perfectly. That's how incredible he was. I'll miss him forever."

That was 1998. Every year after that, I'd call LuAnne and invite her to our year-end performances, and every year she came. When my dancers started to improve to a level where LuAnne would enjoy the classes, I asked her to join us.

She immediately told me no.

"I'm too busy for classes," she explained. "I have too much going on with the kids, driving them around to all their activities. And you know Ronnie works every hour of every day and every week."

I knew that Ronnie's hectic work schedule didn't leave LuAnne a whole lot of time for doing things for herself. Even so, I was determined. When she came to watch us dance each year, I'd hug her and ask, "So when are you coming back to class?"

In 2006, the year we danced at Good Hope Middle School and raised money for the YWCA, LuAnne attended as she always did. But this time her daughter Jessica was in the audience right alongside her.

After the show, I hugged LuAnne and Jess, and we caught up. I'd known Jess literally her whole life, having visited her in the hospital the day she was born. By 2006, Jess had just finished a stint living and interning in New York City and had returned to Harrisburg. She'd gotten engaged to her college sweetheart and was starting a new job at an advertising agency. Jess had always been a pretty child, and as an adult, she had gotten even more beautiful. That night at the performance, her long, light brown hair perfectly framed her heart-shaped face, and she gave me a smile worthy of a movie star. I've always thought that if I'd had a daughter, I would have liked her to be just like Jess.

"Hey, Jess," I said. "Why don't you persuade your mom to start tapping with me again?"

"Vicki, I've been trying to convince her for years," Jess replied, "and I'm still working on it!"

A few days later, to my surprise, I got a call from LuAnne.

"Vicki, I'm finally signing up for your tap class," she announced.

"LuAnne? What changed your mind?"

"Well," she replied, "I ran out of excuses."

"Well, that's true," I pointed out.

"And Jessie's going to come along with me."

I told LuAnne that was the best news I'd heard all year.

I suggested that they sign up for my new summer session. LuAnne agreed, and although I couldn't quite believe it, the following week, there they were at class.

It just so happened that this was the night that a reporter and photographer for the *Patriot-News* had come to observe the class.

Right away, I introduced LuAnne to the reporter.

"I want you to meet LuAnne," I told him. "LuAnne was my star student when I owned Vicki's Studio of Rhythm back in Steelton in the 1960s. It's taken me awhile, but I finally persuaded her to return to dance. This is the same LuAnne who came to Philadelphia with me and won an award for the Best Jazz Dancer in the student teacher category in 1966."

LuAnne blushed from all the attention.

Meanwhile, Jess blurted out, "Mom, I never knew you won a dance award!"

"I didn't think it was important," LuAnne said, shrugging.

It was so hard for me to believe that LuAnne had never told Jess about her award. Dance had been so important to LuAnne, and I knew that the trip to Philly had been a big deal for her. What had happened to the outgoing girl I once knew? The woman standing before me couldn't have been more modest or self-effacing.

In an effort to detract attention from herself, LuAnne introduced the reporter to Jess.

"And this is my daughter, Jess. As a little girl she took tap, ballet, and jazz with Vicki's former student Forry at his studio in Harrisburg."

Like everyone else in our area, LuAnne knew that Forry was the best teacher out there. And she knew that because Forry had taken dance with me, Jess would be learning our style. Jess went to classes for about five years, and loved them, before she was forced to stop. She explained to the reporter that at the age of nine, she began to have acute pain in her knees and was diagnosed with tendinitis. The doctor advised LuAnne, "If you want your daughter to walk, pull her out of dance class." Jess was devastated that she could no longer dance, but she had no choice. She learned to enjoy other activities, like cheerleading, and put her dancing days aside. Now here she was, more than ten years later—thankfully, with her knee trouble well in the past—lacing up her tap shoes again.

As the class began, LuAnne and Jess nervously took their places, instinctively retreating to the back line. We began our warm-up and then moved on to some simple time steps. I could tell just by looking at Jess that she had been taught by Forry. Her feet fell easily into the sequences I showed her. The same ones that I'd taught to Forry all those years ago, he had taught to her. Jess had our style.

But it was LuAnne who stole the show. From the moment she put on her shoes, it was clear that she hadn't forgotten a single step. Muscle memory is an incredible thing. It had been thirty years since LuAnne took a dance class, but she tapped like she'd never stopped. It was no surprise to me that LuAnne was still such a fabulous dancer, but Jess's eyes grew wider and wider as she watched her mom. That's when it occurred to me: Jess had probably never seen her mom dance before.

Jess kept her cool. She obviously didn't want to embarrass her mom by gushing during class. About halfway through the hour, however, I asked the dancers to tap across the room one by one so that I could hear how they were doing with the steps. When it came time for LuAnne to tap, Jess finally blurted out, "Mom, you can really dance! How did you just *do* that?"

LuAnne blushed and shrugged again. By the end of class, LuAnne was still pink in the face, not because she was feeling modest this time but because she'd been dancing so hard. She came over to me, and we gave each other a hug. Then my old friend whispered in my ear, "Order my shoes, teach."

FOR the next six weeks, LuAnne and Jess came to every class. It turned out that Jess had her own reasons for encouraging her mom to start dancing again. LuAnne was emerging from a very difficult year. The summer before, her older brother Dave had died suddenly of a heart attack at the age of only sixty. It had been a shock for the whole family, and particularly for LuAnne, who was extremely close to her brother. Dave was just nine years older than LuAnne, and for the first time, she found herself facing thoughts of her own mortality. My friend suddenly found herself becoming panicky and anxious in all kinds of situations that wouldn't have been a problem for her before. She'd be shopping at the supermarket and start gasping for breath because the thought of driving home was too terrifying. She'd pretty much given up going out because social situations made her freeze up, unable to think about what to say next.

Meanwhile, Jess and her fiancé were looking for a new home in Lancaster, forty-five minutes away. Jess knew she was going to be living farther away from her mom than she'd like, and she was worried. At least if LuAnne had tap class to go to each week, Jess would know that she had something to look forward to every Wednesday.

Jess's original plan was to come with LuAnne for just the first six weeks, to encourage her. But before she knew it, Jess was hooked. Toward the end of the summer session, after one of our classes, I called LuAnne and asked her to put Jess on the phone.

"Jess, you did great tonight," I said. "You've come a long way in tap class these past weeks. I'm proud of you. You're dancing like a real Tap Pup!"

"Oh, thank you, Vicki, that means so much to me!"

Jess paused.

"It feels like coming home."

I told her I knew exactly how that felt.

Jess signed up for the September session along with her mom.

Soon after, the article about the Tap Pups appeared in the *Patriot-News.* It included a giant color photograph of my dancers, with LuAnne and Jess included in the background, and the following headline:

Tapping into Fun: Dance Class Lets Women Cut Loose a Step at a Time

The article was great, perfectly capturing the atmosphere in the class and the camaraderie between the dancers. Looking at the photo and the words the reporter had written about us provided an amazing validation both for me and for the dancers, LuAnne and Jess included.

Soon after, I received a call from *Harrisburg Magazine,* which also wanted to publish a picture and article about Vicki's Tap Pups. Normally, I would let the rec centers manage registration, but I decided to include my phone number in the articles so that I could explain the program to future students, tell them where to purchase shoes, and make sure that each was in just the right class for his or her abilities. With two articles coming out back to back that September, my phone rang for two weeks straight, with students wanting to sign up for the new session. I couldn't believe all the inquiries I was getting. I'd even get calls from women sitting in doctors' offices who had just read the article and didn't want to wait until they got home to call.

Now that I was talking to prospective students directly, I came to learn that everyone had her own unique story about how and why she decided to pick up that phone and sign up for tap class.

"I rushed my knee replacement surgery so I could be ready to be a Tap Pup."

"My husband cut your article out of the paper and put it by my phone to encourage me to get involved."

"I went to a foot doctor today, and she told me she tap-dances with you; sounds like fun."

"My daughter and I saw the article. How great that we can do this together."

I discovered that there were dancers in their fifties and sixties who were taking tap classes with children and teens because they didn't know that adult-only tap classes existed.

"Can you imagine, a grown woman dancing next to an eight-year-old?" one caller told me. "Why didn't I find out about you before?"

By the beginning of September, every class was full, including three additional classes for New Beginners. I was emailing Brian with updates every day, and we were both excited. For the first time, I was taking ownership of my program, making my own decisions, and calling the shots. With a few tweaks, my program was growing—just as Brian knew it would.

As the months went by, I watched LuAnne blossom. She may have been self-effacing outside of class, but in the dance studio, she literally tapped back into her old self again. One day I looked over at my friend, and I saw the LuAnne I'd known from Steelton days, happy and comfortable in her own skin.

In many ways, LuAnne and I were learning the same lesson. It's not always easy to say yes when someone wants to help you, especially when that person is your child. It means giving up control and admitting that you can't do everything alone. But in the same way that I was trusting in Brian and accepting his help with the program, LuAnne had trusted in Jess and come along to class with her. It was the beginning of a period of amazing growth, not just for the program but also for me, with my old friend LuAnne by my side.

· ·

"42ND STREET"

WATCH LUANNE AND JESSICA PERFORM ALONG WITH THE OTHER ADVANCED DANCERS.

www.youtube.com/vickistappups

· ·

Chapter 12

• • •

Sunday, June 12, 2011

1:00 PM

IT'S AN HOUR AND A HALF UNTIL SHOWTIME.

As I walk past the open doorway to the men's locker room, I see a group of Intermediate dancers having a dance-off as a way to warm up. They're in two lines, going back and forth, each dancer showing off her best steps, bouncing along to the beat coming from the boom box.

Dancing in the middle of these women is Trish, age sixty. She is tall, with wide brown eyes and dark blonde hair. Trish first came to me five years ago after she saw the newspaper article about the Tap Pups. She thought, "Well, those women look like me! I think I could fit in with this group."

Trish is a seamstress by profession, and when the other dancers in her class learned this, they started bringing their suits and dresses to class for her to tailor. There was only one problem. Trish had magic hands, but it seemed she just might have two left feet—two left feet attached to a pair of the straightest legs I've ever seen.

When Trish told her sisters that she was signing up for tap class, they couldn't believe it.

"Are you sure, Trish?" they asked. "You know you can't dance!"

Trish was determined to prove her sisters wrong, but as hard as she tried, she couldn't do even the most basic step, called a slap (when you brush the ball of your foot and then drop it on the floor). Her legs were so stiff, she might as well have been wearing knee braces. As a result, her feet scuffed and stuck. And without being able to pull off a slap, it's almost impossible to do anything else in tap.

"Don't worry, you'll get there," I told Trish. "Everyone has their 'click week.' Just be patient, and it will click for you too. It might not be today and it might not be tomorrow, but it will happen."

This was something that I always said to New Beginners: you need to hang in there until you can loosen up your legs and feet, transfer your weight from your heels to your toes, and flex your knees without bouncing. At that point, tap becomes so much easier and a lot more fun.

However, despite our best efforts, Trish was taking longer than anyone else I'd ever taught. After two months of classes, she still couldn't execute a basic slap.

"I know you're wishing I would quit," Trish said to me one week.

"No, Trish," I said firmly, "I'm just wishing I could find a better way to help you get this!"

I didn't want to give up on Trish, especially because I knew how much the classes meant to her. Trish had grown up loving to watch the old Hollywood musicals on television. "If I could do one thing in my life and do it well," she thought, "I'd like to be able to dance like that." Trish's family didn't have the money to send her to classes, and it wasn't until Trish was fifty-three that she came to her first class. I quickly learned that Trish was going through a difficult time. She was adjusting to an empty nest after her kids left for college, as well as grieving for her mother, who had passed away the previous summer. Tap was a way for Trish to do something for herself that would take her mind off how much she missed her mom and her children. It was also a nice tribute to her mother, who'd loved the Hollywood musicals just as much as Trish did.

Although I was determined to transform Trish into a dancer, I have to admit that by the end of her second month of lessons, I'd begun to wonder if I could. Then, one evening, right before Christmas break, the class was dancing one by one across the room. When it came time for Trish's turn, her first few steps were tight as usual. Suddenly she loosened up. Oh, my! I heard her make a proper slap sound for the first time. She did it! Then another. The transition was so smooth that Trish didn't even notice she was dancing correctly until she reached the middle of the room. Then she heard it. She suddenly stopped.

"I got my click week!" Trish shouted, jumping up and down. "I got my click week!"

When Trish looked around, the whole class was jumping, clapping, and smiling along with her. She ran over to me and gave me a huge hug. From that point on, Trish continued to improve. Now that she had her slap, she was able to do everything else. Trish was a tap dancer.

When you're younger, you take it for granted that you'll be able to learn a new skill. It's expected that you'll be able to figure something out, whether it's reading, writing, or learning to swim. Then at a certain age, the expectation is that you just stop, that you've already learned everything you're going to learn. You're established. The problem with this attitude is that you shut yourself off from the joy that comes from mastering something new. It's easy to feel satisfaction when you get something right the very first time. But true satisfaction comes when you try something really challenging and you finally succeed at it after failing many times in the process. For Trish, figuring out how to perform a slap made her happier than anything she'd achieved in years. Yes, it's harder to learn a new skill when you're in your fifties, but that makes the triumph all the sweeter when you finally figure it out.

My girl Trish, who had struggled so much in the beginning, danced three routines in that year's spring show. At the end of the performance, I called her onstage to receive our annual Most Improved Dancer Award. Her sisters were in the audience, cheering for the sibling they thought would never be able to learn how to dance. That night Trish put an end to the "two-left-feet syndrome" in her family once and for all.

Over the next few years, through a lot of hard work and effort, Trish moved up through the levels. In our show today, she's dancing with the Intermediate dancers in some of the most complex routines she's ever performed—and even sharing the spotlight in two numbers with the Advanced group. Although she made me question at times whether I was ever going to crack the code for her, Trish taught me a valuable lesson: we all have our own pace, and although some are quicker than others, the important thing is that we get there in the end.

· ·

"JUMP JIVIN'"

MEET TRISH AS WELL AS OTHER INTERMEDIATE AND ADVANCED DANCERS.

www.youtube.com/vickistappups

· ·

BY the time my sixtieth birthday came into view on the horizon, I had shaken off any lingering doubts about my future and retirement. My program was growing. I was feeling happy and fulfilled. My energy level was back. Around this same time, things started falling into place for Brian too. He'd started a new job, one that fit his skills perfectly and challenged him in new ways.

To cap off everything, just a few months before I turned sixty, I met someone.

It was Saint Patrick's Day weekend, and I had gone up to New York City with my Wednesday night girlfriends Andrea, Jenna, and Susan. Brian was away for the weekend, so we could stay at his place. The evening of Saint Patrick's Day, we were at a bar on Twenty-third Street when I spotted a guy out of the corner of my eye who looked about my age. He had on a business suit, a starched white shirt, and—yes—tasseled loafers. I immediately thought, "Who is *he*?"

I was wearing a long light brown blazer with a pair of black leggings and tall black and brown leather riding boots. I felt good. Everyone has those nights now and again when you feel like yourself and you feel glamorous, all at the same time. This was one of those nights. I once read in a magazine that if you want to meet a man at a bar, you should stand next to him and order a drink. It actually took me awhile to work up the courage to try this, but when I did, of course, the man in question didn't even look my way. "Oh well," I thought. "Obviously I should stop reading articles about how to meet men." But then, to my surprise, when the bartender slid my glass toward me, the man turned around, put his hand on mine, and said, "Let me help you with that."

We talked for about fifteen minutes. He wanted to know if I lived in the city. I told him that I was visiting with friends. I learned that he lived in Manhattan and worked nearby. When the stool next to him opened up, he immediately slid over and invited me to sit with him. His name was Dan. He was a New Yorker, of Irish descent. "Vicki," I thought to myself, "you've been there, done that with an Irish New Yorker. Do you really want to know more about him?" Of course I did. Over the next few hours, we talked and laughed, completely comfortable in each other's company. Meanwhile, my friends were having a good time with a group that they'd met on the other side of the bar.

When it was time to leave, Dan asked me how long I was going to be in New York. I told him that I was in town for two more days.

"If it's okay with you and your girlfriends, I'd love to take you out to dinner tomorrow evening," he said.

After he'd gone, I told my friends that the handsome man at the bar had invited me to dinner the following night. "But that wouldn't be right," I said, "since I came to New York to spend time with all of you."

Susan was the first to speak up.

"Are you crazy? *Of course* you have to go to dinner with him! We'll be fine."

"Okay!" I agreed. "I guess you talked me into it!" She didn't need to twist my arm.

Dinner the next night was very romantic. Dan was attentive. He seemed genuinely interested in learning about me and my life. For most of the evening, we kept making eye contact. A few times, he reached for my hand.

I knew the girls were having a drink nearby, so at the end of the meal, I suggested that we go meet them to finish the evening.

After we found my friends, Dan stayed for a drink. The girls were obviously impressed with him. He asked them lots of questions about their weekend and cracked a few jokes to make us laugh. Then we said good night.

Susan couldn't believe it.

"Vicki, you met a man who is perfect for you, and you're coming home with us?! You should have gone back to his place! Now you'll never hear from him again."

"Oh, Susan," I said. "You know I'm not that kind of girl."

The next day as we were driving home to Pennsylvania, my cell phone rang just as we were exiting the Lincoln Tunnel. I saw who the caller was, so I held up the phone so that Susan could see Dan's ID before I answered.

"Okay," she conceded, "I guess you proved me wrong."

I answered my phone and said hello.

"I knew what time you were planning to leave," said Dan. "I'm hoping I timed it well enough to say good-bye while you are still in New York City."

"Your timing is perfect. I'm just about to leave the Lincoln Tunnel," I told him, a huge smile on my face.

In the coming weeks, Dan kept calling. I went back to New York City to see him, and he traveled to Harrisburg to see me. The relationship was going so well, the thought even crossed my mind that maybe I'd finally met the handsome Irish New Yorker I'd dreamed of all those years ago. There was so much that I liked about Dan. He was fun and smart. He had a house on Long Island, right on the beach, and enjoyed spending time there with friends. He was athletic and dynamic, regularly running marathons.

One day after we'd been dating for a few months, Dan told me that he was going to Ireland that summer to run an international marathon that was taking place in Connemara. His goal was to run a marathon in every continent. Dan asked if I wanted to go with him, and I told him I'd love to. I'd always wanted to go to Ireland, and I thought it would be a lot of fun to see someone prepare for a marathon.

Dan's idea to go on a trip gave me another idea. "You know what'd be great?" I suggested. "How about when we get back, you come down to Harrisburg, and we can go golfing together?"

I knew that Dan wasn't a golfer, but I thought it would be fun to do something that I loved to do and show him around town.

Dan didn't even hesitate before answering:

"Not in this lifetime."

Those were his words: "Not in this lifetime." I waited for an explanation. He didn't offer one.

My heart sank. The least Dan could have done was pretend to be interested. "Not again," I remember thinking to myself. "Not another guy who wants me to give but doesn't want to reciprocate." In the past, I'm sure I would have let a comment like that pass. I would have told myself, "I'm sure Dan meant something else. Maybe if I went to Ireland with him, he'd realize that he wants to come to Harrisburg to spend time with me on a golf course after all."

The problem wasn't Dan. It was that I'd already wasted too much time on men who cared more about themselves than about me. Did I really have the energy to enter into another relationship with someone who might turn out to be selfish? On the edge of sixty, I knew I didn't have the time or the patience for another self-absorbed guy in tasseled loafers.

After taking a deep breath, I said, "You know what, Dan? Don't call me anymore."

"W-What?" he stammered.

"I believe that a relationship should be give-and-take, and I've spent too many years being the one who does all the giving. I think it's best if we go our separate ways. Oh, and just to make sure you are clear: this has nothing to do with golf!"

I'd stuck with Mike. I'd stuck with Larry. I'd stuck with so many men who weren't right for me. I no longer had any interest in being with someone just for the sake of it. My whole life, I had been waiting. Waiting for that special guy to find me. Waiting to find a partner to make me feel fulfilled and complete.

I didn't feel that way anymore.

Up to this point, the thought of retiring alone had always terrified me. But now when I visualized my retirement, I didn't see a big black hole. I envisioned a scene full of friends, laughter, and responsibilities, good ones. My classes were already overflowing. I had gone from teaching 50 dancers to 250 in a matter of months, and I barely had enough time to cope with this new demand. I had a lot going on in my life, and if Dan didn't want to share some of that with me, then it was better that we parted ways.

Far from feeling depressed after ending things with Dan, I felt strong and in charge. Just four years ago, after my breakup with Larry, I'd had a hard time getting up from the couch. Now I was so busy that I spent my evenings either teaching or catching up on emails and phone calls. I almost never had time for TV.

At the age of sixty, it was becoming clear to me that I needed to retire from my day job to look after my business full time. There weren't enough hours in the day to keep up with my responsibilities at work and look after my program. I typed up my letter of resignation. I took a deep breath and told my boss that I wanted to retire the following spring.

In fact, I ended up retiring even earlier.

On March 16, a few weeks after I handed in my notice, we had an unexpected snowfall, about six inches in total. My son Michael, his daughters, Olivia and Savanah, and their dog Finnegan slept over for the weekend. The next day, Saint Patrick's Day, it was warm and sunny and all of our snow melted. That night, Michael went out with his friends, while the girls and I went out to dinner and rented a movie. It was freezing cold and windy.

Around eleven thirty, Finnegan started barking to be taken for a walk, and I wanted to be the one to walk him. I got bundled up in my coat and started toward the end of my driveway. It was dark out, much too dark to see the patch of black ice right past my car.

When I fell, I hit the ground hard, and I heard my leg crack three times.

Since it was Saint Patrick's Day, I thought that the hospitals might be a little busy, so I decided to take a chance that my foot was just sprained. I hobbled up my stairs, collapsed on the bed, and propped up my left foot with an ice bag. At four in the morning, I called to wake my mother.

"Mom, I'm okay, but I think I need a ride to the hospital," I told her. "Looks like I might have broken my leg. Michael will stay with the girls."

By the time I got to the hospital, my entire leg was throbbing, and my foot had swollen up like a balloon. Clearly, something was very wrong.

The doctor's diagnosis wasn't pretty. I'd broken my left foot, ankle, and leg.

"Your bones are fractured so close to the tendons that if you put even one ounce of pressure on that leg, I'm going to have to get you back in here to put plates and screws in your foot and your ankle," he informed me.

"I can't have you do that!" I told him. "I'm a dance instructor. I won't be able to move my foot properly!"

"Then you'd better keep your weight off that foot" was all he said.

I went home with crutches and strict instructions to keep my leg elevated continually until the bones were fully healed. The doctor estimated that I would be laid up for five or six months.

Needless to say, I wasn't too happy about this scenario. It's devastating and no fun being a dance instructor who can't dance. I felt very fortunate to have friends and family who were willing to take care of me—especially because I needed help doing every single little thing. My mom came by every day to cook my meals and to help me around the house. My sons visited on weekends. My neighbor brought in the mail. My friends from Tap Pups were over every day, bringing me lunch, checking up on me. Susan stopped by with a borrowed wheelchair for me. Andrea and Jenna agreed to pick me up for classes and wheel me in. They also offered to be my feet in class, demonstrating the steps for the dancers. Meanwhile, my right foot (the good one) would be moving around like crazy as I tried to demonstrate tap steps while I sat in my chair.

"Mom, look on the bright side," Brian pointed out. "At least you have some free time on your hands to start thinking about the next spring show!"

And so that's what I did. While I waited to heal, I found a venue, and started planning the choreography and the costumes. Proceeds were again going toward the YWCA Domestic Violence Shelter, and we would use the event to continue to raise awareness for the cause. We knew that we had too many dancers for a middle school auditorium, so we switched to a local nightclub called Champions Sports Bar and Grill, with a stage, lights, and a sound system. Brian designed a Tap Pups logo that we put on everything: invitations, T-shirts, tickets, fliers, and the programs. He kept insisting that everything needed to be branded and look and feel as polished and professional as my dancers tapped.

"Mom, you all deserve to look like a million bucks. After all, that's how you feel, right?"

Breaking my leg in three places should have been the worst thing that ever happened to me. Instead it turned out to be one of the best things. From March until September, I was in my wheelchair or on crutches, teaching, planning, reorganizing, and thinking ahead. All that time away from the office forced me to really prepare for leaving my job in a way that I never would have been able to do otherwise.

This year, when Brian told me that he was sending out a press release, I didn't even think to stop him: I'd learned by now that my son knew exactly what he was doing. A reporter was coming to write a feature story, and one of the local TV channels was going to run a segment. We had 50 dancers in the show, and they all rehearsed their socks off. I was blown away when 250 guests squeezed into the nightclub on a Sunday afternoon to see us perform. This was the year that Trish won the award for Most Improved Dancer.

The show was our most professional to date. The crowd was whooping and cheering during every number. We exceeded everyone's expectations, even my own. And we raised more than $2,000 for the shelter, compared to $350 the year before. I left that night feeling invigorated, like I had just been given the energy boost that I needed to start this new chapter of my life.

By September, my leg had finally healed completely, and I was able to return to my day job. The next day, our accountant at my work called me with some news.

"Vicki," she said, "you have to leave tomorrow. You've accrued so much vacation leave over the years that unless you go now, you won't be able to use it all before you retire."

I had enough vacation days to take off the next five months, right up to the day I was due to retire. I went in to see my boss and told him that I had good news and bad news.

"The good news is that I'm back and fully healed," I said. "The bad news is that tomorrow is my last day."

My boss laughed, looked at me, and said, "Congratulations. We'll miss you." That afternoon, I put my boxes of personal belongings in the backseat of my car and drove out of the parking lot for the last time after thirty years. I was now sixty-one years old, and as I headed home, I knew that something had shifted for me. For so long now, retiring had been such a scary prospect, both in emotional and financial terms. After all those years, I didn't know what kind of person I would be outside of my job, especially if I was going to be single. I was so worried about what would happen to me when I wasn't earning a fixed income. But now I was moving on to the next phase of my life, and instead of feeling scared, I'd never felt so certain that I was heading in exactly the right direction.

Chapter 13

• • •

Sunday, June 12, 2011

1:45 PM

BEFORE THE SHOW BEGINS, I RUN OUT TO CHECK ON HOW EV-
ERYTHING IS GOING AT THE FRONT OF THE HOUSE. OLIVIA AND
SAVANAH HAVE SET UP THE TABLES OUTSIDE THE DOOR TO THE
AUDITORIUM, LAYING OUT INFORMATION ABOUT THE YWCA AND
THE 3R PROJECT AND BEAUTIFULLY ARRANGING THE T-SHIRTS
AND DVDS. I BLOW THEM BOTH A KISS.

"We've got everything under control! Now go back and get ready!" they
reassure me.

On my way backstage, I stop to give a hug to Jeanne, who's helping the
girls with the merchandise. Usually Jeanne would be backstage with all the
other dancers, getting ready for the show. Sadly, this year, she had to miss
classes because of illness in her family, so she elected to help sell T-shirts
instead.

Just two years ago, Jeanne was having health issues of her own. She's
been in remission for breast cancer for more than a year. Her hair has grown
back thicker and fuller than ever, her eyes are bright, and her skin is clear.
At sixty-three, Jeanne is tall and striking, a woman who's had a lifelong,

successful career in local government. Before she retired, she was chief of protocol for the State House of Representatives and the director of special projects for four Speakers of the House.

Jeanne first heard about the Tap Pups five years ago. She was at a meeting when one of her colleagues got up from her seat and dashed out the door, saying, "Gotta run, I'm late for tap class!"

Jeanne thought, "Tap class?" and was immediately intrigued. A ski instructor and active boater, she had recently noticed that she felt a lack of confidence in her balance when skiing and walking from the dock onto her boat. When she heard about tap class, she thought that maybe it could help correct her imbalance issue. Like many Tap Pups, she enrolled alone but soon introduced two friends to the program. It wasn't long before Jeanne was addicted, taking her class, then staying for the one after it.

Jeanne had been with me nearly three years and we had become quite close when she came to me to tell me that she had found a lump in her breast and that the cancer was already advanced. I wish this was a rare conversation for me to have with a dancer, but, sadly, I'm very aware of cancer and its impact on women our age. "I found a lump . . ." "They're doing a biopsy . . ." "I have to go for surgery . . ." Yes, we'd all like to feel invincible, but there's no getting around the fact that nature has other ideas. Too many of the ladies I meet through classes have gotten sick, and two of them, my old friend Kay included, have fought so hard to win their battles but have lost. At one time in my life, I'd open up the newspaper right to the bridal announcements to see if anyone I knew was getting married. Now I find myself reading the obituary section, praying that I don't see a name I recognize.

Naturally, I was devastated to hear Jeanne's news. But Jeanne being Jeanne, she did her best to try to ease my concern, telling me that she had already made an appointment with one of the best oncologists in Philadelphia. She kept tapping for as long as she could, until the chemo robbed her of her strength. I told Jeanne that she was still welcome to come to class and watch from the sidelines, and many times, that's what she did.

Thankfully, the treatment was completely successful. These days, I'm happy to say, Jeanne is back to her old self. She has to wear a sleeve on her arm to stop the swelling after the mastectomy, but it's a small price to pay for survival. She's dancing again and enjoying life. And if she ever feels tired or worn down before class, she looks to our other cancer survivors in the Tap Pups for inspiration to keep dancing—women like Debbie, Linda, Elsa, Colleen, Kris, Kathy, Annetta, Susan, Nancy, Sandy, and Mary Lou. That's the amazing thing about the Tap Pups. No matter what you're going through, there's always someone who knows exactly how that feels.

THE year after I retired turned out to be a huge turning point for me and for the Tap Pups. Brian always said that as soon as I stopped working my day job, I would begin to discover all kinds of new ways to teach and run my classes.

"Brian," I used to tell him, "I've been teaching dance since I was eighteen. I know exactly how I want to do this!" Yet Brian turned out to be right again.

One of my biggest revelations took place in one of my New Beginner classes. As I watched a group of beginners struggle with the basic slap step, I suddenly noticed that the dancers were concentrating too hard. They were clenching their feet and legs, and this was stopping them from making the proper noise.

"Relax your big toe," I told the dancers, just to see what would happen. Right away, almost every foot in the class came down firmly on the ball. The sound they made was as clear as a bell. All these years of tap instruction, and I'd come up with a new and ingenious way of teaching a simple slap! I couldn't believe it. Up until now, I'd been so busy rushing from the office to class that I never gave myself time to relax and absorb what was happening in front of my own eyes.

It wasn't that my life was any slower. In fact, the opposite was true. I've never been busier—but I've never been happier. The big difference was that now all my energies were focused on my program.

By now the Tap Pups were everywhere around town. Only a year ago, I was teaching 60 dancers in a week. Now I was teaching 60 dancers in one evening, with nearly 350 dancers in total. I asked LuAnne and Jess to come on board as instructors, as I was going to have to add two new locations to accommodate so many dancers. It was apparent that I was outgrowing my arrangement with the rec centers. I was still teaching in school cafeterias and auditoriums. Obviously, if I wanted to run my business on my own terms, I needed a place of my own.

I started to look around for a space that would work as a dance studio. The following spring, right before our annual show, I was buying material for last-minute accessories at a fabric outlet store in Lemoyne, an area on Harrisburg's West Shore. The complex was large and had several different businesses under one roof. I asked the clerk if she knew of any vacant rentals in the building. Within minutes, the owner was showing me an available space. It was a former horse stable, built in 1913, raw and unfinished—in short, a complete mess, with wires hanging from the ceiling. But I knew that it was everything I needed and wanted. It had a large open space with brick walls, and two rooms to the side, which I pictured being my office and a dressing room, with a small bathroom off the dressing room area. To seal the deal, the landlord had just finished putting in a raised sprung floor. Perfect for a dance floor. I told him I'd get back to him.

I could hardly wait to get in my car to call Brian. When my son heard me say that I'd found my studio, and I wanted him to come and see the space right away, he was skeptical; he simply couldn't believe that the first place I saw was the right place. But the moment he walked inside, he knew we'd found the Tap Pups' new home.

On the way back to my house that day, we were both excited. We couldn't believe it. At the age of nearly sixty-two, I found myself in a unique position: should I sign a lease for my new dance studio or sign up for Social Security?

I chose the studio.

The next few months were spent transforming a horse stable into an elegant dance studio. Brian and I handled the designing and planning. At my request, the landlord installed glossy black tiles over the sprung floor. We added mirrors all along the brick walls and gave the remaining walls a fresh coat of bright white paint. We had an Amish family make custom benches for the dressing room, and a good friend of mine from high school hand-painted a beautiful sign for the front of the building.

The old horse stable was now a shiny, modern loft space with an exposed ceiling revealing the original beams. We decorated the front area of the studio with sleek furniture arranged around a stylish aqua short shag rug, below a huge, sparkling chandelier. The dressing room had a zebra-print rug on the floor, and I hung an aqua boa on the back of the bathroom door to add to the atmosphere. Everything was clean, spacious, elegant, and, above all, feminine. This was a dance studio for grown-ups, a place where my ladies could escape from their daily lives and feel completely at home.

"A woman must have a room of her own," a wise woman once wrote. That's true of dancers too. Ever since I was a little girl, dance studios have been my own version of a sacred space. When I was three years old, staring up at the pink door of the studio where I was about to take my first class, it was like I was standing on the doorstep of a personal fairy tale. At Miss Bette's studio, I was in my element; when the weekly lesson was over, I never wanted to leave. At my Studio of Rhythm back in Steelton, when we gathered for Saturday morning classes, it was our time to express ourselves, to be happy, and to be together. We were in our own little world, where it wasn't important how much money you had, or what clothes you wore, or what your parents did. It was about getting those steps right and learning to shine. Now, all these years later, I couldn't believe that I was finally going to be able to give this same experience to the adult dancers in my program.

In August 2008, Vicki's Tap Pups Studio and Cultural Center was ready for its grand opening. That afternoon as I drove over for the party, I had to pinch myself. Less than a year ago, "going to work" meant driving to my job as an office manager. Now it meant going to my brand-new, beautiful dance studio and teaching my students. I was sixty-two years old and starting all over again. But at the same time, I was coming full circle, finally fulfilling the dream I first had for myself as a seventeen-year-old girl.

I climbed out of the car, walked across the parking lot to the front door, and put the key in the lock. *Click!* "Look at me now," I thought. "This is what I'm going to be doing for the rest of my life." My heart was filled with gratitude and pride.

About 250 people came through the studio that afternoon and evening. We drank champagne, ate chocolate-covered strawberries, and my Advanced dancers performed. In the course of the evening, I must have kissed, hugged, or shook hands with every person in the room. I remember thinking it was a perfect night.

Later, when everyone else was gone, Brian and I stayed behind to clean up and close the studio. I had a stack of new registration forms under my arm, and as I turned off the last light, I let out a deep, deep breath.

"We did it," I told Brian. "I actually have my own studio again. After all these years." Brian was just as proud. This was a huge step for both of us, and we'd done it together. Almost forty years to the day that I closed my Studio of Rhythm and left Steelton to start my marriage, with the help of my son,

I'd reclaimed my life. It had taken awhile, but I was finally back. I was Vicki Grubic again.

Over the coming year, our numbers grew until there were five hundred dancers in the program. Tap Pups was becoming a phenomenon. At some point, Brian wanted to update our website to reflect our new numbers, so he asked me, "Mom, do you think you have the largest adult tap studio in Harrisburg?"

I laughed. "Well, yeah! No one has adult tap studios around here besides me."

"So you think you're the largest in Central Pennsylvania?"

"Of course we are!" was my response.

"Oh my God, Mom!" Brian exclaimed. "Do you think you're the largest in the state?"

"Well, I don't know," I replied. I really didn't. I'd never thought about what kinds of classes people were teaching elsewhere in Pennsylvania.

Brian told me he would dig around and call me right back. He hung up. Ten minutes later, the phone rang.

"Mom! I looked everywhere online," said Brian. "Are you ready for this? I think we're easily the largest adult tap group in America. And from what I'm seeing, there's nothing else like this in the world!"

Brian and I started laughing in disbelief. It had never occurred to us that we would create the largest *anything*. This was crazy!

But in the coming months, it was clear that Vicki's Tap Pups was taking off in a major way. Tap dancers were everywhere I looked. Whenever I left the house—at the supermarket, the salon, the mall, the movie theater—I was running into ladies I knew from classes.

I realized something was going right when one of my All-Star dancers, Tiny, started writing me checks for classes with the word "therapy" in the subject line. Tiny is seventy-four and she started dancing when she was two years old. Her grandfather would take her to his local beer joint on Fridays after he cashed his paycheck, put money in the jukebox, then stand her up on the bar and get her to dance in return for peanuts. These days, Tiny can be found working as as a receptionist at a local dentist's office. She was at her job one day when a man came into the waiting room.

"Okay, who's the Tap Pup here?" he asked. "I saw the magnet on one of the parked cars outside."

Many of my dancers have the Vicki's Tap Pups logo on their cars. Ladies tell me that when they see it on a car in front of them on the highway, they speed up and honk like crazy to say hi to a fellow Tap Pup; or if they see a car with a magnet parked in a mall or on the street, they leave a note on the windshield.

Tiny raised her hand, with a huge smile on her face, and proudly shouted, "That's me!"

But as soon as she got the words out, one of the patients in the waiting room said, "I'm a Tap Pup too!"

The woman sitting beside her, also waiting to see the dentist, said, "So am I!"

And the man who asked the question said, "Well, so is my wife!"

The four of them got caught up in a discussion about who took classes where, and what level they were in, and which night of the week they attended. The community of Tap Pups was growing, and it was bringing people together all across town.

In fact, I started getting students from further and further away. People were traveling forty-five to sixty miles for a weekly tap class, and I started to get emails from women in other states asking me to open something closer to them. One of my newest Tap Pups, Randi, age sixty-seven, lives near Princeton, NJ, and travels three and a half hours one way by train to take two classes every Thursday morning. Every week, a different Tap Pup picks

Randi up from the train station and brings her to the studio. According to Randi, it's worth making such a long trip to do something that makes her so happy, especially at her age.

That same year I opened the studio, we danced and marched for the second time in Harrisburg's annual Saint Patrick's Day Parade. We were by far the largest group marching, all of us wearing our black Tap Pups sweat-shirts or black satin jackets, everyone in red lipstick and gold hoops. We literally took over the parade, covering an entire city block with tap dancers. We had four drummers marching with us to keep the beat, and every few blocks, we'd stop to perform a routine in unison. The spectators' ecstatic response confirmed that Tap Pups were becoming part of the Harrisburg culture. A crowd of twentysomethings standing outside an Irish pub shouted out, "We love you Tap Pups!" People were yelling, "You go, girl!"

At our annual show, we performed for the first time at the Forum in front of more than a thousand friends and family members, and raised more than $6,000 for our local domestic violence shelter. Then, in the spring of 2009, we got more good news. We were asked to open for Joan Rivers at the Whitaker Center for Science and the Arts in Harrisburg as part of a women's health conference. During the day, the women at the conference were going to be treated to spa sessions and classes—and I was going to be one of the instructors. And on Saturday evening, the All-Stars were going to perform right before Joan did her show.

Like so many of my dancers, I've been a huge fan of Joan's since her stand-up appearances on the *Ed Sullivan Show* and the *Tonight Show* in the 1960s. When the big night arrived, my fourteen All-Star dancers were still in their dressing rooms, and I was waiting for them by the stage door. All of a sudden, Joan's car pulled up. I was the only one there at that moment, so I waved and told her I was a big fan. Then as I turned, Joan heard the click of my tap shoes.

She pointed to my feet. "Tap dancer?" she asked.

I nodded and smiled. Then I explained that my group was going to be her opening act tonight.

Five minutes later, I was waiting in the wings with the dancers ready to go onstage—dressed in their satin jackets with the Tap Pups logo embroidered on the front and back—when someone handed me a message. It was from Joan.

"Please ask that tap teacher to wait until I get into the audience. I'd love to see the performance."

We waited, and a few minutes later, out came Joan. She waved and took her seat. That night, the Advanced group performed to perfection.

"Are you freakin' kidding me?" Joan said to us afterward. "All this talent here in freakin' Harrisburg? You ladies belong on Broadway!"

"Can I quote you on that, Joan?" I asked.

"You bet your ass you can!" she replied.

That summer, we received another invitation to perform. Jeanne, my dancer who worked as the director of special projects for the Speaker of the House, asked me if the Tap Pups would like to perform at the closing event of a five-day conference in Philadelphia. This was the National Conference of State Legislatures, and it was going to be attended by members of Congress and key staff from the fifty state capitals.

"What do you think, Miss Vicki? Can you pull it off?"

She explained that the theme of the show was "honoring Philadelphia" and that the performance was going to take place on the steps of the Philadelphia Art Museum, in front of an audience of seven thousand. On top of that, we would be opening for Chubby Checker and Patti LaBelle. Was Jeanne kidding? Of course I said yes!

It was a short turnaround, though. I was going to have to choreograph the routine and assemble the dancers in less than a month. The performance was on a weekday, and it was summer. How many tappers could I really expect to show up with such short notice? As it turned out, a lot. I sent out an email, and within no time, I had commitments from 130 dancers. Enough to make an impact. I began choreographing a special routine to the *American Bandstand* theme song. This was going to be our tribute to the city of Philadelphia, home of Dick Clark's *American Bandstand*, the show that we loved so much growing up.

As we prepared for the big event, there was only one logistical problem. My studio is large, but it still wasn't spacious enough to rehearse with 130 dancers. Luckily, right outside the studio is a large parking lot. Three times before the show, I got all the ladies to park on the street, and we rehearsed outside. All of us were wearing tennis shoes so that we wouldn't hurt our knees dancing on cement, and I brought a boom box outside to blast the music. Our neighbors up and down the block set up chairs on their porches and gathered around to watch the free show. By the end of three rehearsals, the routine had come together, the ladies dancing jitterbug style, in pairs, snapping their fingers and swinging their arms as they tapped.

The day of the performance, 130 dancers climbed aboard two buses that were going to take us to Philadelphia. Two hours later, we found ourselves driving up the wide tree-lined boulevard that leads from city hall to the Philadelphia Museum of Art, perched on a hill overlooking the entire city. It was such a thrill to know that later we would be dancing on a stage set up in front of that very museum.

At the top of the steps leading to the museum is the famous spot where Sylvester Stallone's Rocky Balboa punches the air and jumps up and down in the scene from the movie. After we got off the bus, of course, every dancer wanted to climb the steps and do the "Rocky pose" while her friends snapped photos. That afternoon, I watched as 130 dancers rehearsed their

Bandstand routine outside one of the most famous landmarks in the country. Tourists stopped to watch. People snapped photos. "Hey, who are you ladies?" someone in the crowd shouted.

I couldn't help but remember the Tap Pups' first performance in 1998: 17 dancers performing at a local nursing home for about 20 audience members snoozing in their wheelchairs. I turned to Brian, and he beamed a smile right back at me. He knew as well as I did how far we'd come: from that retirement home to watching these ladies tapping with the beautiful backdrop of the Philadelphia skyline behind them.

The evening's performance was at seven o'clock. By six fifteen, every Tap Pup was in her black pants and aqua-colored polo shirt.

All of a sudden, Jeanne came running in.

"You're going on fifteen minutes early!" she exclaimed. "There is a terrible storm heading our way—we want to get you out there before the rain starts."

Brian and I quickly rallied the dancers. Outside, the sky was dark and imposing, and the wind was gathering force. Luckily, we were ready to go when Jeanne came back a few minutes later.

The museum security guards were yelling at everyone to "get in place," and to "stop running—you can't run in the museum!"

"We need to get you out there now!" Jeanne yelled. "Hurry up!"

All in a line, we began marching out the door, walking—not running— as fast as we could.

Then one of the security staff came toward us with his palms held out in front of him.

"Stop! Go back!"

He explained it was an electrical storm. There was no way we could walk out onto a stage filled with sound equipment. We could hear the rain thundering on the roof of the museum, and outside the windows, the sky was flashing. We turned back and waited, crowded in our holding room, trying to make the best of the situation. Brian got to work taking group shots of all the dancers, hoping to create a fun distraction.

We were there for about an hour. Finally the rain let up, and we received news that they were preparing the stage. I looked around, but for some reason, I couldn't see my son anywhere.

"Where's Brian?" I asked Jeanne.

"He's already outside trying to dry the dance floor so that the dancers can perform!" she replied. Sure enough, Brian was out there with a huge industrial-size squeegee in his hands, fearlessly trying to mop down the buckled dance floor.

At last Jeanne returned to give us the verdict: it was too dangerous to turn on the sound system. The rain had flooded the stage, and they were worried that any electrical equipment might short.

Amazingly, Jeanne had already come up with a solution.

"Why don't we send out the Advanced Tap Pups, and they can do their a capella routine?"

This is the signature routine of the Advanced dancers, and since it's performed without music, we wouldn't have to worry about the sound system blowing up on us. I agreed with Jeanne. Better to send out the Advanced dancers than none at all. Of course, everyone else was disappointed. We'd traveled all this way. We'd spent hours rehearsing our routines. The dancers were dressed and ready to go. But if anyone felt let down, the feeling lasted approximately three seconds. While the Advanced dancers prepared to perform, everyone else went straight out into the audience to support them.

When the dancers finally walked out onstage and took their places, the entire audience of seven thousand people fell silent. I held my breath as Rick made his two loud scrapes and stamps to signal the beginning of the dance. The audience was listening so intently that you could hear yourself whisper. I've seen my dancers perform this routine many, many times, but that night, they danced so well, I actually thought I saw sparks fly under their taps. Then, a second after they danced their last step—throwing their arms out in a big V shape in front of them—the crowd erupted in applause. It was deafening, even louder than the storm that nearly threatened to stop the show. One of the senators attending the conference was standing next to me. "Are those your dancers?" she asked. "They're incredible!"

After the dancers left the stage, it was time for Chubby Checker. During his set, he gave a shout-out to the Tap Pups and asked them to come onstage to dance the Twist while he sang. So many ladies ran to go up that the security guard had to hold half of them back. There was a sea of aqua Tap Pups shirts onstage, and immediately below were all the rest, dancing away and having the times of their lives.

Brian put his arm around my shoulders. "Mom, just think," he said. "These ladies thought they were just signing up for a tap class. Look at them now!"

• •

PHILADELPHIA REHEARSAL FOR CHUBBY CHECKER

WATCH VICKI'S TAP PUPS PREPARE AND PERFORM

IN PHILADELPHIA.

www.youtube.com/vickistappups

• •

During Patti LaBelle's performance, she told the crowd that she was shivering from the cold, so one of the dancers handed her a Tap Pups jacket. I have photos of Patti wearing it while singing "Lady Marmalade."

On the bus trip back, we celebrated the Advanced dancers and their performance. We toasted Jeanne, who'd made all of this possible. We toasted all the dancers who weren't able to perform but who were definitely the evening's loudest and most enthusiastic audience members. The party went on all the way back to Harrisburg. Later, Jeanne, who had stayed behind in Philadelphia, told me her one regret was that she didn't get to come home with us on the party bus.

It was two months later when Jeanne received her breast cancer diagnosis. Word quickly spread throughout the Tap Pups. Because of the trip to Philly, everyone in the program knew Jeanne, even if they didn't take classes with her. Over the next few weeks, she received hundreds of get-well cards and email messages. Dancers even called offering to drive her to her chemo sessions.

"Thank you so much for the offer, but my husband can drive me," Jeanne told them.

"Okay, so what kind of soup do you like?" came the reply.

Jeanne found herself showered with affection and concern. A dancer named Sabina, who is an attorney for the US State Department, offered to help with any legal issues that might come up. Trish, our resident seamstress, told Jeanne that she would make her a special blouse to slip over her head after surgery, when it would be difficult to lift her arms.

Deb—one of our "Three Musketeers"—decided that she wanted to do something special for Jeanne as well. Although Deb had never met Jeanne before the trip to Philadelphia, when she heard about her diagnosis, she got to work. In no time at all, she had made Jeanne a hand-sewn quilt decorated with fabric cutouts of our black-and-white tap shoes. Each pastel-colored square on the quilt represented the colors of the T-shirts that the Tap Pups wore at our spring show that year. Deb brought the quilt to my studio with a felt marker and asked me to make sure that every dancer in each class and location signed it with a message of support.

I knew that Jeanne was going to be blown away by Deb's thoughtful gesture. At Deb's request, I presented the quilt to her one evening at her home.

Jeanne couldn't believe that Deb had done this for her, when the two of them didn't even dance in the same class and had met only once. Jeanne was so moved that she laid out the quilt on top of her piano in her living room so that everyone who came to visit could see it and read the messages. And when she came back from her chemo sessions, Jeanne wrapped herself up in that quilt and thought about this community of dancers who cared so much.

After Jeanne made her full recovery, she came to each one of my classes to say hi and thank everyone for the cards and messages. Each class surrounded Jeanne while the dancers took turns giving her hugs. We were so happy to have her back.

As a group, we've had our fair share of heartache over the years. I've seen the dancers support one another through illness, through separations and divorces, through widowhood, and through financial troubles. We've celebrated the good times too: birthdays, retirements, births of grandchildren, kids graduating college—even when one of the dancers, Roz, got her college degree at the age of sixty-three. It's amazing to watch. It's as if there are invisible threads connecting every one of the dancers, even those who have never met one another before.

Chapter 14

• • •

Sunday, June 12, 2011
2:05 PM

THE PRESHOW MUSIC IS PLAYING, THE LIGHTS ARE READY TO GO, THE DANCERS ARE PREPPED AND LOOKING FABULOUS. THE EN-ERGY BACKSTAGE JUST NOTCHED UP FROM HIGH TO HIGHER. IT'S NEARLY TIME.

My granddaughter Savanah runs backstage to tell me that there's a line of people around the corner waiting to get into the theater. Sure enough, the road that runs alongside is swirling with people being dropped off: men, women, children, babies in strollers. People are carrying signs to hold up— "Go, Claudine!" "We Love You, Nana!" "My Mom Rocks!"—and bouquets of flowers to give to their favorite Tap Pup after the show. Bill Haley is play-ing over the outdoor loudspeakers. The sky overhead is blue, and the sun is shining brightly on the theater—the perfect late spring afternoon. One guy tells me later that he double-checked his ticket to make sure he was in the right place—he couldn't believe that all these people had turned out to see "old ladies tap-dancing."

Ducking backstage again, I head to the wings. Soon enough, I can hear a familiar hum coming from the auditorium: people are filing in and taking their seats. I've always loved the sound of an audience arriving. So many of the people taking their seats today are husbands, sons, daughters, grandchildren, neighbors, and coworkers of the dancers performing. Many of them have been coming out to support us for years now; they're our cheerleaders, our loyal fans. Meanwhile, for the mothers backstage, it's a strange kind of déjà vu: we've spent so many years attending our kids' recitals and sporting events. Now our families are the ones in the audience, ready to cheer for *us*.

At the back of the auditorium is what we call "gentlemen's row." This is where all of the "newbie" husbands end up sitting when they come to the show for the first time. As soon as these guys sit down, they cross their arms and start the countdown until the show is over. They have no idea what to expect. All they know is that they're here to watch their wives tap-dance. "Hey, guys!" I always want to tell them. "Just wait till you see my ladies move! You're not going to believe what you see." Because as much fun as it is for us to dance, it's equally fun to watch us onstage. The sound of the rhythm, the grace of movements, and the energy behind the dancing—all this coming from women old enough to know better—it's impossible to watch without smiling. By the end of the show, these guys are up on their feet and cheering. I remember one man who'd been hiding up in gentlemen's row stopping me afterward to tell me that he would be furious if his wife ever stopped coming to tap class because he loves how happy it makes her.

Dance affects our lives in so many ways, but for at least one afternoon a year, it affects our family and friends too. When we're performing, something magical happens. The happiness that we feel gets projected directly to the people we love—and it comes right back at us through their cheers and applause.

THE year after I opened my studio was an emotional one for our family. In 2009 Mike—my sons' father—passed away from cancer. He'd noticed a small spot on his back for some years but hadn't gotten it checked, and it turned out to be basal cell carcinoma which spread through his body. By now he'd met someone new, he was working and getting benefits, and even had life insurance. Most important, some years before he passed away, he'd made contact again with his sons. Olivia was six and Savanah was three when he met his granddaughters for the first time. After Mike died, I went with the boys to his funeral on Long Island. It was a very sad day for all of us. Mike had been someone with so much potential. Despite the many difficulties of our marriage, I have no doubt that he could have been an amazing father to the boys when they were growing up, if he'd just managed to turn himself around.

For so many years, my own life had seemed like a giant jigsaw puzzle, with pieces that didn't seem to fit together. As hard as I tried, I couldn't figure out the bigger picture. Why me? I used to think. Why did I marry a man who clearly wasn't capable of marriage? As the years went on, and my relationship with Larry didn't work out the way I'd hoped, things only got more confusing. The questions kept going around in my head: Why me again? Why was I retiring alone? I remember having this overwhelming feeling of wanting to go back in time so that I could rearrange the pieces. I wanted the picture to turn out better this time: a happy marriage, a life partner, our golden years together. The problem was, the past wouldn't budge. No matter how I shuffled the pieces, the picture didn't make any sense to me. But that picture was all I had.

After I retired and opened my studio, everything changed. The pieces of the jigsaw had finally fallen into place. For the first time, it all made sense. Mike was the reason I gave up dancing, but he triggered a chain of events that had brought me to the present moment. *Of course* I had to marry Mike, because without him, I wouldn't have my boys. Michael and Brian were the reason I came back to dance, because I needed to support my family. And then so many years later, my boys were the reason I pushed myself to the next level with my dance program. Forty years later, it all added up.

Now that I had my studio, my day-to-day life was transformed. I wasn't spending my waking hours going through the motions in a job that was a means to an end. I no longer had to teach in spaces that weren't designed for dancing. I didn't have to start the evening by breaking down tables and chairs, or sweeping cookie crumbs from the cafeteria floor. In the past, my ladies had danced around stacks of chairs and tables—even two big poles in the center of the room. One time I had to teach my class in a kitchen because someone had forgotten to tell us there was a meeting going on in the main room of the firehouse. Many of my dancers can still remember learning their first time steps around a stainless steel kitchen island. All those years of teaching in borrowed spaces made me truly appreciate my own studio, this "room of my own."

My studio was also giving me a lot more visibility around town, and as a result, I started coming back into contact with more of my students from the past.

The evening I opened my studio, a tiny brunette, dressed smartly in a blazer and summer dress, came toward me, smiling like a long-lost friend.

"Miss Vicki!" she said, throwing out her arms.

"Oh my goodness, Liz Smith, is that you?"

"Yes, it's me."

The woman standing in front of me must have been in her fifties, but she had the exact same brown eyes as when I taught her to dance at the age of eight. It was little Liz, the girl from my Studio of Rhythm days whose mother had told her she couldn't come back to class because her parents couldn't afford to send her anymore.

"So are you going to come back to tap class, Liz?" I asked her.

"I'm going to think about it, Miss Vicki," she said. "I've been away so long. I'm not sure I can dance anymore."

"Sure you can," I said. Sure enough, by the end of the night, she filled out a registration form.

Liz joined my Beginner 3 class. Lucky for her, she chose to dance next to Marji, one of the most outgoing and friendly dancers in the class. I had met Marji through golf, and we'd become fast friends. Marji is a bubbly brunette with fair streaks in her hair and a ton of energy and enthusiasm, a real people person. Soon enough, Marji took Liz under her wing, and they started spending time together outside of class. Marji and Liz bonded for various reasons. They worked near each other, and they both had grown sons living at home again.

Liz and Marji always took class with me on Thursday evening, my last class of the week. Every Thursday, I started to host my own little gathering in our new lounge area at the studio, mostly as a small end-of-the-week reward to myself. I began by asking my students if anyone would like to stay for a glass of wine. Nine times out of ten, the answer was yes. Those evenings under the chandelier usually consisted of Liz and Marji, as well as Linda, Betsy, Marcia, Carol, Peg, and the Three Musketeers. We'd discuss everything: first crushes, how we met husbands, new recipes, our children and grandchildren.

When I was working with Brian to design the studio, I knew that I wanted to find a way to encourage the friendships I was seeing in my classes. I wanted a studio with a beautiful dance floor, but I also wanted to give my dancers a place for connecting with one another. That's why we created the lounge. We placed striking white lacquer furniture around a large mirrored coffee table and hung a large crystal chandelier above. I bought an elegant vase and filled it with Twizzlers, my favorite candy. One of my last purchases for the studio was a small brushed-gold minibar, which fits perfectly in a corner of my office. Ideal for a dance studio for adults, I thought.

My studio had been open only a few weeks when I realized that the area under the chandelier was becoming almost as crowded as the dance floor. Dancers started arriving a half hour before class so that they could gather and catch up with friends. I found myself trying to teach classes over the sounds of giggling and chatter from the lounge.

"Hey, ladies," I'd shout, "keep it down over there!"

One evening, under the chandelier, I thought it would be fun to get the Thursday group to share how they ended up becoming Tap Pups. As we went around the circle, we got to Liz.

Of course, she told everyone how she used to take dance from me when she was a young girl at my Studio of Rhythm.

"But then after Vicki moved to New York and closed her studio, I gave up dancing," Liz explained. "It's taken me nearly forty years to come back to my Miss Vicki again."

"So why did you come back to teaching dance, Vicki?" Marji wanted to know.

"Because I had to," I explained. "I was raising two boys as a single mom. My ex-husband never paid a penny of child support. I didn't have any choice."

As I said this, Liz put her hand to her chest and gasped.

"You?" Liz asked. "That happened to you? Oh, Vicki, I had no idea."

"You probably always pictured me driving off into the sunset to live happily ever after with my handsome husband," I said.

"Of course!" Liz said. "You were like our princess. We all thought you were living a fairy tale. A dream. I never imagined anything else for you."

"So what happened to you after I left?" I asked Liz.

It turned out that Liz had known about my classes for some time. "I always wanted to come back," she admitted, "but it was hard for me to get up the courage. I've spent a lot of time feeling sorry for myself the past few years."

Liz told us that she had separated from her husband seven years ago after a long and difficult marriage. The decision to leave her marriage was one of the best things that had ever happened to her, but it had also raised a lot of doubt.

I knew from my own experience that when a marriage ends, there are so many questions left to answer. Why? Why did I stay all those years? Why wasn't I stronger? Why did I let myself get trapped in that situation?

"I don't tell a lot of people about what happened to me," she admitted. "Sometimes it just feels easier to keep things to myself."

I reached out to give Liz's arm a squeeze. I thought about Andrea, Jenna, and Susan, my original friends from tap class, and how much I'd learned from spending time with them. Thanks to these ladies, I finally got it. I didn't have to hold myself up to the standard of "perfect mother," "perfect wife," "perfect life." My friends were the ones who told me, "It's okay, life is messy; your struggles are part of what makes you *you*." I credit my girlfriends from dance class with showing me that it is possible to accept yourself on your own terms, whatever age you are.

Over time, Liz's group began to do the same for her.

"I always felt I had something to hide in the past," she told me later. "I used to be shy, I was never outspoken. Other women always intimidated me. But coming here every week has brought me out of myself, just as dance did when I was a little girl. I've made wonderful friends. They give me great advice. They support me. It's changed me. I have people in my life constantly telling me, 'Liz, you can do it.'"

Liz is just one of hundreds of dancers who have found solace from being in this group. We're surrounded by women who support us and tell us we're not alone. And she wasn't my only student from the Studio of Rhythm to come back to me either.

In the summer of 2010, the Moure sisters returned: Darla, Cathy, and Vicki Lee. All three had been students of mine at the Studio of Rhythm. Their mother had been friends with my mother, so I'd agreed to take them even though I knew she was a single mother and wouldn't be able to pay for their classes.

"Miss Vicki, it's me!" Darla said when she called. She had seen an advertisement in a local magazine and called me right away. "Do you mind if I call you Miss Vicki? I can't imagine calling you anything else."

"I would love it if you called me that," I replied.

Darla came to class the next week, and her sister Vicki Lee was right behind her. The girls told me that their sister Cathy was also going to join as soon as she'd recovered from a knee injury.

Then about six months later, I reconnected with another little girl from the Studio of Rhythm, Debbie Cuckovic. She was the shy little girl with dark-brown hair who loved to escape to the studio to get away from the rough-and-tumble of her three brothers at home. At the beginning of 2011, we got back in contact again through Facebook. When I clicked on her profile and saw that she still lived in the area, I sent her a message:

"Debbie, why aren't you a Tap Pup?"

"I don't know," she quickly replied. "I've been wondering the same thing myself."

She started classes the very next week. Debbie told me that she never expected to be here. At the age of twenty-four, she'd suffered a brain aneurysm, and her doctors had told her she'd never walk again. But over a period of years and with a lot of physical therapy, she'd proven them wrong.

"You have no idea what it means to be to be back dancing with you again," Debbie told me after her first class.

I told her how much I loved having my original dancers at my new studio. It gave me a feeling of finishing something I'd started a very long time ago. Now that Debbie had joined, I had six students from the old days: the Moure sisters, Debbie, Liz, and, of course, LuAnne.

In the spring of 2011, we decided to get together for a minireunion and a glass or two of wine at my studio. Brian went out of his way to come to Harrisburg that weekend so he could meet my "originals."

Our gathering took place on a Saturday afternoon, just like we used to spend Saturday afternoons together at my Steelton studio. When I'd first taught them, I was barely an adult, and they were children. Now time had leveled the playing field. The little girls were all in their fifties, with grown-up children of their own, and in some cases, grandchildren. As the ladies walked into the studio, everyone embraced, holding out their arms to get a better look at one another, with expressions that said, "Really, is that you? After all these years?"

That day, I'd brought the album my mother had given to me before I closed my studio and left Steelton for New York. It was bound in brown leather, with gold trim. The words "Miss Vicki" and two roses were hand-painted in aqua across the front. In the corner of the cover were the words "I love you" written in the shorthand that my mother, a secretary, knew I would understand.

The spine was cracked. The pages were stuck together, their edges torn and faded. Many of the photos had fallen out. Somehow the album had managed to survive the flood in New Jersey. And now, forty years later, we opened the pages. Inside were photos of the dancers as little girls, taken at the photo studio owned by Forry's parents. Every year, around the time of the recital, I'd get the dancers dressed up in their costumes and pose them in front of a plain white backdrop.

"I grew up looking at this photo album!" Brian told the ladies. "I can't believe I'm getting to meet the girls in the photographs."

We gathered around, taking turns to point out the photos of ourselves in each of the group and individual shots, shrieking, "That's me!" and then laughing at how we looked back then.

"Oh my goodness! Remember the 'William Tell Overture' routine?" asked Vicki Lee, looking at a picture of herself wearing a little peaked hat and a red vest with a short skirt, meant to look like a riding outfit.

Then Debbie shared something that she had brought along to the studio: her old costumes. We couldn't believe it. The little outfits she pulled out of her bag were the exact same ones that we were looking at in the photos: the striped, one-shouldered black-and-white leotard with the bright red fringe across the front, from one of our jazz routines; the green-and-white twirling outfit with a big white V for Vicki on the chest.

"These costumes meant so much to me that I kept them all these years," she said.

We began to reminisce about all the different outfits we'd worn.

"Remember the fishnets?" Darla asked.

"Do I ever," said her sister Vicki Lee.

That's when I remembered. I'd bought fishnets for the Moure girls so that they would be able to wear them for their recitals.

"When we put on those fishnets you gave us, Miss Vicki, we felt like queens. That's what you taught us. You taught us to hold our heads up. We didn't have much to be proud of going to school back then—but after we started dancing, we could go to school and say, 'I'm in a recital, I'm in a parade.' We were part of Vicki's Studio of Rhythm."

"That's something I never could figure out, though," said Vicki Lee. "How our mother could afford to pay for classes. There were three of us, and all those costumes."

At that moment, I realized that Nancy, their mother, had never told them that I didn't charge them for their classes. They had no idea.

Everyone was so busy looking at the photos that only Vicki Lee and Darla heard me as I caught their eyes and told them quietly that their mother never had to pay, that I'd taken care of their lessons.

"I never knew," said Vicki Lee, eyes tearing. "I never said thank you."

"That's okay," I told her. "You're thanking me now. Just by being here."

Meanwhile, Brian was quizzing the other ladies about what I used to wear to teach class back then.

"She always wore everything matching," LuAnne told him. "Matching tights and matching leotards, with a little chiffon skirt."

"She was like our princess," Debbie said, smiling. "I can even remember your scent. You always wore Chantilly?"

I smiled and nodded.

"I remember thinking, 'As soon as I'm old enough, I'm going to get that perfume!'" remembered Debbie. "I had no idea that you could buy it at the drugstore. As far as I was concerned, you were ordering that scent from Paris!"

Then she stopped and frowned. It was the same frown she used to make as a little girl concentrating on her steps.

"I can still remember the day of your wedding," she said. "August 24, 1968."

"Debbie," I told her, "I can't believe you remember that date."

"I'll never forget it," she replied. "That was the day you went away from us."

"Oh my goodness, I will never forget your wedding either!" LuAnne agreed. "I was inconsolable!" Suddenly LuAnne started crying and repeating the words "You left us . . . you left us . . ." She continued: "My mother took me to a few other dance studios after that, but I refused to go back. It wasn't the same."

All this time I had known LuAnne and I never realized how much it had affected her when I'd left. As I looked around the room, every woman around that table had tears in her eyes. I realized that even after forty years, the memory of my studio closing was painful for them. Of course, I had to grab a few tissues for myself.

These women gave up dancing after I left Steelton. LuAnne taught dance for a while, but gave it up when she had her children. Debbie had taken classes with Forry for a time after college, but for the most part, dance had gone out of their lives. That afternoon, they kept telling me how much I'd done for them. What they didn't realize was that they've done so much more for me. If my students enjoy their classes and become better dancers, then that's the best validation I can have as their teacher.

To have my son there to witness this reunion made it all the more special for me. Brian had been the one to point out that my days running the Studio of Rhythm held the key not only to my past but to my future. He saw the teacher in me and pushed me to follow my calling. There were days when I thought Brian's ideas for my business were unattainable, but now here I was, getting the ultimate do-over and feeling like the luckiest dance instructor in the world.

Driving home that day, Brian turned to me.

"Mom, do you realize that everything you used to do for those little girls at the Studio of Rhythm, you're doing for your ladies now?"

"I know, Brian," I said. "Teaching dance is who I am."

It had taken me so many years to acknowledge the importance of those words, but now I knew it with all my heart.

As I write these words, I can't help but think of my granddaughters and what their stories will be. My heart fills up with my hopes for them. Both girls are so talented and have so much to offer. I hope that they can continue to carry themselves as they do today, with such commitment and confidence. I hope that they can see how much dance has given to me and how much I lost when I let it slip away. If these two girls take away anything from my story, I want it to be these words: Lead with your strengths and don't be afraid to follow your passions. You can never be too young, or too old, to find something you love that helps define who you are. This is what will give you strength to make the best choices in your life, no matter where it takes you.

EPILOGUE

• • •

SHOWTIME

LET ME DANCE
I WILL
FEEL RHYTHM AGAIN.
I WILL
BE HEALTHIER.
I WILL
GET OFF THE COUCH.
I WILL
MAKE NOISE.
I WILL
FINALLY DO SOMETHING I'VE ALWAYS WANTED TO DO.
I WILL
MAKE TIME FOR MYSELF.
I WILL
BE HAPPY.

VICKI'S TAP PUPS

THESE were the words from our most recent advertisement in all our local papers. The ad also gave us the theme of this year's annual spring show: Let Me Dance. My dancers tell me that these words sum up everything that inspires them to come to class. I have dancers who cut out the ad and stuck it to their refrigerators, or on their bulletin boards at work, or who carry it around in their wallets. It makes me very proud that my little business—something I started to keep me and my boys afloat—could have such a physical and emotional impact on the women of my community.

What many of my dancers probably don't realize is that the words in that ad touch on the exact same issues that I've been dealing with myself. At fifty-six, I was so anxious about the future, scared of growing older alone, lacking in confidence in my changing body. I didn't see the potential in my dancing and my teaching to shift me forward. I assumed that my best years were behind me. Ten years later, I can see that by finally focusing on my passion, I found my rhythm again. I'm in exactly the right spot, doing exactly what I should be doing.

At every pivotal moment, dance has been there for me. When my boys became teenagers and needed me to be a strong mother, dance got me through. When my heart was broken after they left home, it got me through. From small beginnings, my program has grown and grown, and now that I've reached retirement, it continues to sustain me and to lift me up. I'm still single—still hoping that one day I'll get to meet that prince of mine, someone with whom to share all this excitement—but I know that thanks to dance, I will never feel alone again.

As I step backstage one last time before the show begins, I see LuAnne, my old friend, my lead instructor. I shoot her a wink and a thumbs-up.

"Here we go," she says. "Just like old times."

"Knock 'em dead, girl!" I tell her, and we hug.

Out in the audience, everyone is seated. The music is turned up high, and the crowd is clapping and whooping. Lights are sweeping across the stage, and Brian, Michael, and my granddaughters are throwing glowing beach balls out into the auditorium for the audience to bat around while they wait for the show to begin.

The fourteen All-Star dancers quietly take their positions in the wings. A few hold hands to help bring down their nerves. They're wearing black pants and black blouses with our logo embroidered on the left chest and a thick band of white sequins down each sleeve. The same band of white sequins sparkles down each side of their legs.

The lights go down in the auditorium and onstage. I wait in the wings so that I can direct the dancers and they can see me if they need help.

The All-Stars walk out onto the pitch-dark stage. They strike the same pose. Each dancer lunges forward with the right foot, her thumb and fingertip grasping an imaginary hat brim, the other arm extended behind. Ready to go.

Then *boom!*

The big V-shaped light flashes on in bright aqua, and at that moment, the dancers appear, silhouetted with their white sequins sparkling on black.

I hold my breath, waiting for the sound of the first three steps.

It's showtime.

ACKNOWLEDGMENTS

• • •

WRITING A BOOK ABOUT MY LIFE AND THE PEOPLE IN IT WAS AT TIMES A DAUNTING EXPERIENCE, TO SAY THE LEAST. REEXAMINING PERSONAL ASPECTS OF MY PAST TO HELP TELL THE STORY OF HOW I CREATED SOMETHING THAT I'M INCREDIBLY PROUD OF DOING WAS BOTH A PRIVILEGE AS WELL AS A GIANT THERAPY SESSION. BUT I GOT HERE AND I COULDN'T HAVE DONE IT WITHOUT ANY OF YOU.

Brian S. Riordan, my younger son, the most loving, unselfish, and insightful person beyond his years; the mastermind behind the growth of Vicki's Tap Pups. Everyone needs a Brian, but you'll have to get your own, this one is mine!

Michael Riordan, my older son, who is there for me with deep love and those much needed special hugs and personal insights when I need them most. Olivia Riordan and Savanah Riordan, my baby dolls and beautiful granddaughters who bring joy to my life every single day of the year. Jennifer Riordan, the mother of my granddaughters, you will always be my daughter-in-law.

My mother, Charlotte Grubic Gustin, for a lifetime of unconditional love and strength and for being a world-champ mom and Grammie Char. In memory of my father, Victor T. Grubic; I miss you, Daddy. In memory of

James M. Gustin, the best Jimmie Pap for my sons and one of the most caring and loving people in my life. In memory of my aunt Dutch Brubacher, who was like a second mother to me. Christopher Strazzella, for always stepping in and being there when I need you the most. My cousin Rev. Dennis Brubacher, my first best friend and confidant. My uncle Russ Brubacher, thanks for always making me feel so special.

Msgr. Brendan P. Riordan, for your consistent love and support and for being the older brother I always wanted. Msgr. Alan Placa, a brilliant sounding board, who offered his excellent legal guidance, love, and support. Ed Riordan, who would have known we would actually end up being friends? Janie Riordan, only you could have gotten me through those years in New York. My niece, Doreen Riordan Hughes, you'll always be my girl. My nephews, Michael and Christopher Riordan, I love you dearly. John and Jane Bretagna, my wonderful friends, thank you for helping to take off my rose-colored glasses.

Eve Claxton, thank you for all the hours you spent away from your family to continually add your unique sense of rhythm and style to the stories of my life. Amy Tannenbaum, my editor at Atria Books, for knowing just the perfect way to edit my words; you must have known me for a lifetime, you certainly don't miss a thing! The team at Atria Books: Judith Curr, Peter Borland, Diana Franco, Hillary Tisman, Isolde Sauer, Kimberly Goldstein, Alysha Bullock, Philip Bashe, and Dana Sloan, for believing in my vision and helping to make it come to life so beautifully. Fletcher & Company, my agents, Christy Fletcher and Grainne Fox, for helping guide me through the creative process of book writing. Anita Rao, thank you for kindly assisting in the editorial stage. Swanna MacNair, Creative Conduit, for your friendship and strong insight and conviction that my story should be a book.

Tom Papas, for always making our graphics look so sharp. Only you could have figured out how to put my actual signature on our logo; you are solely responsible for so many women and men wearing a giant aqua "V" on their chests.

My two best friends, Mary Morrone and Ellen DePalma, who are like sisters to me. I couldn't have survived without either of you in the most pivotal times of my life. Peter Velencia, my buddy then, my buddy now.

To all of my dancers: Vicki's Studio of Rhythm, 1964–1968, I started it all for you. Forry Gehret, "Steelton's own Gene Kelly," wish you were here dancing with me today. My fifties/sixties dance classes, remember not to move your lips when you count your steps. Country Line Dancers: your boots were made for dancing. To all of my Tap Pups through the years, you make me feel like I'm truly the luckiest dance instructor in the world. Vicki's Tap Pups All Stars: Linda Beaver, Tiny Burns, Andrea Catlin, LuAnne Davis, Jenna Dishong, Deb Hamilton, Rick Hoover, Sandi Komaromy, Pam Kaylor, Heather Long, Lynne Ritter, Joan Sandherr, Jessica Simmons, and Janet Tommasini, I couldn't ask for better dancers to represent my style. The significant others of Vicki's Tap Pups for the love and support you give to each one of my dancers to help them shine even brighter outside of the studio.

My Instructors, my friends: LuAnne Davis, Jessica Simmons, Rick Hoover, Andrea Catlin, Jenna Dishong, Sandi Komaromy, and Janet Tommasini, for their passion and devotion they give so that each Tap Pup truly finds happiness through tap.

Carmen Williams, director, West Shore Recreation Department, a million thanks, look what you started! Brent Smith, Swatara Recreation Department, for always making things easy for me; Jennifer Johns, Derry Township/Hershey, Recreation Department, for making sure we were always in the studio for classes.

To my honorary Tap Pups: Derek Euston, my "music man" at the Green Room. Chris Freitas, who is like my third son, for his years of friendship and all of his handywork helping me to build my studio. Jason Naugle, our first music man and for making our Tap Jams so much fun at Champions Sports Bar and Grille.

My Manhattan Contingent: Pete Borba, Wendell Brown, Trevor Burgess, Dana DeVito, Mark Fichera, Gary Hess, Eric J. Johnson, Eric L. Johnson, Julie Levin, Lincoln Palsgrove, Phil Parotta, Michele Pokowicz, and Zak Profera—for never getting tired of hearing Brian and I talk about the Tap Pups. We love you all.

Brad Kenyon and Darren Iovino, Aurora Creative Group, for the stylish editing and video production that brings Vicki's Tap Pups to a larger audience. Dave Weaver, Mr. Bobbin Embroidery, and Milo Stavely, Moore Graphics, for impeccably producing all of our T-shirts, jackets, bags, and costumes, even when I get the order in later than I should. Vance Malone, Film Director, W. Hollywood, and Michelle Towse, Line Producer, NYC, for your invaluable time spent in Harrisburg.

Mary Ann Havalchek and Pamela Rhoads, YWCA of Greater Harrisburg, I look forward to a continued wonderful relationship and helping the women of our community through your Domestic Violence Program. Sally Krasevic for helping to lead us in the right direction with the YWCA of Greater Harrisburg.

AFSCME Council 13 and Council 89 for not having a problem with letting me follow my dream of being a dance instructor after work hours; Michael Fox and Norma Braidigan, two great bosses, who quickly became my friends.

Executive Women's Golf Association, Central PA Chapter: to all of my golfing friends that help me to forget everything except hitting that darn white ball.

• • •

TAP PUPS ROSTER

(Don't ever stop giving me goose bumps!)

•

All Stars

Linda Beaver, 69, Ret, Game Commission • Tiny Burns, 74, Receptionist in Dental Off • Andrea Catlin, 61, Actress/Tap Pup Adm/Instructor • LuAnne Davis, 58, Admin Asst/Tap Pup Instructor • Jennifer Dishong, 62, Owner Window Designs/Instr • Deb Hamilton, 59, Adm. Asst/Travel Agent • Rick Hoover, 65, Ret French Teacher/Tap Pup Instr • Pam Kaylor, 57, Blk/White Tap Shoe Sales Assoc. • Sandi Komarony, 58, Teacher/Tap Pup Instr • Heather Long, 30, Journalist/Editor • Lynne Ritter, 56, Legal Secretary • Joan Sandherr, 81, Ret. Bell Telephone of PA • Jessica Simmons, 30, Mkt-Branding/Tap Pup Instr • Janet Tommasini, 56, Phys Ed Teach/Tap Pup Instr

Advanced

Faith Archambeault, 39, Nurse • Holly Bahnick, 39, Software Engineer • Natalie Baker, 43, Owns Dance Studio • Viki Baker, 61, Ret. Teacher • Linda Beaty, 59, Homemaker • Donna Blessing, 59, Nurse • Kathy Bratic, 61, Business Owner • Sharon Caba, 62, Retired • Sylvia Cagle, 31, dancer/actor • Susan Cunningham, 60, Ret. Lt. Col. USMC • Amanda Cyr, 30, Consultant/Graphic • Michelle Day, 37, Physician Asst. • Susan Del Monte, 42, Self-Employed • Pam Doll, 36, Finance Manager/Zumba Instr. • Sheila Earhart, 52, PA House of Leg/Admin. Asst. • Stephanie Fisher, 39, Mental Health Caseworker • Shelley Goldstein, 30, Editor • Kelly Gore,

34, Teacher • Suzi Guyer, 60, Legal Secretary • Jacqueline Hall, 49, Nurse • Marsha Hall, 63, Ret. Accountant • Linda Heilman, 65, Ret. Dental Asst. • Greta Ingraham, 57, Social Worker • Karen Kelly, 64, Ret. Teacher • Crystal Kerns, 60, Retired • Linda Lemmon, 63, School Superintendent • Jennifer Leshniowsky, 43, Ballet Teacher • Sherrie McCartney, 55, VP Countertop Sales • Diane Miller, 69, Ret. Teacher • Joan Peck, 77, Ret. Art Teacher • Tracy Reinl, 52, Business Analyst • Deb Shelley, 55, Owns Insurance Agency • Heather Spaan, 31, therapist • Annie Standley, 46, Ret. CPA • Joan Stehulak, 58, attorney • Erin Verano, 38, Atty. Comm. of PA • Patrick Wallen, 54, Business Consultant • Barb Warfel, 63, artist • Deanna Wealand, 35, Marketing • Morgan Williams, 26, Intern Community Action • Patti Williams, 62, Ret. Teacher

Intermediate

Nicole Bassounas, 38, RN • Luann Bird, 54, Owns Insurance Agency • Jennifer Bistline, 57, Activity Coordinator • Terri Bretz, 55, Sr. Director • Karen Brown, 60, Ret Real Estate Paralegal • Connie Carey, 65, Hershey Company Employee • Karen Christie, 55, VP Finance, Delta Group • Kathy Cont, 50, Admin Asst • Rita Dallago, 64, Realtor • Dina Duffy, 36, Teacher • Trish Edmiston, 60, Owner Seamstress Business • Jackie Fagan, 38, Homemaker • Jim Fisher, 33, GAP Manager • Tina Freeman, 38, Teacher • Rita Gardner, 32, RN • Sue Hamilton-James, 58, Nurse Practitioner • Lydia Hammand, 62, RN • Erin Hankey, 29, Speech Therapist • Marsh Harris, 68, Ret. School Teacher • Judy Hempt, 68, Accountant • Stephanie Hench, 51, Office Manager • Marsha Hertweck, 59, Works in Dental Office • Sabina Howell, 57, Attorney, Comm of PA • Vicki Hutchison, 61, Homemaker/ Rides Harley • Debbie Johnson, 58, Accts Payable Clerk • Mary Jane Jones, 67, Ret. Typist • Jill Kelley, 56, Military • Connie Kennedy, 55, Mental Health Consultant • Sonya Kennedy, 61, Retired • Kathryn King-Solon, 55,

Reading Specialist • Becky Kishbaugh, 30, Realtor • SueAnne Knowlton, 59, RN • Diana Koleck, 51, RN • Jayne Kopko, 44, Computer Analyst • Erica Kunkle, 32, Acct. Manager • Maria Lavelle, 43, RN • Charlotte Lefevre, 33, Homemaker • Marian Lefevre, 60, Pinnacle Health • Kim Lehman, 40, Mother of Twins • Vickie Leko, 38, Homemaker • Dolly Leonzo, 65, Exec. Asst. • Carol Long, 51, Accountant, Family Business • Jen Love, 46, Medical Transcriptionist • Cindy Maurer, 61, Ret PA Dept Public Welfare • Patty McCown, 50, Quality Assurance • Diana Mihailoff, 64, Ret. Comm of PA • Amanda Miller, 24, Service Representative • Christine Mummert, 66, Retired/Aerobic Instr • Joanne Neimer, 61, Retired Teacher • Therese Newcomb, 55, Information Management • Shirley Newhart, 60, Ret. Music Education • Diane Schaeffer, 57, Microbiologist • Dara Pachence Schmick, 34, Speech Pathologist • Nicole Schonewolf, 33, Nurse • Darlene Shaffer, 60, Retired PA Labor & Industry • Karen Shaffer, 31, Sales, Medical Equipment • Jody Sheffer, 54, Retired Acct/Owns Yarn Business • Mary Shettel, 71, Ret. Holy Spirit • Molly Shook, 23, Actuary • Dorian Skrinak, 32, Dept. Auditor General • Kortni Smith, 23, Education • Tina Solomon, 41, 5th Grade Teacher • Hope Sterner, 41, Office Manager • Christine Stewart, 48, Auditor • Dianne Tiboni, 66, Ret. Training Mgr. • Loni Warholic, 30, Campus Dining Mgr. • Helen Weigel, 48, Director, Dept. Auditor General • Alexcia Wheeler, 36, Speech Pathologist • Laura Wildman, 32, Admin, Asst, Family Business • Karen Williams, 43, Speech Pathologist • Stacy Wolf, 46, Education Consultant • Bert Zumoff, 76, Allergist

Beginner 3

Bridget Abbott, 50, Nurse • Margie Adelmann, 54, President Nat'l. MS Society • Betsy Baker, 54, Part Owner of Appliance Store • Pat Banzhoff, 58, Therapist • Claudine Battisti, 35, PR Dir, PA Dept of Health • Elaine Bender, 55, Administrative Asst. • Marji Beyer, 59, Ret. Ex. Asst. Labor & Industry •

Mary Jo Bianco, 59, Learning Support Teacher • Peg Biasucci, 63, Retired Teacher • Deb Bielek, 59, Retired Teacher • Claire Birney, 28, Hair Stylist • Marise Brennan, 29, Nationwide Ins. • Joanne Bupp, 56, Office Clerk • Mary Jo Capuano, 52, Claims Analyst • Dominique Carta, 29, Medical Sales • Sally Cawthra, 67, Ret Acc't/Grant Mgmt • Natalie Chango, 34, Child Life Specialist • Brenda Clark, 55, Ret. Spec. Agent • Vicki Clark, 56, Hair Stylist • Susan Cohen, 66, Ret WomenArts/Freelance Writer • Dotti Cole, 66, Ret. • Beth Cornell, 65, Consultant PA Dept of Ed • Joan Costello, 76, Retired • Kristin Daniels, 42, Homeland Security • Pat Davis, 68, Ret. Dir. PA Food Bank • Terrie Davis, 52, RN • Jen Delozier, 64, Ret. Insurance • Lisa DiVittore, 47, M.I.S., AFSCME C13 • Jackie Doyle, 49, UPS, Adm. Asst. • Marcia Egan, 57, Artist/ Trainer • Joan Foley, 57, Nurse • Margie Fultz, 58, RN Instructor • Beth Goldstein, 62, Elem. School Counselor • Jan Haas, 62, Provider Rep, Blue Cross • Alice Harris, 63, Comedian • Beth Hess, 32, Marketing, Family Business • Millie Hitz, 84, Ret. Accountant/ Piano Teacher • Karie Hoffer, 29, RN • Nancy Hoffman, 60, RN • Elaine Hoover, 65, Ret. Bell Atlantic • Tommy Hostetter, 63, Artistic Dir. Emeritus • Joyce Howells, 59 • Grace Huber, 63, Ret. School Librarian • Gail Jackson, 57, Director, Data Center Geospatial • Nicole Kaiser, 32, Podiatrist/Surgeon • Dorothy Kardos, 58, Hearing Specialist • Linda Kautz, 61, Insurance Verifier • Kim Kelly, 55, Drafting Coordinator • Carol Kennedy, 66, Retired • Denise Kennedy, 56, Travel Agent • Annie Kerrigan, 70, Business Owner • Michelle Kingsbury, 57, Ret. Secretary • Kristi Klinger, 21, RN • Liz Kolonoski, 56, PA Dept Auditor Gen Asst. • Winnie Kostoff, 65, Ret PA Senate • Cindy Kuentzler, 56, Owns Hair Salon • Virginia LaFond, 68, Antique Clock Sales • Joan Langendijk, 64, Sign Language Instr. • Sandy Leyh, 65, Travel Consultant • Anni Lodge, 59, CFO Publishing Co • Alberta Luther, 66, Ret. US Navy Depot • Ricki Lyter, 63, Ret. Professor • Jenni MacNamara, 34, Case Mgr. • Diane Markley, 55, Ret. Banker •

Jodie Martin, 49, Harrisburg City Police Officer • Linda Masoero, 56, Para Educator • Joyce Match, 57, PA Dept. Public Welfare • Jean McDonald, 75, Homemaker • Barbara Meehan, 69, Ret. Marketing • Lana Meidinger, 62, Owner, Tack/Horse Supplies • Deborah Minner, 57, School Bus Driver • Dot Mitchel, 86, Retired • Judy Moffett, 68, Ret School Bus Driver • Elly Morrison, 52, RN • Susan Mountz, 69, Ret. RN • Megan Mumma, 26, Business Off, Health Care • Melody O'Donnell, 38, Mkt Cord/Fitness Inst • Missy Patterson, 45, Central PA Food Bank • Nancy Pavelic, 61, 2nd Grade Teacher • Deb Pitzer, 60, Weight Watchers Consultant • Margaret Puliti, 69, Ret. State Investigator • Dr. Susan Richman, 70, Ret. Professor • Betsy Riter, 60, Teacher of the Gifted • Karen Robbins, 53, Insurance Underwriter • Judy Rohacek, 62, HACC Adm. Secretary • Sue Rynex, 65, Ret Medical Receptionist • Victoria Sahonic, 65, Ret. Dept. of Defence • Dawn Schaef, 52, Admin, Officer. Comm of PA • Jeanne Schmedlen, 64, Ret. House of Reps • Judy Schmidt, 64, College Professor • Kathy Seipe, 58, Office Mgr. • Deborah Shellenberger, 57, Happy Housewife • Mary Sholley, 57, Training Specialist • Roberta Silver, 58, Attorney, Comm of PA • Kristin Sinkovitz-Radle, 32, Art Teacher • Constance Sokalsky, 63, Ret. Convention Services • Ellen Spaulding, 70, Yoga Instructor • Lisa Swope, 31, Financial Analyst • Kate Sukley, 58, Legal Clerk • Mary Lou Swartz, 64, Financial Analyst • Elena Taylor, 48, Paraprofessional • Kitti Taylor, 68, Retired • Carol Tyndale, 61, Owner Tyndale Flag Service • Gail Urich, 59, Teacher's Assistant • Darla Via, 56, Legal Clerk • Vicki Via, 59, Exec. Admin, Coor/3 Mile Island • Sheri Virnig, 50, Database Manager • Melinda Walker, 60, Ret Attorney • Kristy Webster, 35, Rite Aid Surplus Analyst • Jacquie Whitcomb, 61, PA House of Representatives • Justina Williams, 54, Sr. Programmer Analyst • Bonnie Willis, 69, Ret Banker • Georgi Willis, 69, Ret Travel Agent • Barb Wilton, 64, Ret Lab Tech • Susan Zartman, 46, IT • Tina Zimmerman, 43, Teacher • Amy Zuvich, 29, Budget Analyst

Beginner 2

Sherry Abraham, 66, Ret. Teacher • Jane Adams, 64, Homemaker • Paulette Alexander, 60, Real Estate Spec. • Michelle Armour, 47, Paralegal • Becky Bacher, 55, Banker • Roz Ball, 63, Recent College Graduate • Kathleen Bard, 61, Retired Teacher • Susie Haas Bates, 47, Writer • Jenny Beck, 63, Ret Teacher • Kyleen F. Bender, "old," Retired • Yvonne Bevilacqua, 65, Ret Telecom. • Carmel Bilko, Business Owner • Nancy Bohn, 59, CT Scan Tech • Ellie Boyer 73, Ret. Music Teacher • Amanda Brendlinger, 35, Safety Trainer • Carla Brokenshire, 66, Retired Legal Secy. • Doug Brown, 59, Therapist • Jama Calabro, 61, Asst. Teacher • Tammy Carter, 55, US Navy Logistics • Cynthia Clippinger, 67, Ret. Elem. Teacher • Yvonne Cody, 76, Ret. School Secy. • Joan Connor, 77, Realtor • Eleanor Conrad, 72, Retired • Rickie Cook, 67, RN/Marketing • Robert Cook, 66, Retired • Gwenn Curry, 54, Physician • Stephany Davidson, 66, Ret. Elem. Teacher • Sherry Deane, 62, Secry/Receptionist • Kristy Demsey, 60, Teacher • Jody Diehl, 61, Homemaker • Elsa Doyle, 71, Ret. Comm. of PA • Sandy Dupkas, 59, Machine Operator • Melodee Durff, 62, Social Worker • Kathy Ebersole, 65, Retired • Sherry Eichelberger, 49, Receptionist • Lisa El Haddad, 47, Legal Admin Asst • Vicki England, 51, Teacher • Lindsay Ewing, 29, Spanish Teacher • Sherrie Feldman, 55, Dermatologist • Justine French, 53, Personal Trainer • Rita Fulton, 49, Substitute Teacher • Susan Ganhann, 57, Mgt Dept of Public Welfare • Sue Gardner, 59, Retired Teacher • Sue Garrett, 60, Trainer • Terry Gawlas, 60, Trainer • Kirk Gibson, 70, Sales • Sally Gibson, 61, Adm. Asst. • Linda Goodhart, 69, Ret. Pinnacle Health • Grace Gornik, 74, Ret. Owner Rest/Bar • Vicki Gray, 56, Adm. Asst. • Joyce Gustavson, 65, MD • Jennifer Hande, 57, RN • Jean Healy, 69, Ret. Teacher • Tobi Heise, 34, Team Leader, Mary Kay • Bunny Highfield, 65, Ret. Banker • Tara Hostetler, 39, Penn Carpet & Flooring • Sharyl Houser, 65, Retired • Shannon Howell, 35, Supv., Health Solutions •

Nancy Hunsberger, 56, IT • Nancy Ives, 70, Ret. Teacher • Gerry Ivkovich, 65, School Teacher • Sally Kitchen, 62, PA House Legislative Asst • Cheri Klipa, 56 Ret, Comm of PA • Chris Klipa, 53, Respiratory Therapist • Sandy Kohler, 61, Medical Coder • Deb Kreiger, 55, RN • Kathy Kuhn, 63, Dir. Christian Ed • Chris Lahr, 52, Budget Manager • Darleen Limburg, 55, IBM Corp • Sally Marisic, 64, Retired, Elem. Teacher • Bev Maynard, 66, Dental Hygienist • Marlene Miller, 59, Secretary • Polly Miller, 69, Owner Hair Salon • Janet Moses, 61, Teacher • Tina Mushalko, 59, Medical Secretary • Beverly Paine, 59, Education • Marge Panettieri, 66, Retired • Barbara Pinto, 62, Owner, Peter Alan House • Jana Poole, 54, Occupational Therapist • Peggy Purdy, 72, Travel Consultant • Bonnie Reichenbach, 56, PA Dept Public Welfare • Bonnie Rhoads, 60, Ret Comm of PA • Linda Ries, 59, Archivist • Lisa Ritter, 48, CPA • Jane Robinson, 52, Homemaker • Ali Rodrigues, 26, Music Teacher • Deb Rodrigues, 56, Statistician, Comm of PA • Lurlei Rutkowski, 41, Hollywood Casino • Nancy Rybicki, 62, Clinical Social Worker • Donna Savage, 55, Baker • Pat Schofield, 72, Ret. Adm. Asst • Jacqueline Sheaffer, 58, Accounting Mgr • Pat Sheibley, 57, Adm. Asst. • Lynne Shellenberger, 59, RN • Pat Shofield, 70, Retired • Linda Shopes, 66, Freelance Editor • Annetta Simington, 63, Ret. High School Principal • Linda Starr, 62, Insurance Acct. Ex. • Gloria Stewart, 82, Ret Teacher • Barbara Stone, 59, Secretary • Carol Sunderland, 59, Computer Tech • Jeanne Thomas, Abstractor • Joyce Thomas, 63, Ret. RN • Susan Thomas, 60, Retired • Tappin' Tanya Thomas, 64, State Tax Agent • Peggy Porr Toms, Retired • Donna VanZandt, 65, Business Owner • Jan Vernam, School Counselor • Denise Wade, 58, Administrative • Beth Wagner, 31, Teacher • Judy Warner, 59, Ret. Teacher • Colleen Weaver, 57, Consultant Telecom Spec. • Mary Lou Williams, 71, Ret. Med. Office Mgr. • Linda Zawacki, 60, Purchasing Asst. • Michelle Ziegler, 44, Ass't. Gen. Mgr. Hotel Industry

Beginner 1

Kristine Barney, 42, Office Supervisor • Donna Benson, 51, Special Educator • Tracy Black, 41, Legal Secretary • Kristal Blake, 58, Retired Consultant • Barbara Bloom, 63, State Government • Karen Bloomingdale, 57, Off. Mgr. AFSCME C13 • Sandra Book, 68, Retired Supv of PC for US Navy • Denise Bowen, 60, Delta Dental Ins. • Marilyn Breed, 61, Retired Teacher • Susie Brehm, 59, Special Ed Teacher • Rebecca Bremer, 46, Administration/Actress • Cheryl Brubaker, 63, Ret. Elem. Teacher • Carole Capriotti, 65, Ret. School Principal • Carmen Castillo-Zerbe, 42, College Professor • Jennie Cheeley, 28, Student • Kate Chescattie, 37, Professor • Sue Clausen, 64, Retired Clerical Supv • Karen Close, 61, Homemaker • Debbie Coffee, 57, Adv. Sales • Vonnie Cressler, 70, Ret. Teacher • Susan Croushore, 61, Ret Dir Health Admin • Mary Daubensperk, 54, Teacher • Pat DeBon, 60, Intervention Spec. • Marcia Dessett, 63, Teacher-Instr/ Aide • Renee DiCarlo, 41, Homemaker • Wendy Diem, 50, Homemaker • Becky Doble, 39, Civil Engineer/Actress • Lesley Dunkerley, 62, Ret. Store Manager • Lora Etter, 30, Real Estate Agent • Blaine Fasnacht, 55, Owner Hair Salon • Gordana Fasnacht, 57, Patient Transport • Aggie Freeland, 85, Ret. Weight Watchers • Judy Grzymski, 66, Bank Teller • Barbara Fox, 73, Retired • Elizabeth Fox, 66, Retired Accountant • Paula Gibson, 48, Product Development • Roxy Gies, 55, Spec, Ed Educator • Linda Gorka, 42, Lines Underwriter • Lisa Graham, 43, Sales • Jacqueline Granite, 68, Ret. Therapist • Diane Granoff, 51, Insurance • Barbara Groce, 66, Retired • Rhonda Gutshall, 56, School • Cindy Hallman, 56, RN • Candy Harris, 60, Ret. Supply Tech • Julie Kane, 36, Higher Ed Administrator • Marian Keller, 70, Retired • Mary Kerr, 53, Programmer Analyst • Nancy Knecht, 56, Finance Clerk • Sandra Kohr, 63, Ret Human Resources • Ann Korb, 36, HR Analyst • Mary Kost, 53, RN • Randi Kulik, 67, Ret. Commutes to class from NJ • Maryanne Lewis, 55, Deputy Atty. Gen. • Candy McDaniel,

68, Retired Legal Secy. • Mary Morrone, 65, Owner Hair Salon • Kaitlin Mussomeli, 55, RN • Diane Neiper, 62, Ret. Teacher • Kelly O'Connor, 29, Nurse • Linda O'Connor, 57, Educator • Roxane Pace, 52, Educator • Gretchen Petri, 73, Ret. Computer Trainer • Claudia Pritchard, 67 • Colleen Rice, 41, RN • Anneke Richcreek, 34, Medical Asst. • Dana Shanaberger, 31, Legal Asst. • Ann Stewart, 56, Writer/Facilitator • Karen Storm, 58, Sales Administration • Cicily Waeger, 65, Ret. Health Counselor • Jeanne Wagner, 68, Teacher • Carol Walker, 60, Ret. IT Specialist • Mary Warner, 64, Ret. Reporter • Jacquie Waters, 64, Ret. Secretary • Lisa Watson, 36, Attorney • Allison Watts, 53, Professor • Shelley Watts, 58, FCS Teacher • Lisa Wayne, 34, Hair Stylist • Nancy Weikel, 61, Teacher • Kerri White, 57, Jewelry Artist • Pat Williams, 65, Retired • Lisa Woodburn, 36, Attorney • Dawn Yeager, 40, Ret. Visual Specialist

New Beginner

Gwen Alsedek, 63, Theater Designer • Dixie Anderson, 67, Retired • Kim Anderson, 28, Homemaker • Eric Leonardo Bailey, 20, Temple Univ. • Elaine Baumbach, 64, Retired • Earline Bellaman, 56, Data Entry Clerk • Janet Bohnert, 56, RN • Steve Booker, 51, Verizon • Mary Brenner, 55, Teacher • Alex Burke, 36 • Judy Buszka, 66, Ret. Teacher • Barbara Byrne, 70, Retired • Sherry Caldwell, 64, Ret. Hershey Company • Margie Cannon, 66, Ret, Navy Base • Ali Cassel, 32, Attorney • Sherilyn Clark, 72, Piano Teacher • Barbara Clawson, 59, Sales Consultant • Barbara Closky, 62, Retired • Lynn Conklin, 60, Office • Angie Connaghan, 51, Blue Chip FCU • Bonnie Cooper, 49, Medicine • Christine Corrigan, 47, Asst. Golf Pro • Debbie Christian, 67, Bus. Mgr, Comm of PA • Debbie Culley, 48, Labor Mediator • Karen Culley, 69, Ret. Office Adm. • Linda Davis, 67, Erie Insurance • Mary E. Davis, 73, Ret. US Army Security • Pat Deniston, 75, Ret. Professor • Debbie Diller, 61, Ret. Principal • Patti Dilley, Ret. Technical writer/

editor • Ginny Duncan, 61, Catholic Diocese of Hbg • Sharon Durst, 50, LPN • Mary Eckman, 60, Fabric Store Sales • Lisa Effinger, 21, Child Care • Maryland Ferretti, 57, Legal Asst. • Karan Fink, 57, Payroll/Tax • Bill Fisher, 36, United Concordia • Jill Frank, 60, Teacher • Jane Fuller, 51, Library Assistant • Christine Getz, 59, Teacher • Anne Marie Gill-Re, 40, Respiratory Therapist • Rhonda Gutshall • Ashley Davis Hale, 33, Acct. @ Steel-High • Janet Harter, Sales • Dot Hartman, 52, Retired • Sue Heist, 51, Retail Owner • Lisa High, 53, Librarian • Naida Huber, 84, Ret. Library Clerk • Deb Joyce, 50, Golf Pro • Jeanne Kandra, 57, Dietitian • Joanne Keim, 61, Retired • Cari Kennedy, 51, Accountant • Mary Kinsinger, 62, RN Supervisor • Elaine Kistler, 68, Ret. Teacher • Linda Klutas, 63, Secretary • Kurt Krusen, 52, Veterinarian • Pam Kutchman, Regional Manager • Chris Laughman, 58, Capital Blue Cross • Carol Leach, 62, Ret. Teacher • Patricia Lego, 65, Ret. RN • Caitie Link, 27, Music Teacher • Marian Linnell, 53, Programmer • Betti Lusk, 59, Office Mgr • Tina Luth • Karen Mallah, 42, Psychologist • Elena Man, 45, Pediatrician • Kathryn Marlier, 57, Rental Mgr. • Carole Martin, 67, Ret., United Concordia • Christine Mason, 46 • Lenora Mauro, 63, Surgical Tech • Deb McClain, 51, Ins. Acc't. Ex. • Shirley McCormick, 63, Ret. Accountant • Jill Miller, Travel Agent • Tami Minnici, 59, Appraiser • Margie Mitchell, 70, Ret. Teacher • Mary Modical, 53 • Sandy Mohall • Trudy Moore, 48, Asst. Dir./USDA • Dona Joy Mosser, 60, Ret. Teacher • Jan Myers, 58, Sales Rep • Jeffrey Myers, 61, Ret. Ins. Adjuster • Maria Noss, 33, Respiratory Therapist • Janice "JP" Paul, 60, Ret. RN • Kathi Pendleton, 61, Met Life Sales • Gail Perez, 55 • Mickey Perez, 62, Accountant • Mary Plasic, 63, Office Manager • Eve Platkin, 62, Cust. Ser. Giant Foods • Dede Ramm, 71, Ret. Medical Rep • Phil Raudensky, 67, Mkt. Mgr. • Lisa Robinson, 47, RN • John Rubisch, 59, Susquenita Counselor • Shelby Sammartino, 30, Teacher • Mardi Sawyer, 58, Administrator • Laurie Schuneman, 52, Ret. Education Coach • Susan

Seneca, 49, LPN • Judith Shenk, 51, Business Owner • Jennifer Skoff, 47, Legal Secy. • Lisa Solomon, 60, Human Services Comm of PA • Julie Spotts-Katona, 49, RN • Denise Stamm, 46, Dietitian • Sherri Sternberg, 47, Stay-at-home Mother • Maria Stoner, 30, Teacher • Bonnie Suggs, 67, Ret. • Rhonda Summery, 49, RN • Linda Surak, 62, Retired • Jody Tay, 57, Business Analyst • Susan Torres, 56, Attorney • Jocelyn Troup, 54, Clerk Typist • Jennifer Troutman, 54, Insurance Agent • Sharon Waraby, 63, Ret. • Choy-Foong Wong, 42, Portfolio Mgr. • Liz Yarnell, 59, Legislative Research Analyst • Dottie Young, 56, Bookkeeper • Kathy Zoladz, 59, Massage Therapist

Rocket: Our mascot who makes everyone smile.

Printed in the United States
By Bookmasters